ELUSIVE KINSHIP

CHRISTOPHER KRENTZ

Elusive Kinship

Disability and Human Rights in
Postcolonial Literature

TEMPLE UNIVERSITY PRESS
Philadelphia • Rome • Tokyo

TEMPLE UNIVERSITY PRESS
Philadelphia, Pennsylvania 19122
tupress.temple.edu

Library of Congress Cataloging-in-Publication Data

Names: Krentz, Christopher, author.
Title: Elusive kinship : disability and human rights in postcolonial
  literature / Christopher Krentz.
Description: Philadelphia : Temple University Press, 2022. | Includes
  bibliographical references and index. | Summary: "This volume analyzes
  the figure and representation of disability in postcolonial literature,
  unpacking how depictions of disability both reflected and directly
  impacted the growth of disability human rights in the latter half of the
  twentieth century"—Provided by publisher.
Identifiers: LCCN 2021046379 (print) | LCCN 2021046380 (ebook) |
  ISBN 9781439922217 (cloth) | ISBN 9781439922224 (paperback) |
  ISBN 9781439922231 (pdf)
Subjects: LCSH: Disabilities in literature. | People with disabilities in
  literature. | Postcolonialism in literature. | Human rights in literature.
Classification: LCC PN56.D553 K74 2022 (print) | LCC PN56.D553 (ebook) |
  DDC 823/.914093527—dc23/eng/20220211
LC record available at https://lccn.loc.gov/2021046379
LC ebook record available at https://lccn.loc.gov/2021046380

Printed in the United States of America

9 8 7 6 5 4 3 2 1

For Michelle

Contents

ELUSIVE KINSHIP

Introduction

In an unusual series of more than thirty video interviews posted to YouTube in 2012, young disabled Africans offer revealing accounts of their personal experience and outlook. Called the African Youth with Disabilities Network, the videos feature interviewees who frequently recount societal prejudice, barriers to education, and dealing with a lack of resources.[1] For example, Nicolette Pieters, a mobility-impaired woman from Namibia, states that her primary school had no ramps, so classmates had to carry her up the stairs; she was so poor during college that she sometimes foraged through trash bins for food. Robert Ssewagudde, a deaf man from Uganda, reports that people in his home area perceived him as stupid and looked at him "like I was nothing" until his mother sent him away to a school for deaf students, where he found an empowering community of sign language users. Other interviewees talk about how society sometimes hid disabled children; remark on sexual violence against disabled women, especially in war zones; and address how disability can overlap with local cultural traditions such as female genital mutilation. Despite such challenges, or because of them, all the interviewees express firm dedication to serving as advocates for disability rights. "Every child has the right to go to school," Lawrence Mute, a blind Kenyan, asserts. One is struck not just by the obstacles the interviewees face, but also by their humanity, energy, and commitment to making the world a more just place for disabled Africans.

The videos are also notable for the way they give a direct voice to Black disabled people in the Global South, which does not happen often. While disabled people everywhere have dealt with barriers to making their views known, those in the Global South, who are usually people of color, have long been largely unheard, despite numbering more than half a billion people.[2] Like other socially and politically disempowered people in the Global South—one thinks of groups such as refugees, migrants, and orphans—they have often been voiceless in Gayatri Chakravorty Spivak's terms and anonymous in public discourse. As Nirmala Erevelles has pointed out, disabled people in the Global South are hidden from view in media in the North: "Third-world disabled people . . . face the social, political, and economic implications of being invisible," she says (*Disability* 133). Such invisibility underscores how disabled people and those close to them in the Global South have commonly been afterthoughts, deemed unimportant and disposable.

The disregard for disabled people in the Global South unfortunately has become even more pronounced during recent nativism in the United States, Great Britain, Germany, Italy, and other countries in the North. This nationalist wave is typically built on grievances against immigrants and refugees (usually of color) from other places. Even before the disastrous coronavirus pandemic, accompanying economic distress, and outcry for racial justice, U.S. President Donald Trump's "America First" slogan epitomized how his administration increasingly turned the country inward, embracing walls and immigration restrictions and discounting others. In 2020, his administration's heavy-handed response to largely peaceful protests for racial justice even drew a warning from the United Nations Human Rights Office (O'Grady).[3] Human rights around the world—the notion that all people deserve to live lives of dignity free of abuse—were not a priority.

Yet as is often the case when leaders pursue misguided policies, the humanities—and, specifically, literature in this case—offer an important if gentle corrective. Disabled people are definitely not invisible in prominent postcolonial literature in English, where they regularly have a compelling presence. *Elusive Kinship* takes on the proliferation of disabled characters in this fiction, a topic that is ripe for inquiry. It shows that since the mid-twentieth century, and especially since 1980, figures of disability occupy central places in work by celebrated authors such as Chinua Achebe, Salman Rushdie, J. M. Coetzee, Anita Desai, Jhumpa Lahiri, Edwidge Danticat, and others, and that such representations do important cultural work.

This study has several overlapping aims. I seek, first, to enhance our appreciation of key texts in the Anglophone postcolonial literature of the Global South by uncovering the myriad ways they gain energy, vitality, and metaphoric force from characters with extraordinary bodies or minds. At the same time, *Elusive Kinship* explores how this work confirms, challenges, or expands on existing theories of disability in literature developed in North America and Western Europe, nudging us toward a fuller understanding of disability worldwide. Moreover, I view this corpus through a human rights lens, showing how it depicts injustice with disabled characters and raises awareness of human rights. Finally, I argue that the works increasingly help to create connection and care for disabled people in readers' imaginations—what I call "kinship" in the title—that are a crucial first step to achieving meaningful disability human rights in the world, even if some fiction implicitly cautions that human rights alone are not enough for justice. As suggested by the titular "elusive," such connection is not direct or consistent, but it does seem to happen and deserves attention.

Because 80 percent of the world's disabled people live in so-called developing countries (Stein "Disability" 76), disability is much more common in the Global South than in the North (although, as Helen Meekosha and Jasbir Puar argue and I discuss below, the North has played a decisive role in creating disability in the South). So in one sense it is not surprising that disability often turns up in this literature. Yet authors are not just reflecting reality; they also deploy characters with exceptional bodies to advance a countless number of topics. From the one-legged woman associated with the Igbo clan's formidable war medicine in Achebe's *Things Fall Apart* (1958) to Coetzee's cognitively disabled Michael traversing a war-torn South Africa in *Life & Times of Michael K* (1983), from Saleem's incredible telepathic nose and cracking body in Rushdie's *Midnight's Children* (1981) to My Luck, the boy soldier who has had his vocal cords severed in Chris Abani's *Song for Night* (2007), from the beloved Haitian American sister's missing forearm in Danticat's story "Caroline's Wedding" (1996) to Animal, the exuberant boy in India who has a bent spine and goes around on all fours as a result of a chemical plant disaster in Indra Sinha's *Animal's People* (2007), notable Anglophone literature from Africa, Asia, and the Caribbean frequently depicts, and seems structured around, memorable characters with impairment.

Although these representations are quite varied and heterogeneous, collectively they make disabled people in the Global South more visible and significant. I should clarify that I am not suggesting that such depictions substitute for disabled people speaking for themselves. For starters, the authors are mostly nondisabled (as far as I know). Still, these representations, even magical realist ones, provide powerful witnessing. They allow the reading public to traverse seemingly vast distances (whether geographic, cultural, or chronological or related to differences in race, class, gender, or disability status) and connect with others through their imaginations, which leading human rights advocates have seen as important. As Samuel Moyn points out in his well-

TABLE I.1. CHRONOLOGY OF FICTION IN THIS STUDY AND MAJOR HUMAN RIGHTS INITIATIVES

Year	Major International UN Human Rights Declarations and Treaties	Fiction in This Book Published	UN Disability Events, Declarations, and Treaties
1948	Universal Declaration of Human Rights (UDHR) for "all human beings"		
1958		Chinua Achebe, *Things Fall Apart*	
1960	Declaration on the Granting of Independence to Colonial Countries and Peoples		
1965	Convention on the Elimination of All Forms of Racial Discrimination		
1971	Declaration on the Rights of Mentally Retarded Persons		Declaration on the Rights of Mentally Retarded Persons
1975	Declaration on the Rights of Disabled Persons		Declaration on the Rights of Disabled Persons
1979	Convention of the Elimination of All Forms of Discrimination against Women (CEDAW)		
1981		Salman Rushdie, *Midnight's Children*	International Year of Disabled Persons
1982			World Programme of Action Concerning Disabled Persons
1983		J. M. Coetzee, *Life & Times of Michael K*	
1983– 1992			Decade of Disabled Persons
1984	Convention against Torture and Other Cruel, Inhuman, or Degrading Treatment or Punishment		
1989	Convention on the Rights of the Child		
1990	Convention on Protection of the Rights of All Migrant Workers and Their Families		
1991			General recommendation 18 to the CEDAW asks nation-states to report on status of disabled women
1993			UN adopts Standard Rules on the Equalization of Opportunities for Persons with Disabilities

1994		Edwidge Danticat, *Breath, Eyes, Memory*	UN Committee on Economic, Social and Cultural Rights adopts General Comment on Persons with Disabilities
1995		Edwidge Danticat, "Caroline's Wedding"	
1999		J. M. Coetzee, *Disgrace*; Anita Desai, *Fasting, Feasting*; Jhumpa Lahiri, "The Treatment of Bibi Haldar"	
2004		Chris Abani, *GraceLand*	
2006	Convention on the Rights of Persons with Disabilities		Convention on the Rights of Persons with Disabilities
2007		Chris Abani, *Song for Night*; Indra Sinha, *Animal's People*	
2015		Petina Gappah, *The Book of Memory*	

regarded history of human rights, *The Last Utopia*, in the 1960s human rights activists recognized that a crucial initial step in the ascension of human rights in general was not laws or treaties but winning people's "*imagination*, first and foremost" (5, emphasis added). Imagination is, of course, a realm of fiction: by compelling readers to engage with physical, sensory, and cognitive difference in their minds, the literature of the Global South often directs attention to disability and makes it human, relatable, and exciting in ways that cold statistics do not. (For a chronology of when the fiction covered in this study was published vis-à-vis human rights initiatives, see Table I.1). By depicting an oppressed group that too often is left out of conversations about rights, such works have significant consequences not just for this corpus and narrative theory, and not just for global power dynamics and a host of other subjects, but also for the actual lived experience of disabled people in the Global South.

Theoretical Background

With this focus, *Elusive Kinship* seeks to bring together three dynamic interdisciplinary fields: postcolonial studies, studies of human rights and literature, and literary disability studies. While the former two have had important and rewarding exchanges, they have both largely bypassed disability. First, disability and postcolonial studies have developed largely independently over the past several decades. In disability studies, scholarly explorations of the roles of disability in Euro-American literature have flourished, emphasizing a nonpathological and liberatory approach.[4] But the prominence of disability in the Anglophone literature of the Global South has only recently begun to receive notice. Concurrently, while postcolonial scholars have made many incisive and valuable interventions in literature about oppressed people in former European colonies, they have not had much to say about disability. When they do comment on it, they have tended to focus on metaphoric meanings, choosing not to engage with the material presence of disability in the text or connections to actual disabled people (Hall *Literature* 50). In *Relocating Postcolonialism* (2002), Ato Quayson and David Theo Goldberg note that "the potential theoretical overlaps" between postcolonial studies and disability studies are "quite immense" and call for the two fields to work together. "It is necessary to pursue joint projects of agitation for justice that would embrace the disabled equally with the racially ordered, gendered, and postcolonial subject," they write, not only affirming disability studies scholars' contention that disability is an identity category that should be placed alongside race, class, and gender, but also adding postcolonial status to the mix (xvii). Both postcolonial theory and disability studies are about power; they concern populations that are oppressed and typically disenfranchised. Disabled people collectively remain one of the most vulnerable populations in the world. How does literature imaginatively begin to counteract the situation by giving disabled characters a more visible, consequential presence in the public imagination?

A few pioneering studies on disability in literature about the Global South have recently indicated how fertile this area is for inquiry. Quayson published *Aesthetic Nervousness* (2007), which explores disability in Coetzee's and Wole Soyinka's work alongside literature by prominent European and American authors. He contends that these literary treatments of disability from disparate places work on a multiplicity of levels, creating an anxiety not just between characters, but also between texts and readers, leading to what he calls a crisis of representation. In the first book-length study of the topic, *Postcolonial Fiction and Disability* (2011), Clare Barker contests the notion of a narrative crisis. She argues that portrayals of child disabled characters in literature from Zimbabwe, Nigeria, India, Pakistan, and Māori New Zealand serve as both metaphoric critiques of "dominant (post)colonial or national ideologies" and empathetic depictions of disabled experience (26). For his part, Michael Bérubé, in *The Secret Life of Stories* (2016), discusses intellectual disability as a narrative force in Coetzee's fiction alongside that of select Western writers and filmmakers. Journals have devoted special issues to the subject.[5] More broadly, disability scholars as varied as Michael Davidson, Nirmala Erevelles, Eunjung Kim, Shaun Grech, Julie Avril Minich, and Jasbir Puar have advanced disability theory on a transnational level in recent years, while anthropologists such as Benedicte Ingstad and Susan Reynolds Whyte have published on disability in local and global contexts.[6]

Alongside such developments, the project contributes to a third nascent field: studies of human rights and literature. Inaugurated by such scholars as Joseph Slaughter, James Dawes, and Elizabeth Anker, this field emerged around 2007 and has grown since then, calling attention to the relationship of literature to rights abuses around the world, although it, too, has had little to say about disabled people to date.[7] Slaughter points out that, through its emphasis on the individual in society, fiction (and in his case especially the bildungsroman, or coming-of-age novel) and human rights are mutually reinforcing ideological constructs that work toward the same ends, addressing individuals' relationship to their societies. Scholars in the field use human rights as an analytic lens with literary works, contending that fictional works can forcefully reveal and testify to rights issues. As Pramod Nayar puts it, "Literature . . . offers a key route into the very idea of the human and insights into those excluded from this idea" (v)—illumination that, he maintains, legal discourse and political commentary alone do not adequately provide. He cites a range of commentators who agree.

Yet while acknowledging the value of bringing literary studies and human rights together, critics have pointed out that doing so is not easy or straightforward, especially because of the contradictory nature of human rights. Dawes and others have pointed to paradoxes underlying rights or how they are problematic or even complicit with global power structures and corruption. Although human rights as promulgated by the United Nations strive to be universal, pertaining to all people wherever they are, a fundamental contradiction is that those rights depend on nation-states for enforcement, and those nation-states may themselves be human rights violators. Moreover, Michael Freeman acknowledges the fear some people have that the promotion of human rights as universal might lead to the hegemony of dominant world powers (121). Some have associated rights with neocolonialism or global capitalism, another component of the current world order that often leaves people behind.

Reading literature carefully can make these difficult contradictions clearer and allow us to explore them. For his part, Dawes has pointed out that, to address human rights violations, we need to tell stories about them to make them known, but such stories raise vexing questions about how to narrate the unspeakable, who has the authority to write them, and the danger of retraumatizing survivors by telling their stories. In addition, according to Elizabeth

Swanson Goldberg and Alexandra Schultheis Moore, scholarship in the field is characterized by an "aura of contestation," as well as by "a deep desire for social justice" (1). Though typically critics have taken on literature depicting gross violations such as torture, genocide, and violence to probe the relationship between narrative and human rights, Nick Mansfield points out that even fictional representation of the seemingly everyday can have significance in this area. "Literature's most valuable contribution to human rights discourse comes . . . from domains where rights may not be mentioned or even recognized as an issue," Mansfield says, an observation that applies to this study as most of the works it discusses do not explicitly refer to rights (213).

The field's goal of social justice and dignity for all people clearly converges with the aims of both disability studies and postcolonial studies, yet so far disability has been mostly overlooked by scholars working in human rights and literature. A few recent exceptions exist. Crystal Parikh gestures toward disability in her discussion of wellness toward the end of *Writing Human Rights* (2017); Moore brings it into "'Disaster Capitalism' and Human Rights," her chapter on Sinha's *Animal's People*; and the *Journal of Literary & Cultural Disability Studies* had a special issue on disability and human rights in 2017 (Greco and Di Giovanni), publications that hint at what a deserving and rewarding area of inquiry this can be.

Methodology and Argument

Building on such groundbreaking work, *Elusive Kinship* puts these three fields into conversation with one another. After exploring the idea of connection between readers and characters more in the next chapter, I proceed in largely chronological fashion, starting with Achebe's *Things Fall Apart* at the mid-twentieth century and working into twenty-first-century literature, the better to show how these literary depictions evolved and their striking relation to emerging international disability human rights instruments during the same period. Instead of trying to cover all disability aspects in each work, I focus on those features that seem especially prominent and significant.

These provocative representations add unruly energy and meaning to their stories in ways reminiscent of David Mitchell and Sharon Snyder's influential theory of narrative prosthesis. They trenchantly show how Euro-American literature often depends on disability as a device to inaugurate and move narratives forward. As Mitchell and Snyder put it, disability frequently appears as an "interruptive force" and adds "disruptive punch" to texts, phrases that certainly describe depictions of disability in the literature of the Global South in English too (*Narrative Prosthesis* 48–49). According to the theory of narrative prosthesis, typically disability is removed at the end of Euro-American narratives, ultimately shoring up some notion of normalcy elsewhere, a removal, as I show, that we can sometimes find in narratives of the Global South. However, Mitchell and Snyder have refined the theory over the years. In *The Biopolitics of Disability* (2015), they state that, if modernity sought to eradicate impairments, the postmodern neoliberal age stresses *"exceptionality,"* where disabled bodies are made into sites of *"cultural rehabilitation,"* profitability, and normativization (205). Some literary disability scholars have critiqued this analysis extensively, and we could add in depictions in postcolonial literature here. Although in works from the Global South disabled characters certainly are exceptional, they are almost never rehabilitated; in fact, Saleem Sinai in *Midnight's Children* depicts medical intervention as damaging and Animal in *Animal's People* explicitly rejects medical treatment at the end. Especially since 1990, disability in this literature is often not eliminated or rehabilitated. It just remains at the conclusion, which seems to add another twist to Mitchell and Snyder's theory.

Along these lines, I also strive to examine how such representations relate to existing theories of disability in literature that were developed in North America and Europe. As scholars have pointed out, Euro-American understandings of such concepts as autonomy, normalcy, and minority identity cannot simply be exported and applied to locations in the Global South that have distinct cultures and histories. Pushpa Naidu Parekh, for instance, calls for theoretical "re-visioning" in global contexts to analyze "historical and cultural-specific meanings of disability" (150). Added to this need is the complication that cultures usually contain more than one view of disability, which may well show up in fiction. Due to the accelerated forms of human movement and contact associated with globalization and migration since World War II, not to mention the current era of social media and technological connectivity, attitudes in any given culture toward disability are not necessarily uniform but may be intermixed and in dialogue with one another. To make matters even more complicated, almost all of the authors under consideration here could be called transnational, with experience living in both the South and the North. Accordingly, I try to practice the kind of "situated critical reading practices" that Clare Barker and Stuart Murray advocate, which attend as far as possible to the nuances of specific local situations (228). In the process, I endeavor to place each work in its historical context. Well aware of the Euro-American tendency to display cultural arrogance in such matters, I do not pretend such a task is an easy enterprise, but I do think it is an important one. Mindful of what Jean and John L. Comaroff call the "polymorphous, mutating ensemble of signs and practices" of modernity in Africa and, by extension, throughout the Global South, I take the rich, inventive literature itself as my main guide (7).

Finally, *Elusive Kinship* argues that dynamic postcolonial literature often helps to create the imaginative connection required to implement meaningful human rights and justice for disabled people. Instead of just producing a victims' literature of passive suffering or outrage, authors occasionally use figures of disability to create something innovative and surprising, something that, while testifying to the agonizing harms initiated by colonialism and global capitalism, or destructive abuses originating in the home nation-state, indicates disabled people's worth and humanity. Again, not all such literature conveys this value: depictions vary widely and are multifarious and even contradictory. Nonetheless, some influential instances affirming the value and dignity of disabled people exist. Moreover, this literature sometimes offers a meaningful bond between reader and disabled character. As I discuss more in the next chapter, such works subtly uphold compassion, connection, and mutual dependence in the face of vulnerability and oppression, which coincides with the arguments for global disability rights and for the capabilities that, Martha Nussbaum asserts in *Frontiers of Justice* (2006), all people deserve, whether they can reciprocate or not.

In making this argument, I might seem to follow a view articulated by scholars such as Lynn Hunt that links the evolution of the novel with the evolution of human rights by stressing literature's capacity to promote sentiment and humanitarian feeling. However, such sympathy historically has not extended to disabled people. Elizabeth Anker points out that Enlightenment-based liberalism often imagines a person with rights as invariably possessing a body that is "whole, autonomous, and self-enclosed" (*Fictions* 3).[8] Euro-American canonical literature, especially in the eighteenth and nineteenth centuries, generally reflects this attitude. As disability studies scholars such as Lennard J. Davis and Mitchell and Snyder have shown, it typically has marginalized disability while upholding notions of normalcy. Contemporary postcolonial literature in English adds to its vitality by emphasizing disabled people's experiences and often making them central to postcolonial existence. By pointing this out, *Elusive Kinship* seeks to bring disability more forcefully to the critical conversation on the relationship between human rights and literature.

The Move to Global Disability Rights

The situation of disabled people in the Global South is a real issue. They are among the world's most disenfranchised citizens. In *Disability and Poverty:*

A Global Challenge, Arne H. Eide and Benedicte Ingstad emphasize what scholars have long recognized as the "vicious circle" that often connects disability and indigence, in which disability leads to poverty and poverty leads to disability, reinforcing each other (1). While most nations of the Global South are disproportionately poorer than their counterparts in the North, their disabled citizens typically endure "poverty within poverty": they have limited access to health care and housing and are among the first to perish from food shortages, natural disasters, and other emergencies (3). Persistent problems include not just widespread hardship, but also the fact that disabled people everywhere are often perceived as useless and unable to reciprocate adequately for benefits they may receive. In the Global South they have much less access to education, employment, and social activities. A very low percentage of disabled children in these areas receive schooling at all (Stein "Disability" 76). Disabled women and girls are especially vulnerable. While reliable statistics can be hard to come by, some researchers estimate that literacy rates for women with disabilities globally may be as low as 1 percent; moreover, disabled women are more often the victims of violence (including rape and domestic abuse) (UN "Women"). Contextual conditions beyond people's control shape these distressing circumstances, including the destructive legacies of colonialism, war and internecine conflict, and prevailing neoliberal ideologies that favor free-market transnational corporate practices and in effect perpetuate an enormous gap between very rich and extremely poor people.[9] The novel coronavirus pandemic that is currently unfolding will almost certainly add to this precarity, creating millions more disabled people in poverty, for again disabled people are typically among the first victims of disasters.

The encouraging news is that disability is finally on the world's agenda, a transformation that, *Elusive Kinship* argues, Anglophone postcolonial literature helped to bring about. Since the 1970s, the United Nations has gradually undertaken a series of increasingly forceful initiatives aimed at improving the situation of disabled people across the globe (see Table I.1). Such efforts culminated in the United Nations' landmark Convention on the Rights of Persons with Disabilities (CRPD), adopted in 2006 and ratified in 2008, which has sought to ensure the worth of disabled people everywhere. The CRPD's guiding principles include respecting the dignity of disabled people, nondiscrimination, access, and effective participation and full inclusion in society (UN "Guiding"). Unlike most other United Nations human rights treaties, with the CRPD, the stakeholders—disabled people—were directly involved in negotiations, in keeping with the international disability rights slogan "Nothing About Us Without Us."[10] Although most of these disabled participants did come from the North in the period leading up to the convention, probably because of travel costs (Stein "China" 16), communities organized on a global scale using social media and other virtual technologies, showing worldwide engagement (Meekosha 679). The CRPD helped unite the global disability community. As of 2020, the CRPD had been ratified by 182 nations (out of 195), showing broad international support.[11] To many disabled people, the ratification of the CRPD meant that they were finally recognized and acknowledged to have rights, too. Some activists feel empowered. The South African deaf leaders Bruno Druchen and Wilma Newboudt-Druchen optimistically call the CRPD "a potent new weapon in the fight for access" (Cooper and Rashid xi). As I investigate in the final chapter, real limitations have emerged, and disabled people in the Global South often still live lives of grievous precarity. But the dynamic literature of the Global South has made an important and often overlooked contribution to a change in how disabled people are perceived worldwide, from shameful objects of pity to fellow human beings with rights.

On "the Global South," "Disability," and "Human Rights"

Before proceeding, I should pause to explain exactly what I mean by "the Global South," "disability," and "human rights," keywords that are both indispensable to this study and frequently questioned. The first two terms cover enormously diverse groups of people and contain many ambiguities, while the third, while hopeful, is surrounded by contradiction and controversy.

"The Global South"

The phrase "Global South" has become increasingly widespread as a quick way to refer to poor nations of the world, replacing earlier terminology such as "third world" and "developing" countries. The idea of a Global South goes back at least to the mid-twentieth century but gained notice especially in the early 1980s with the publication of the Brandt Report, which called attention to the stark disparities in wealth and standards of living between the world's Northern and Southern hemispheres.[12] It points to drastic inequalities in economic development, industrialization, use of technology, stability of government, and military power. Historically, colonizing nations were usually in the North, and colonized countries were in the South, which often has left a legacy in the South of poverty, exploitation, and economic dependence.

Because the term "Global South" expresses such inequities, some scholars have found the concept empowering and to have advantageous value in resisting hegemonic forces (Hollington et al.).

Yet, as commentators have pointed out, the term "Global South" is a simplistic, reductive way to describe the stunning variety of humanity in these areas. (At the same time, we should note that the Global North, too, is quite heterogeneous, and that nations in the North have sometimes taken contrary positions.) The term "Global South" elides the fact that wealthy groups and nations exist in the South (in places such as China and Argentina), and numbers of disenfranchised people, including ethnic minorities, refugees, and immigrant communities, live in the North. Moreover, it can obscure the traumatic history of colonialism, not to mention the increasing interdependence and global forces that bind the North and South together. Jean and John L. Comaroff find the label "inherently slippery, inchoate, unfixed," with "complex connotations" (45). They argue that from the beginning, modernity was a North-South collaboration (think especially of how the North and South were linked and mutually changed through colonialism). They also argue that, since the South is often the first to feel the effects of global historical forces, it can serve as a harbinger of the North's future; this could be said, for example, with regard to climate change. Thus, the Global South has much to teach those of us in the North. The term "Global South" often does not convey this nuance and value.

Still, better nomenclature is elusive. While acknowledging the need to attend to the rich meaningfulness of the South, I have found the term a useful rubric for this study. At times I use "Global South" elastically to refer to diasporic and migrant communities who may be living in the North, allowing me to discuss, for example, Danticat's depiction of immigrants from Haiti in the United States. I also refer to postcolonialism to discuss the harmful effects of colonialism and its afterlives, which are so important in this literature. Perhaps at times Immanuel Wallerstein's terms "core," "periphery," and "semi-periphery" to describe the world system can be helpful, but they give central importance to Europe and North America and seem to make it harder to posit a full and sufficient self in the "peripheral" other parts of the globe, which runs against the thrust of much great postcolonial fiction.[13] The phrase "the Global South" may serve as a more neutral space for these populations to exist on their own terms, even as we acknowledge enormous differences between them and the continuing impact of the North in a profoundly interconnected world. Rather than trying to define it, I employ the phrase as a concept and resource in this study.

"Disability"

For its part, as scholars in disability studies know (and they may want to skip over this section), the term "disability" has a complex etymology, and its meanings have been "shifting . . . and sometimes contradictory" (Adams et al. 5). "Disability" has been in the English language since at least the sixteenth century, yet what counts as a disability has changed over time. Moreover, the definition of "disability" has varied from place to place.[14] Michael Ashley Stein, who participated in the drafting of the CRPD in the early twenty-first century, recalls a "wide divergence in self-reported prevalence rates of disability amongst" nations, including wild variations "from less than one percent in Kenya to twenty percent in New Zealand, even as the World Health Organization utilized a baseline assumption of ten percent and the World Bank estimated ten to twelve percent" ("China" 15). Such fluctuation points to the fact that disability, like all human variation, is a social construct. Its significance can vary tremendously across cultures. Notions of disability are further complicated by its inherent instability. Anyone can become disabled at any moment, making it more porous and fluid than most other identity categories. "Disability" became the preferred term globally during the twentieth century, but because the category is now so capacious, it has a certain ambiguity: it covers an extensive range of conditions that may be physical, sensory, or cognitive; temporary or permanent; and visible or invisible.

Along with such slipperiness, in the past "disability" has almost always been fraught with negativity, which has sometimes led people perceived to be disabled to distance themselves from the label. As Erving Goffman explains in his classic *Stigma* (1963), disability has so often been stigmatized socially that people with an impairment have gone to lengths to hide it from view or at least minimize its presence. In addition, the word "disability" has frequently been used figuratively (and, many disability studies scholars would aver, almost unthinkingly) in a range of contexts to signal disadvantage or disqualification. No surprise, then, that people broadly perceived as disabled—such as some deaf people who use sign language or dwarfs—have rejected the moniker.[15] Paradoxically, as Alison Kafer and others have shown, "disability" thus encompasses people who may not themselves identify with the term or agree on a shared definition. Many people with disabilities do not want a cure, while others do. Moreover, until the second half of the twentieth century, they typically did not see themselves as part of a coherent group.

The rise of the disability rights movement in the United States and United Kingdom in the late 1960s—which largely coincides with the period under consideration in *Elusive Kinship*—began to challenge these dynamics as activists expressed a unified disability identity and even disability pride. By turning attention from the individual body to ways that societies marginalize disabled people, discriminate against them, and deny them dignity, they helped to create a viable identity among those with widely varying bodily conditions.[16] They also fostered self-respect among disabled people. As they staged sit-ins and demonstrations, consciously following the Civil Rights Movement, protestors displayed both impatience with social oppression and a liberating collective sense of empowerment.

In the late twentieth century, scholars in the emerging academic field of disability studies joined the struggle, picking up on these galvanizing tenets of the disability rights movement and carrying disability as an illuminating category into a range of disciplines. Like activists, they emphasized a unified, inclusive disability identity, as well as the social barriers that prevent disabled people from flourishing.[17] Like activists, they fought against notions of disability as shameful. With the title of her manifesto for the field, *Claiming Disability: Knowledge and Identity* (1998), Simi Linton recast the disability label as something to be embraced, not disavowed. A growing number of critics employ the affectionately defiant word "crip" (popularized by Robert McRuer and others) to resist ableism, much as "queer" had become a revolutionary word of pride in queer theory.[18] In addition, disability theorists stressed that disability is an important part of being human. Because anyone can become disabled at any time, and just about everyone knows a disabled person, it is relevant to every person.

Together, these varied efforts have had a transformative effect on the meanings of disability in ways that have rippled across the globe. First, they have associated disability with rights, as mentioned above. In the United States, activism helped lead to the successful passage of the Americans with Disabilities Act (ADA) of 1990, which ensured equal rights to disabled citizens. On a global scale, as discussed above, efforts helped to produce the landmark UN Convention on the Rights of Persons with Disabilities (CRPD), ratified in 2008, the first human rights treaty of the twenty-first century. While traditional negative ways of thinking about disability unquestionably persist in all parts of the world, such conventions and laws helped disabled people to be perceived as a disenfranchised group with rights.

Along the way, activists and scholars sparked recognition that disability is a product of the environment as much as of the individual body. While early efforts first emphasized the overlooked social, nonmedical aspects of disability, more recently, disability theorists including Tom Shakespeare and Tobin

Siebers have called for a more nuanced approach that includes both social and biological factors. Siebers terms this linkage "complex embodiment" (25); others, such as Davis and David Morris in their essay in *The End of Normal* (2013), have referred to it as a "biocultural" notion of disability. Notably, both the ADA and the CRPD include social factors in their definition of "disability." The CRPD, for instance, states in its preamble that "disability is an evolving concept," and "disability results from the interaction between persons with impairments and attitudinal and environmental barriers that hinders their full and effective participation in society on an equal basis with others." By acknowledging the pivotal role of social forces, this definition creates space for variation in cultural meanings and goes well beyond the classic definition of 1547, which limited disability to the body. Today the meanings of "disability" are so manifold and flexible that some scholars maintain a simple explanation is not possible.

With "debility" in *The Right to Maim* (2017), Jasbir Puar adds a compelling new element. She explains the term as "a needed disruption" to triangulate the ability-disability binary and convey "the slow wearing down of populations," which include vast numbers of people who are not commonly seen as disabled, but are not able-bodied, either (xiv–xv). Using a provocative intersectional approach, Puar argues that debility is a common feature of neoliberal capitalism, and that Black and Brown bodies, especially, become disabled or debilitated so capitalist entities can extract value "from populations that would otherwise be disposable" (xviii). Saying that disability and debility often overlap and distinctions are not clear, Puar dramatically expands the scope of disability studies and provides a useful way to approach some of the representations of disability in the Global South that we will see. While her arguments are insightful and provocative, one significant reservation is that she consistently treats disability as something negative, which, unfortunately, reinforces the widespread ableist bias that disability studies scholars in the North have worked so hard to resist.[19] In her understandable focus on preventing debilitation, she seems to miss how productive and valuable disabled identities can be, how they are part of the spectrum of human difference in every society. In any case, as with "the Global South," I seek not to define "disability" as a firm category but, rather, to explore it as a concept.

"Human Rights"

Aided by globalization, the late twentieth and early twenty-first centuries have been called the era of international human rights. Such human rights are now, as Michael Ignatieff put it in 2001, "the lingua franca of global moral thought" (53), or in Samuel Moyn's words, "the last utopia," the remaining site of hope for dignity and justice for all people across the world, although controversy about rights persists. Of course, concern for the dignity and well-being of other people goes back to ancient times.[20] The idea of state-sanctioned rights dates back at least to the eighteenth century, but such Enlightenment-based ideas hinge on the right of a group of people to be members of a sovereign state that in turn protects them. The notion of *human* rights, in contrast, springs from the concept of an international covenant that rejects violence, oppression, and other abuses of people that occur inside a sovereign state (Ganguly 11). Human rights appeared on the world stage in 1948, with the United Nation's Universal Declaration of Human Rights, which were for "all human beings," that year; subsequently, the United Nations produced more specific conventions to eliminate racism and discrimination against women, to protect the rights of children and migrant workers, and the like. According to Moyn, the international rights movement did not really become a global force until the late 1970s, when other widespread emancipatory ideologies, including communism and postcolonial nationalism, increasingly appeared unsuccessful. The literary works I discuss were published at a time when the world increasingly directed its attention to protecting people from torture, genocide, oppression, economic disenfranchisement, and other violations of human dignity.

Human rights conventions have sometimes been met with suspicion and criticism, not least because they are occasionally perceived as vehicles for imposing Euro-American values worldwide, complicit with the imperial and neoliberal forces that cause poverty and suffering in the first place. With regard to people with disabilities, Puar is critical of rights discourses, maintaining that they privilege some disabled people while ignoring many others; as she trenchantly points out, rights rely on the same global systems (neoliberalism, imperialism) that sanction the debilitation of others (such as people who are affected by war or terrible labor situations). Puar's criticisms are important, given the way whole populations are now treated as second rate, and pair well with Moyn's recent work arguing that rights by themselves are insufficient in a neoliberal age. I explore the limitations of human rights in more detail using twenty-first-century literature in the final chapter. In the Epilogue, I briefly consider some possible ways forward.

To figure out how best to proceed, we need first to understand the momentous changes with regard to thinking about disability since the emergence of human rights. One essential component of that remaining labor is the need for scholars to pay more attention to disability issues in the Global South and, when necessary, reformulate theory developed in the North. I hope that *Elusive Kinship* will help with that project by exploring how, since World War II and especially since 1980, the vibrant fiction of the Global South in English both subtly shaped and reflected the international turn in how disabled people are seen.

Obstacles

Given such complexities, writing about disability rights in the Global South presents challenges that help to explain why the figures of disability in Anglophone postcolonial literature have not received more academic notice. Scholars in postcolonial studies may feel disability is uninteresting compared with many other pressing issues, while those in literary disability studies located in the North often confront the difficulty of literature describing circumstances that are dauntingly different, arising from places where theories and methodologies developed in North America and Europe may not apply.

Challenge 1: Global Income Inequality

In approaching the issue, a few disability theorists have insisted that one must start at the macro-level with the pivotal economic inequality between North and South. For example, Michael Davidson argues that scholars working on disability in global contexts should first consider "the unequal distribution of wealth" (*Concerto* 172), while Meekosha states that "a southern theory of disability and human rights must inevitably question international inequities" (678). Such matters are not a new concern. For more than half a century, social justice advocates, from Moses Moskowitz in 1968 to Nussbaum in 2006 and beyond, have been decrying the stunning inequality dividing the planet's populations. The gap between countries' wealth has been increasing inexorably over the past two hundred years and shows no sign of slowing or narrowing. In 2000, Americans were nine times richer than Latin Americans, seventy-two times richer than Sub-Saharan Africans, and no less than eighty times richer than South Asians (Hickel). The anti-poverty charity Oxfam reported in 2016 that the richest sixty-two people in the world had as much wealth as the entire bottom half of the human population, or 3.6 billion people ("Richest"). Ironically, alongside such wealth disparity are some hopeful signs. According to one report, the rate of global extreme poverty shrank by almost half between 2010 and 2019, with the rate declining from 15.7 percent to 7.7 percent (Lawler). China and India were primary drivers of this good news, although nations as varied as Cambodia and Ethiopia also saw success ("Millions"). Such figures give optimism that the United Nations can achieve its ambitious goal to "end poverty in all its forms everywhere" (UN "Sustainable"). Still, the current COVID-19 pandemic endangers decades of growth, with low-income countries and those dependent on tourist money at particular risk, and the global inequality crisis threatens many vulnerable populations and requires more attention.

The North actively contributed to this troubling economic divide. While globalization promises to lift more people from poverty and ensure greater access to health care, critics point out that global capitalist free-market policies frequently actually foster inequality. Before around 1960, European powers conquered or controlled lands in the Global South through colonialism; extracted natural resources to enrich themselves; and often produced violent conflict, corrupt leaders, and dependence. Colonialism also smoothed the way for the more recent rise of neoliberal free-market globalization. Wealthy nations have formed, in Nussbaum's words, "a powerful global economy [that] makes all economic choices interdependent and often imposes on poorer nations conditions that reinforce and deepen existing inequalities" (*Frontiers* 19). Money still flows from the poorest to the richest countries. From transnational corporations to the debt system, free-trade agreements, and tax havens for the wealthy, a neoliberal world system of capitalism, supported by nations in the North, shapes the immense international disparity in wealth.[21] Such causes are together so pervasive and enormous that they can be difficult to perceive clearly, but their effects are readily apparent to anyone who makes even a cursory inquiry.

Challenge 2: The North Causing Disability in the South

As Puar and other critics have shown, just as the North has contributed to the impoverishment of the Global South with its economic policies, so it has produced more people with disabilities there. Even leaving aside the common adverse side effects of poverty, such as malnutrition and lack of access to health care, one does not have to look far to see actions that have increased the number of disabled people. Most wars since World War II have occurred in poor countries, producing many more people with mobility, sensory, or cognitive impairments. Davidson reports that there are more than 110 million land mines in sixty-four countries, including 1.5 mines per person in Angola (where 120 people per month become amputees) and one mine for every two people in Afghanistan (*Concerto* 170–171). In addition, Meekosha notes that the United States and United Kingdom are leading suppliers in the international arms trade (with China and Russia also becoming influential players), selling arms, which presumably are used to cause more disabilities, to poor nations around the world. She also mentions unsafe factories and sweatshops, the export of pollution to the South, and the testing of nuclear weapons as other examples of ways that "impairment in the Global South is often the result of the *continued* dependency on the northern metropole" (677). Accompanying all of these factors is the very real psychological trauma, a cognitive disability, that accompanies violent conflict (including ethnic strife, torture, and rape), poverty, and hunger. Because people in the Global South affected by such actions are typically anonymous in media, they often have been marginalized, deemed unimportant in world affairs.

Challenge 3: Balancing the Biological and the Social

Therein lies a fundamental challenge for scholars in disability studies, one that helps to explain the field's relative dearth of work on disability in global contexts. As noted above, scholars in the North, like disability rights activists, thus far have focused on moving beyond the medical model (which positions disability as an individual biological problem on the body in need of a cure) to emphasize social barriers and advance the positives of a disability identity. In the process, they have vividly shown the dreadful history of eugenics in the late nineteenth and early twentieth centuries in North America and Europe, which featured forced sterilizations of thousands of disabled people and led to the horrific Nazi campaign (what the Nazis called their T4 Program) that murdered about 200,000 physically and cognitively impaired people in Europe during World War II. Given this appalling history, as well as the continued dominance of ableist ideology, scholars in the field understandably have been loath to return to the medical model. They have avoided discussing topics such as contemporary causes or prevention of disability, except in current bioethical discussions, such as those on prenatal and genetic testing. Similarly, founding work in disability studies does not acknowledge trauma and loss, as James Berger has pointed out. Despite many theorists' move around 2006 to embrace the notion that disability arises from both biological and environmental factors, most disability scholars still resist discussing biological specifics out of apprehension of allowing society to return to the narrow medical paradigm that has been so pervasive, preferring to focus on challenging ableism and affirming disabled identity instead.

Many disability scholars continue to subscribe passionately to this approach, with good reason, yet several critics have recently explored this issue in thoughtful ways that engage with the complexity of disabled people's lives. Siebers acknowledges that disability has both positive and negative connotations in the field; disabled people may be comfortable with who they are but not want to acquire additional disabilities, for example. Still, he avers that "the central purpose of disability studies is to reverse the negative connotations of disability" and adds that "this pursuit tends to involve disability as an identity category rather than as a physical or mental characteristic" (4). Even as he acknowledges the presence of biological factors, Siebers places primacy on social matters such as combating negative connotations of disability and forming a shared identity. Noting the advantages of claiming disability, he says that people who identify positively rather than negatively with their disabled status tend to lead more productive and happier lives. Similarly, Alison Kafer, while acknowledging her own lack of desire to acquire further disability, nonetheless argues against the popular outlook that disability is the sign of not having a good future and for a political view of disability that embraces rights and justice.

Applying such complexities to the Global South, one wonders whether a collective identity is feasible anytime soon for disabled people there, who frequently live in dire circumstances. Forming a larger identity requires a community with similar people and a positive sense of self. Is this collective sense of self-worth available to disabled people across the Global South who frequently endure stigma and lack of access to such basics as protection, education, and employment? As psychologists and sociologists have repeatedly shown, widespread oppression is easily internalized. In Chapter 2, I explore how Okonkwo in *Things Fall Apart* displays some of the grievous results of such internalization. Disabled solidarity around international initiatives such as the CRPD offers grounds for optimism, as do the African Youth with Disabilities Network and disabled people's own local organizations, interest groups, and agitation in the Global South.[22] My recent experience in Sub-Saharan Africa gives me hope, as well.[23] The potential for empowerment exists. Yet the present vocabulary in Euro-American disability studies makes it difficult for the field fully to acknowledge and condemn terrible causes of disability such as war and poverty or the mass trauma that frequently accompanies disabilities and debilities acquired from such dreadful circumstances—causes that frequently appear in my literary archive. "There is a productive tension," Puar accurately points out, "between embracing disability as a universal . . . and combating the production of disability acquired under the duress of oppressive structures" (*Right* 70). Given this tension, existing theory of the North often appears conceptually inadequate with regard to a full analysis of disability in the Global South.

In view of such obstacles, a few scholars have proposed supplementary terms or called for new approaches. Anthropologists and others in the social sciences have offered "social suffering" to describe not personal tragedy but, rather, hardship that comes about because of unjust economic, political, cultural, or other social forces. Scholars such as Eide and Ingstad find the concept useful as a reminder that the difficulty experienced by disabled people in the Global South is not primarily their responsibility (10). Another possibility is Puar's "debility," a notion that I employ especially in the final chapter. With both "social suffering" and "debility," users insightfully seek to direct attention to the unique social circumstances and politics surrounding disability. Others have urged a change in disability studies' theoretical paradigm in ways that may be both productive and controversial. For example, scholars such as Quayson, Barker, and Murray have urged attention to trauma and loss in global environments; Davidson has called for more "fruitful alliances" with nongovernmental organizations (NGOs), political action campaigns, and local community organizations advocating for disability rights (*Concerto* 195); and Meekosha argues that the field must "make a stand against suffering" and advocates considering prevention and joining forces with peace movements as ways forward (679). Such calls make sense, but how scholars can fulfill them without endangering hard-won gains against ableism in the North remains an open question. Acknowledging the presence of trauma in the lives of disabled people would seem to open the way once again for constraining disability as negative and inferior, conflicting with much work for disability empowerment and, indeed, the whole thrust of the disability rights movement to direct attention to problems of social attitudes and barriers. What is clear is a consensus that disability theory needs to expand and shift if it is to engage meaningfully with global disability. Puar offers one invigorating example of how this might be done, even if her mindset seems to resist disability pride. *Elusive Kinship* seeks to advance such engagement.

Challenge 4: Powerful Local Beliefs That Position Disability as Evil

A concomitant impediment confronting scholars who want to take on disability in the Global South concerns the presence of powerful local spiritual beliefs that can cause discrimination or worse against disabled people. Such ideologies are, of course, not limited to the Global South; disability theorists sometimes refer to a moral model of disability that refers to how societies all over the world have periodically interpreted disability as evil, a curse, or punishment for sin. While the moral model has receded in the North as other models, including the medical, social, and biocultural, have ascended during the modern period, such thinking still dominates in some regions of the South. Anita Ghai, for example, refers to a "common perception" in India that "views disability as a retribution for past karmas (actions) from which there can be no reprieve" (89). While many people in India may understand disability as a divine curse for past offenses, the Songye of Zaire perceive albino children as "not even human beings" who are "in contact with the anti-world of sorcerers" (Devlieger 96). In Ethiopia, villagers may simply expel disabled people. Ingstad has argued persuasively that social circumstances such as poverty often shape such attitudes (Eide and Ingstad 137). When disability means that people will be economic liabilities, that they cannot gain an education or job, it becomes an ever more stigmatized burden in societies that have scarce resources. Such matters provide tricky terrain for critics. I do not wish to be part of Northern interventions in the Global South that trample on indigenous forms of knowledge in the name of rationality and liberty, as Shaun Grech and others have cautioned (Goodley 38). Yet such matters also cannot simply be bypassed by anyone seriously interested in justice for disabled people.

Literature plays a significant role in mediating such formidable questions. The engrossing postcolonial Anglophone fiction of the Global South helps to make these issues vivid and recognizable; indeed, even works not "about" disability derive force from their depiction of them. Like all artists, these authors both reflect and critique their cultures. By reading attentively we can discern how influential literary works, which vary tremendously in form, style, and content, negotiate such factors; posit meaning; and sometimes invite recognition, compassion, and understanding. Along the way, I seek to show anew the value of reading fiction attentively, which some may find anachronistic in our increasingly fast-paced media age.

Scope of Project and Questions of Gender, the Human, and Language

In exploring these matters, I turn to a literary archive that includes works by Nobel Prize winners (J. M. Coetzee), by Booker Prize recipients (Salman Rushdie, Coetzee) and finalists (Anita Desai, Indra Sinha), and by canonical authors of the twentieth century (Chinua Achebe), as well as by some recent acclaimed contemporary writers (Jhumpa Lahiri, Edwidge Danticat, Chris Abani, and Petina Gappah) who together have sold millions of books and prominently feature disability in their work.[24] All of these writers have found international fame and audiences far beyond the borders of their native

countries, and rather than replicating colonial attitudes and racial formations, they often contest them, adding to these works' distinctive energy and
relevance. In the classroom, students respond well to this fiction, which often
provokes useful, fascinating discussions. The selections are not meant to be
exclusive or definitive. Instead, I am trying to advance a critical conversation
by considering works that seem to me especially valuable and illuminating.

The study proceeds chronologically, the better to show how the appearance of disabled characters in this literature relates to the emergence of disability human rights instruments, which leads to an unfortunate gap in the
gender of authors. I first deal with prominent, even emblematic cases (Achebe,
Rushdie, and Coetzee) who happen all to be male, before turning to women
(Desai, Lahiri, and Danticat) who published in the 1990s. For evidence of
male authors being more canonical early on, see Figure I.1.[25] The early male
authors (Rushdie and Achebe in particular) have received far more notice—in
books published in the United States, anyway.

Elleke Boehmer has called attention to variables such as double colonization of women and the marketing and publishing industries to explain
why early postcolonial female writers seem less known internationally than
their male counterparts (*Stories*).[26] Now, with the rise of Tsitsi Dangarembga,
Arundhati Roy, Chimamanda Adichie, and many more, postcolonial female
writers in English have a prominent global presence. In the final chapter, I

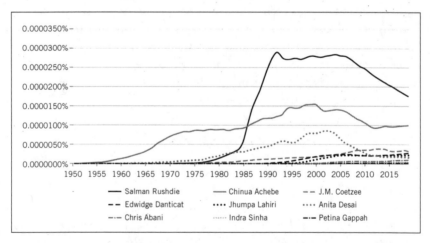

Graph from the Google Ngram Viewer (https://books.google.com/ngrams) showing
the frequency that names of the authors in this study appear in books published
between 1950 and 2019 that have been scanned by Google. The books are written
in English and published in the United States, so the graph does not give a
comprehensive, worldwide picture. Nevertheless, it offers an illuminating view.

look at both male and female authors (Abani, Gappah, and Sinha) who have published in the early twenty-first century around the time the CRPD was ratified.

Some exciting recent scholarship in both disability studies and postcolonial ecocriticism has questioned the primacy of the category of human, especially since people have rampantly harmed the environment and non-human animals.[27] But my archive here, especially after 1981, often works to demonstrate the interiority and humanity of its disabled characters, a crucial part of achieving disability justice. Claiming humanity has been a central part of disability activism, as it has been for other devalued and marginalized groups of people (including racial minorities). It may seem obvious in the twenty-first century that disabled people are people, but we should remember that in 1963 Goffman wrote that people with stigma, including disabled people, were commonly seen as "not quite human" (5). When the American disability rights activist Judith Heumann recently published her memoir, she titled it *Being Heumann*, wordplay with her name that points not just to her autobiography, but also to her humanity and that of all disabled people. Such questions matter. As Crystal Parikh puts it, "If human rights are the rights one has by virtue of being human, the definition of what it means to be human is of paramount concern" (*Cambridge* 8). Adding disability to the category of the human can enlarge notions of humanness. According to Julie Avril Minich, "The inclusion of disability literature in discussions of human rights prompts a more expansive understanding of both humanity and rights" ("Who" 46). Advocating for their full humanity has unquestionably enabled disabled people to achieve rights. I consider how humanism works throughout *Elusive Kinship*, especially with regard to Sinha's *Animal's People*, and return to the important question of posthumanism in the Epilogue, in which I try to look toward the future.

The use of English in literature from the Global South has been explored in much depth in postcolonial studies. In parts of Africa and the Caribbean, authors employing English have sometimes been seen as perpetuating a colonial mindset; English, in this view, is inadequate for truly expressing indigenous cultural identity. In Coetzee's novel *Disgrace* (1999), the white South African character David Lurie believes something similar when musing about the experience of his Black counterpart, Petrus. "He would not mind hearing Petrus's story one day," David thinks. "But preferably not reduced to English. Pressed into the mold of English, Petrus's story could come out arthritic, bygone" (117). In David's view, by its very nature English cannot capture vital truths of postcolonial subaltern identity. We should remember that, like David, we are getting only a sliver of the rich cultures of the Global South through English. Some postcolonial authors, however, might not necessarily consider English foreign. In multilingual India, it has served as a literary language, with authors such as R. K. Narayan, Mulk Raj Anand, Raja Rao, Rushdie, and Roy employing it. Many of the authors I consider here grew up with exposure to English. Others have seen English as something that can be modified, as the expression goes, so that one uses the master's tools to take down his house. With his influential notions of hybridity and mimicry, which disrupt the authority of colonial discourse, Homi Bhabha calls attention to writers from colonized nations using the language in empowering ways to resist the colonizer's control. Moreover, many postcolonial writers include non-English words and phrases in their fiction as a way to evoke their cultural communities. Achebe and Sinha even provide a glossary of Igbo and Hindi words at the end of *Things Fall Apart* and *Animal's People*, respectively. These words might create what Bill Ashcroft calls a "metonymic juncture" in the text, reminding Northern English speakers that, even though most of the work is in English, they are foreigners to the culture being described ("Congo"). In these ways, authors strategically use English to communicate the particularities of their cultural locations.

Chapter Overview

My argument in *Elusive Kinship* consists of six chapters and an Epilogue, moving chronologically from a mid-twentieth-century depiction to a more contemporary moment (2015). After this Introduction, Chapter 1 explores the possible connection between readers and literary characters. Drawing on a range of theorists, I consider how literature sometimes makes it possible for readers to care about disabled characters, an elusive and inconsistent bond of "kinship" that has potential advantages in connection with disability human rights.

With this framework, *Elusive Kinship* proceeds to consider theoretical questions about literature and disability human rights through a series of detailed readings. Chapter 2 begins by examining how, even before the arrival of colonization and capitalism, disabled people in the Global South could be marginalized through local belief systems. The chapter turns to Achebe's justly famous *Things Fall Apart*, which, even as it powerfully portrays the appalling damage of European colonialism, subtly critiques a traditional Igbo privileging of able-bodiedness and consistent bias against disabled people. The novel demonstrates one of the paradoxes of human rights: victims of human rights abuses can also be perpetrators of them. The European missionaries first gain a foothold by welcoming those stigmatized people excluded by the Umoufians, and the narrative upholds compassionate Igbo like Obierika and Nwoye, tacitly endorsing the humane values behind disability justice.

After pointing out that literary magic realism, from Jorge Luis Borges to Gabriel García Márquez, often turns on disability, Chapter 3 focuses on Rushdie's *Midnight's Children*, the first of the novels under consideration to have a first-person disabled narrator, potentially adding a new element to readers' imaginative engagement with disability. Matters are complicated, though, because Rushdie's postmodernist play and his narrator Saleem's claims of having fantastic telepathic powers might actually make it *harder* for readers to identify with him. The novel has a multifaceted, complex depiction of disability, in which disabled people simultaneously are powerful figures who offer hope for the newly independent Indian nation and vulnerable citizens almost always marginalized and victimized by society. Along the way, it expresses the importance of self-determination, a key concept in rights. As it uses disability to describe the postcolonial Indian nation-state, the novel quietly promotes humility toward disabled people, who, it shows, are decidedly not useless or devoid of humor, which aligns with disability dignity and justice.

Chapter 4 addresses the tradition of using disability as a metaphor for something bad or that has gone awry, a practice that has been both prominent in postcolonial writing and controversial in disability studies. It discusses how disabled figures can both be realistic and serve as metaphors for the cruelty and injustice of colonial ideologies. The chapter considers two of Coetzee's novels, *Life & Times of Michael K* and *Disgrace*, to show how the author repeatedly employs disability in ways that not only reveal the lasting damage of colonialism and apartheid, but also convey the real lived condition of disabled people. In *Life & Times* and other early works, even as his white narrators or protagonists struggle to understand his disabled characters (always people of color), Coetzee often treats them with quiet sympathy. This dynamic shifts markedly in *Disgrace*, where a recalcitrant disabled character is much more aggressive and disturbing. Yet metaphorically, he, too, could be said to represent the injustices of apartheid. The white protagonist contends with not just personal violence, but also brutal reckonings of the history of Black oppression in South Africa. Disabled figures raise important ethical questions about human rights in these Coetzee novels.

Turning to disability and gender in the Global South, Chapter 5 investigates how disability functions in works from the 1990s by three contemporary female authors: Desai's *Fasting, Feasting*, Lahiri's "The Treatment of Bibi Haldar," and Danticat's *Breath, Eyes, Memory* and "Caroline's Wedding."

These works frequently depict what we could call a feminist ethic of care regarding disabled female characters, who are often relatives or neighbors of the narrators. To be sure, disability is typically a stigmatized identity, especially in the case of disabled women in India who cannot marry, and Danticat connects disability with trauma. But all three writers depict an empathetic connection and solidarity with disabled women that can be empowering and fits into a disability rights paradigm.

Finally, Chapter 6 explores the limits of human rights by considering the devastating effects of war, global capitalism, and environmental disaster on disabled people in the Global South in recent novels. Abani's *Song for Night* takes place during the Biafra War in Nigeria and is poignantly narrated by a child soldier who has had his vocal cords severed. My Luck, the soldier, emerges as both a sympathetic victim and a perpetrator of human rights abuses, illustrating the paradoxes of human rights in settings of all-out warfare. For their part, Abani's *GraceLand* (2004) occurs partially in a Lagos ghetto and features a one-eyed beggar, while Petina Gappah's Zimbabwean novel *The Book of Memory* (2015) features an albino character who lives in a slum, showing the deleterious effects of poverty (which connects with global capitalism) on their lives. Finally, Sinha's *Animal's People* shows the horrific effects of an accident at an American chemical factory in India (a fictional account based on the real disaster at a Union Carbide plant in Bhopal in 1984 that killed and sickened thousands of impoverished people) through the eyes of a deformed boy who goes about on all fours. Such work emphasizes how the experience of disability in the Global South is often markedly different from that in the North and, in many cases, is caused or shaped by Northern transnational capitalism; it also points to how human rights alone are not enough to counter the deleterious environments in the novels. Yet even as they show the formidable obstacles to disability human rights and justice, all four novels feature disabled narrators or characters who, in the midst of the grimness, show themselves to be witty, active, and indisputably human, deserving of dignity and respect.

The Epilogue recaps the argument of the book and raises the question of where we should go from here for disability justice. As we see, human rights are laudable but insufficient, so I briefly consider possible solutions. To chart the best way forward, the fields of disability studies, postcolonial studies, and the study of literature and human rights must include global disability in their explorations.

These works open the way for the greater cross-cultural understanding that is one of the primary assets of fiction. *Elusive Kinship* acknowledges that the connection between readers and disabled characters is unstable, inconsistent, and contradictory. No seamless dynamic exists here. But it shows that the rich, variegated postcolonial literature in English not only frequently draws its power from disability, and not only depicts many human rights violations, but also sometimes produces a bond in the imagination, a recognition by readers that they share a common humanity with disabled people who may be in distant places and under difficult circumstances, a small but crucial step toward achieving dignity and justice for all disabled people.

1

On Kinship with Literary Characters

The Power of Fiction

Stories matter. . . . Stories have been used to dispossess and to
malign, but stories can also be used to empower and to humanize.

—CHIMAMANDA NGOZI ADICHIE

At the end of "The Danger of a Single Story," her well-known online
TED talk in 2009, the Nigerian author Chimamanda Ngozi Adichie
avers that narratives have important real-world consequences, which
can be positive (empowering and humanizing) or negative (dispossessing or
maligning). They shape how we think about and understand other people
and places.[1] We might add that the stories that people find meaningful and
acclaim have added potency. Such tales are more likely to exert broad influence across cultures and national borders and over time.

People have always tended to delight in a good story, which has made
some critics contend that storytelling could have evolutionary significance.
Stories (including a range of popular forms, including folklore, science fiction, fantasy, and mystery), give us the pleasure of entering the lives of fictional characters, no matter how far away and different their worlds, and of
allowing us to experience their lives and conflicts along with them in our
imaginations. Storytelling shows up in every known human culture extending back in time, a fact that suggests to Blakey Vermeule that "storytelling
is a human universal, that it has a function, and that it is a human necessity" (161). In *Why Do We Care about Literary Characters?* Vermeule asks why
we become emotionally involved with fictional figures whom we know do
not exist. Her essential answer is that literary characters help us to think
and to work out problems. Drawing from cognitive science and evolutionary
psychology, she argues that our caring about fictional characters resembles

our caring about other people, especially strangers we do not know. Literary characters teach us crucial skills of navigating the complexities of different social situations and groups, she asserts. When they face injustice, they inspire indignation and raise questions for us about how things should be.[2] Vermeule and other critics suggest that our penchant for stories could be an evolutionary adaption that is not incidental but a product of natural selection, that it benefits our survival.

Although this adaptationist theory (a recent branch of literary criticism known alternatively as "evocriticism" or "literary Darwinism") is provocative, Michael Bérubé expresses some reservations. For one, he points out that it must remain a theory since it cannot be definitively proved. "There is no evidence that storytelling *in general* conferred an evolutionary advantage on us," Bérubé states in the midst of a reading of the evocritics Lisa Zunshine and Brian Boyd (*Stories* 180). Moreover, Bérubé criticizes how Boyd dismisses literary theory, not to mention culture, history, and the value of examining "the grainy textual details of individual stories" (183). He also resists the way evocriticism does not distinguish between oral and written literature or literature and visual media. Still, despite these disagreements, Bérubé and evocritics concur on essential points: that storytelling appears in every human society and that stories have cultural value, including benefits for our social cognition and understanding of human experience. As Adichie says, stories matter.

These theoretical debates provide a good foundation for approaching the specific topic of this study: how Anglophone literary works by postcolonial authors reflect and have contributed to global disability human rights since 1958. Vermeule especially points to how such fiction can make readers care about disabled characters, regularly causing us to feel a connection—what I am calling a sense of kinship—that leads us to follow their fate. Although imaginative fiction, such works can help us to unravel the complexities surrounding real-life disability in the Global South. They testify to lives that are often invisible and overlooked, depict injustice, and reveal instances of abuse. In a fast-paced, increasingly hyperconnected age, when media rush from one crisis or spectacle to the next, mobile devices are ubiquitous, and attention spans have become ever shorter, these works bring into focus the often hidden predicament of disabled people in the Global South in a way that is reminiscent of Rob Nixon's account of literary testimony to the gradual "slow violence" of environmental degradation that otherwise often eludes public notice. But such dynamics are neither simple nor straightforward; the affective dimensions of reader response need closer scrutiny.

The Capacity of Literature to Make Readers Care

Many commentators have celebrated the ability of literary fiction to make readers feel connected in their minds with the characters about whom they read. Such diverse critics as the nineteenth-century poet William Wordsworth, the historian Lynn Hunt, and the philosophers Richard Rorty and Martha Nussbaum praise literature's ability to teach readers how to understand and connect with others across race, religion, gender, class, nationality, and time, to "[bind] together by passion and knowledge the vast empire of human society," in Wordsworth's phrase (qtd. in Dawes "Empathy"). Along the same lines, an article published in *Science* in 2013 argued that reading literary fiction improves "theory of mind," or a person's understanding of how others feel and think (Kidd and Castano), a thesis that has been supported by follow-up studies.[3] As Rita Felski recently put it, "Many of us have felt a tug of connection with a character in a novel . . . a sense of affinity or shared response" (1). That connection is both frequent and intricate. The sharing of feeling and perspective through narratives continues to receive attention and debate from literary critics, cognitive psychologists, and philosophers studying empathy.[4]

Such acclamation of reader-character connection (which again I am calling kinship) may invite skeptical charges of naivete, easy humanitarianism, or sentimentalism, and I examine key objections below, but crucially such claims of connection do not imply agreement, only some kind of imaginative bond. Felski, for example, asserts that ties between readers and characters "can be ironic as well as sentimental, ethical as well as emotional" and can exist even if the reader also feels conflicted or ambivalent (1). In her estimation, we relate to different literary characters in different ways, and even if we simultaneously have reservations about them. Despite the sometimes potent ties we as readers often experience, we are not in a sense prisoners in the imagination to whatever fictional character, no matter how charismatic, evil, or mendacious, an author puts before us. Even as we savor the immersion into other identities and places, to be successful readers we need to read attentively, actively, and critically to arrive at persuasive interpretations (something we, of course, practice for countless hours in literature classrooms).

Reader-character kinship is not easy or automatic, but it can happen and contribute to equity and human rights everywhere. In "Human Rights, Literature, and Empathy," James Dawes summarizes views of how literature can create caring for others among readers and goes on to incisively probe the contradictory relationship between empathy and rights. After conducting interviews with a variety of fieldworkers at human rights organizations and with local advocacy groups, he reports that his interviewees had a range of seemingly paradoxical theories about empathy. The same person often held these beliefs simultaneously, he says, pointing to the convoluted and conflicting ways the emotion can work. However, the following notion of how empathy can contribute to human rights occupies Dawes's most prominent spot:

> Generating empathy in distant spectators is the *first and most important step* in addressing human rights violations. Human rights is, in a sense, nothing more than the historical expansion of our capacity to empathize: expanding our circle of concern beyond our kin, our community, our region, our religion, our nation-state, expanding it to encompass the globe. ("Empathy" 429, emphasis added)

Dawes's calling empathy "the first and most important step" in human rights recalls Samuel Moyn's saying that human rights activists in the 1960s recognized that people's imaginations had to be won, "first and foremost," for human rights to gain traction (*Last* 5). In addition, Dawes reports that his interviewees see empathy as an important way to recruit people into human rights careers and keep them there: "What brings people to the field is a feeling of empathy rather than the acknowledgment of moral duty" (429). Creating understanding and feeling for others serves as a crucial first step toward broader human rights and can move some people to pursue human rights work.

Stories in general, and fiction in particular, can advance this process by making readers feel kinship with characters far from them and in different circumstances. Stories can spark people's imaginations and help to spread awareness and humanize others, as Adichie, Hunt, Rorty, and Nussbaum have in various ways asserted. Such a connection can lead to social change. Greg Mullins points out that "fiction can generate wider public conversation and even social action, but its energies coalesce mainly in the intensely interior act of reading" (124). A private act usually done in solitude, reading can still have broad social consequences. Taken together, these views point to the potential benefits of reading fiction: in addition to such advantages as sharpening a reader's language and critical thinking, fostering understanding of history and of different cultures, and creating insight and an emotional bond to others in different situations, it has the potential to make the world a better place. These insights reinforce a basic claim of this book: that literature reflects and contributed to the measurable progress in disabled people's rights in recent decades.

Objections and Caveats

Despite such exciting potential, reader-character connection does not always happen (as the "elusive" in my title suggests) or advance an ideology of rights. Dawes makes clear that the dynamic contains any number of possible drawbacks. First, narratives could divert readers' attention from actual human rights violations, giving them the satisfaction that they are compassionate without them doing anything in reality. In the face of often overwhelming challenges, such thinking goes, readers may find it easier just to read a story. Moreover, we should note that we have no guarantee that readers will respond to narratives by behaving in moral versus immoral ways. As Adichie acknowledges, stories have been used to "dispossess and malign" others. The reader-character connection generated by fiction does not necessarily lead to helping behavior, and much depends not on the author or work but the reader's response, which is, of course, shaped by who readers are and the experiences they bring to a text.

In addition to such important cautions, some scholars express reservations specifically about using the word "empathy" to describe readers' experience, which prompts me to distinguish my idea of literary kinship from the more profound connotations of that term. For example, Sander Gilman says the concept of empathy connotes an external understanding of the other's "soul/psyche"; he prefers "projective identification" because that phrase "reflects our subjective creation of the other's internality." Along the same lines, Dawes says that what we call empathy may not be empathy at all but, rather, a more superficial pseudo-empathy. Moreover, in her comprehensive study of literature and empathy, Suzanne Keen even questions whether "reading by itself" can produce empathy "beyond its predictable reach of family, community, and tribe" (108). Like Gilman and Dawes, Keen seems to have a notion of empathy as profound understanding here. We clearly need to separate what I am calling literary kinship from these weighty meanings of empathy. By kinship, I mean the pull of connection between reader and character, a bond or identification that can happen even if readers are ambivalent or conflicted about what they read. Again, studies have shown that reading can improve one's theory of mind, or ability to understand others' perceptions and beliefs.[5] That is different from a deep understanding of a character's soul or psyche. We should hesitate to celebrate literary kinship too readily or easily or to assume that it simply means empathy or always leads to helping behavior. Still, while such reader-character connection can be elusive, it does happen, and I think we should not be shy about acknowledging that it is part of the joy of reading literature.

How Disability Adds Complexity
to the Reader-Character Relationship

Matters become even more complicated in the case of disabled characters since readers either may not connect with them or not perceive them as disabled at all. On relating to disabled characters, Susan Wendell argues that readers can identify with all kinds of characters different from themselves, including with different races and genders, but in the case of disability often resist such identification because of a pervasive deep fear, pity, or even horror of disability. If most readers have not experienced a depicted disability, they may almost instinctively resist identifying with it. Furthermore, as noted in the Introduction, most postcolonial critics have tended to approach disability in the literature of the Global South as metaphorical rather than realistic, as if metaphor precludes the possibility of verisimilitude. When I mentioned Salman Rushdie's Saleem as an example of a disabled character to a postcolonial scholar, they had to look back at *Midnight's Children* to confirm that he is indeed disabled. They just had not thought about that aspect of Rushdie's novel before, although they knew the book well. Such oversight of many readers recalls Paul Longmore's incisive essay in the 1980s about disability in media and film in which he asks, "Why do television and film so frequently screen disabled characters for us to see, and why do we usually screen them out of our consciousness even as we absorb those images?" (132). We could ask something similar here about postcolonial fiction. These factors cause me to call the connection, or kinship, between readers and disabled characters "elusive" in my title because it often lurks out of reach and is hardly sure to happen.

In addition to calling reader-disabled character ties elusive because readers do not believe they are similar or do not perceive actual disability aside from metaphor, I do so because such depictions themselves sometimes recalcitrantly resist understanding or emotional connection. The deployments of disability in these narratives are tremendously diverse, and even other characters struggle to understand and relate to disabled characters such as J. M. Coetzee's cognitively disabled Michael K, who perpetually is out of range of even self-understanding, so readers probably do not understand him, either. As I show in Chapter 4, in writing a novel about Michael, Coetzee holds him up as a cipher and implicitly asks us readers what to make of him, prodding us to consider the ethics of his treatment and fate.

Yet with David Mitchell and Sharon Snyder, we could take a more positive view of the possibility of reader-character bonding. They maintain that literature sometimes offers an intimacy with disabled people that for many readers is rare in their actual lives, opening the way to connection ("Disability"). This closeness seems especially true in fiction that features disabled first-person narrators who draw us into their world; such disabled narrators do not prominently show up in postcolonial Anglophone literature until after 1981, making reader-disabled character connection more likely after that time, which, coincidentally or not, was the period when global disability human rights began to gain notable traction.

With disability especially, other dangers are readerly voyeurism or pity, which both actually reify the powerlessness of disabled people. In *Animal's People*, Indra Sinha confronts the risk of readerly voyeurism directly. The novel takes place in an Indian town where there has been a horrible chemical disaster, very much like the real tragedy that happened in Bhopal in 1984. The disabled narrator, a boy called Animal, says scornfully of an Australian journalist who wants to interview him: "You were like all the others, come to suck our stories from us, so strangers in far off countries can marvel there's so much pain in the world" (5). Animal is cynical about the value of sharing his tale with curious international readers who have vastly different experiences, acknowledging the potentially touristic or exoticized aspects of such depictions, although he does eventually choose to tell his story, which "wants to come out," insisting that it not be edited and addressing it directly to the reader (11).[6] In an interview that appears at the end of the book, Sinha says he hopes the novel will help impoverished Bhopalis in their desperate campaign for adequate care and recompense. If the danger of voyeurism and pity exists, Sinha and authors like him balance that against potential benefits of making the world aware of grievous injustice and moving some readers to action.

Similarly, for centuries, critics of compassion and pity have seen them as connected with narcissism, in that holders of the emotion superciliously position themselves above others. Such suspicion shows up among disability activists in the North. In the documentary film *Vital Signs*, for instance, the late disability activist Harlan Hahn wears a shirt that says, "Piss on Pity," a deliberately coarse signal of his revulsion at the emotion, which often positions the person who pities above the pitied subject. These moments point to the complex politics of empathy in general, and between readers and disabled characters in literature of the Global South in particular.

In these ways, this study calls for a new kind of reading of postcolonial fiction in English. Just as scholars did not address the racist aspects of *Huckleberry Finn* until more than a half-century after it was published in 1884, opening a vigorous discussion of the cultural meanings of that influential, controversial novel as they relate to the harrowing national history of white racism and African American persecution, so should we investigate an important, fresh way of reading these acclaimed Anglophone works. By viewing them through a disability lens, we enrich our understanding both of them and of their cultural significance. We uncover the authors' achievement in a new dimension.

Method

To unpack such intricate matters, I employ a critical methodology that aims to ground large claims in specific details to show the ways that this literature works. In keeping with Bérubé's cautions, I strive to read each of these texts closely, attend to relevant literary theory (while acknowledging that theory developed in the North may not apply to the South), and pay attention to the specific local history—whether it is apartheid in South Africa or the chaos of Hindu-Muslim violence in newly independent India—and culture. Doing so shows how disability adds richness and force to this literature. As with literary depictions of race or gender, images of disability can work simultaneously on multiple levels, sometimes in imbricated or paradoxical ways, adding to the energy and imaginative vibrancy of this fiction. Literary disability studies scholars including Mitchell and Snyder, Ato Quayson, Clare Barker, and Bérubé have shown how disability appears in a variety of narratives, not just in the depiction of disabled characters, but also sometimes in language, metaphor, or even the structure of a narrative's plot, all of which can make fiction more compelling to readers.

In addition to these features, these literary works connect with readers' imaginations simply because they are printed text. Oral storytelling, visual media such as film, and printed literature each have advantages in telling a narrative. For example, oral storytelling offers the fundamental human pleasure of happening live and face to face, connecting the performer and the audience. Oral storytelling is also usually more available to impoverished people in the Global South than printed literature or film, especially if they know only one language. Moreover, oral storytelling and film are accessible to illiterate people—about one-quarter of the adults on our planet, sadly enough—while printed literature is not. For its part, film has the unique capacity for visually showing, making a direct visual impact (on sighted viewers, anyway); it also has a soundtrack that shapes (hearing) viewers' experiences, all of which can produce a powerful and engrossing experience.

But because books do not rely on visuals, they have a special ability to force readers to put together the story *in their minds*. The best printed literature communicates interiority and sparks readers' imaginations, which makes it especially suited for fostering connection and kinship with audiences. As Debjani Ganguly puts it, printed literature offers "the magic of transport to worlds distant and different" and the opportunity "to enter into the lives of myriad fictional characters," pleasant experiences that, for her, remain valuable despite the advent of multimedia, digital technology, and other forms of narrative on screens (ix). Such features are among the most important attributes of printed fiction, distinguishing it from other forms of storytelling. Furthermore, while oral storytelling and films tend to be relatively short, at two hours or less, novels often take longer to read, meaning that they not only require more active commitment but can cover more ground; readers are submerged in the lives of fictional characters, including disabled ones, for a longer time. They require a larger imaginative investment. In these ways, the medium of printed literature has noteworthy capability to make readers care about characters who are not real and the issues of injustice they face.

By featuring characters with disabilities as they tell their stories, this literature collectively contests the widespread notion that disabled people in the Global South are insignificant. To read these works chronologically is to see disabled characters becoming more prominent in fiction and even telling their stories themselves. In depicting what otherwise might seem an incalculably vast and depressing topic in interesting ways, such literature sometimes, and especially after 1981, makes the human rights of people with disabilities more graspable, moving, and personal to readers.

Between Indigenous Beliefs
and Colonial Invasion

The Vital Role of Disability in
Achebe's Things Fall Apart

In the mid-twentieth century, disabled Africans "were routinely pitied, ignored, and not expected to become productive members of society," states
Isaac Agboola, a deaf man who grew up in Nigeria and writes from personal experience (185). At that time, Agboola says, parts of Africa did not have
schools for the general public, and most regions were still European colonies.
He testifies to the almost complete disempowerment of disabled people close
to the moment when the United Nations General Assembly adopted its landmark Universal Declaration of Human Rights (UDHR), which pronounced
that "all human beings are born free and equal in dignity and rights," in 1948.
Michael Freeman notes that the UDHR was a manifesto rather than enforce-
able law, as it "included no right to petition the UN about human-rights violations, and no means to implement the rights that it proclaimed" (47). Despite
these drawbacks, the declaration began the modern era of human rights, with
other, more specific human rights treaties to follow, and diverse people around
the world today celebrate its importance.[1]

Ten years after the UDHR but still near the mid-century, the Nigerian
author Chinua Achebe produced his celebrated Anglophone novel *Things Fall
Apart* (1958), which in many ways serves as an effective starting point for this
study. Although disability has a subtle, easy-to-miss presence in the book—a
much less visible presence than in subsequent works I consider—it nonetheless often drives the plot. Written soon after the start of the human rights era
but set around 1890, at a time well before the establishment of the United
Nations and human rights, the novel depicts issues of equity and abuse that

directly relate to the quest for dignity for all in the UDHR. By portraying disabled characters, Achebe gives a sense of disabled Igbo lives at the end of the nineteenth century, before colonialism brutally changed the Nigerian region. It helps to introduce the momentous transitions that have taken place in many regions of the Global South over the past century and a half. It also reveals the complexities of the topic, including how victims of human rights abuses can paradoxically also be perpetrators of them, and how notions of rights can run up against entrenched local cultural and metaphysical practices. Even as he shows the agonies brought about by foreign colonial incursion, Achebe quietly supports a compassionate view of disabled people that aligns with disability human rights and is sometimes at odds with the practices of the Igbo clan he respectfully portrays.

To back up a bit: impairment, of course, appears in all human populations, but its social significance varies enormously. Postcolonial literature reveals many overlapping factors that shape the social meanings of disability, which demonstrates how we need an intersectional approach to the topic. In addition to such influential elements as time and place, race and ethnicity, gender, class, caste (in India), war and violence, family, and community, these works show that three interconnected factors frequently dominate representations of disability in the South: European colonialism and its neoliberal afterlives, poverty, and the presence of powerful indigenous metaphysical or cultural beliefs. All three are complexly entangled and regularly mold and inform portrayals of disability that readers witness. All three thus connect to disability human rights and deserve close inspection.

Any consideration of the Global South must acknowledge the immense effects of European colonialism, although its connection to disability needs more attention. From the late fifteenth century until the aftermath of World War II, Europe controlled substantial portions of the globe, which caused huge transformation among both colonized people and colonizers and has received massive attention. On the positive side, as Edward Said puts it, "One of imperialism's achievements was to bring the world closer together" (xxi). In making the globe more interconnected, colonialism occasionally made possible symbiotic exchange that benefitted both groups and shaped the development of modernity. But, Said adds, colonialism featured "separation between Europeans and natives [that] was . . . insidious and fundamentally unjust" and led to appalling "horrors, bloodshed, and vengeful bitterness" (xxii). Colonialism caused wars (between Europeans and native peoples and interethnic conflict among native groups, especially after colonialism ended); the imposition of European religious and economic norms on native people who had their own rich traditions; and mass suffering and trauma. As Achebe wrote in 1966, six years after Nigeria achieved independence from Great Britain:

> Without subscribing to the view that Africa gained nothing at all in her long encounter with Europe, one could still say, in all fairness, that she suffered many terrible and lasting misfortunes. In terms of human dignity and human relations the encounter was almost a complete disaster for the black races. It has warped the mental attitudes of both black and white. ("Burden" 135)

In Achebe's view, colonialism was almost entirely a tragedy for people in Africa. Does that include for disabled Africans?

Among the far-reaching consequences of European incursion was the advancement of global inequity. As I show, poverty in places in the Global South often predates European colonialism, but colonialism and its legacies contributed to the contemporary predominance of capitalist, free-market-based globalization and drastic economic inequity between the North and the South, with all of its grievous effects. Sankaran Krishna argues that capitalist development and colonial conquest or domination took place concurrently and produced "prosperity for the few and immiserization for the many," a dynamic that Krishna asserts is enforced by political and military coercion (4). Many scholars, including Krishna, Helen Meekosha, and Nirmala Erevelles, agree that past Northern colonialism was complicit in fostering the contemporary world order and stark global inequity. As Quinn Slobodian shows, neoliberals pursued deregulation of industry and a world system in which capital would be safe from political interference and mass demands for social justice. Although neoliberalism has lifted many people from poverty, its problem, as scholars such as Mark Sherry have pointed out, is that it leaves many others behind, unsupported, and often debilitated, in Jasbir Puar's terms (Sherry "Promise").

Further complicating matters is the presence of potent beliefs, which may or may not be related to poverty. Benedicte Ingstad has argued that social circumstances such as poverty often lie behind poor treatment of disabled people in the South; that what looks from the outside like neglect, hiding, or worse can often be explained by the precarious situations of the families responsible for caring of the disabled person. We could add that even in societies that have achieved economic stability, cultural attitudes originally formed in poverty may linger. While some native philosophies, such as the concept of *unbuntu* in South Africa, may view disabled people affirmatively, as full humans deserving respect and support, other traditional beliefs marginalize them or present them as objects of pity or evil (Ndlovu). Even in an increasingly interconnected, globalized world where multiple ideas circulate, traditional beliefs often hold special sway.

Literature helps to mediate these complex factors and offers a valuable way to begin thinking about human rights for disabled people in the Global South. No one person knows all the countless languages, cultures, and histories in the South. Approaching any topic across such an expansive area requires humility and a willingness to learn from others, including from authors from diverse regions of the world. Fiction makes it more possible to discern how the myriad elements function, how they intersect, and which factors are most relevant in any given situation. Authors both depict the attitudes toward disability in their cultures and often subtly critique these beliefs. Following Clare Barker and Stuart Murray's call for attention "to the local formations and understandings of disability" (219), and heeding Ato Quayson's advocacy of reading that is "alive to the implications of disability," an approach that, he asserts, reveals questions of justice at the "ethical core" of narratives (*Aesthetic* 208), we can begin to uncover how such intersectional factors work.

Quayson's emphasis on an ethical core takes us back to human rights, for the ethical questions at the heart of many narratives frequently concern treatment of other people and groups. Human rights may seem straightforward, guarding all humans' individual freedom and dignity, protecting against discrimination, slavery, torture, and other abuses, but matters become more complex when we encounter different cultural beliefs and entrenched practices. Drawing from its study "The Challenge of Human Rights and Cultural Diversity," the United Nations states that no exceptions exist for cultural beliefs that lead to discrimination against or harm to other people:

> Every person has the right to culture, including the right to enjoy and develop cultural life and identity. However, cultural rights are not boundless. The rights to particular cultural practices become limited at the point where they infringe upon other human rights. This means that cultural rights cannot be invoked as a defence for acts that constitute human rights violations or abuses; and cultural rights cannot be used to justify, for example, torture, murder, discrimination or any of the universal human rights and fundamental freedoms established by international law. (UN "Toolkit")

Such an understanding can help to make sense of human rights in practice. Again, rights have sometimes been controversial as critics have charged that they are falsely universalist, the product of Europe and North America imposing its values on the world. Some historical evidence supports this idea. For example, the UDHR did not include the right to self-determination because European colonial powers did not want to embolden their colonial subjects. But core human rights covenants in 1966 included this right in their first articles, and evidence of broad support for rights lies in how many nations have ratified subsequent treaties. That the decisive majority of nations (182 out of 193 in the United Nations as of 2021) from all parts of the world has ratified the 2006 Convention on the Rights of Persons with Disabilities (CRPD) shows that, with regard to the rights of disabled people, broad consensus exists (among governments, anyway), even if in practice many people with disabilities remain marginalized and stigmatized.

To begin unraveling such complicated matters and considering their relationship to disability human rights, I turn to Achebe's classic *Things Fall Apart*. In the novel, Achebe illustrates the ways that normative ideologies, strong metaphysical beliefs, colonialism, poverty, gender, and other factors intersect and overlap to shape the social meanings of physical, cognitive, and sensory impairment in one specific setting in the Global South: an Igbo clan in southeastern Nigeria near the end of the nineteenth century. In Umoufia, as the village is called, disability is occasionally a sign of fearsome power and, more often, disqualifying difference and inferiority, but never are disabled people just people in these pages. They are invariably stigmatized and set apart as different. Achebe manages both to depict this outlook and subtly to critique it in ways that shore up the rationale for disability justice, although he leaves some matters unresolved.

Things Fall Apart through a Disability Justice Lens

Published two years before Nigerian independence from Great Britain in 1960, *Things Fall Apart* offers a rare depiction of an Igbo clan before colonization and the upheaval that ensues when British colonizers arrive, apparently near the end of the nineteenth century. Achebe discussed how he wanted to counter the inaccurate representations of Africans in European novels such as Joyce Cary's *Mr. Johnson* (*Morning* 123) and Joseph Conrad's *Heart of Darkness* and to show that before colonization Africans had dignity. "It is this dignity that many African peoples all but lost in the colonial period, and it is this dignity that they must now regain," he wrote five years after he published the book. "The worst thing that can happen to any people is the loss of their dignity and self-respect" ("Role" 8). He portrays the beauty and value of such Igbo traditions as the ritual greetings and breaking of the kola nut, negotiations of bride price, wrestling matches, public addresses, successful farming, and the effective justice administered by the *egwugwu* (masked ancestral spirits), all through written English that has Igbo words and proverbs seamlessly woven in.[2] Robert Wren and Simon Gikandi assert that, in researching his novel, Achebe drew on both Igbo and colonial sources, while Carey Snyder details how the narrator of *Things Fall Apart* oscillates between being a participant in Igbo culture and an observer looking in from the outside. As scholars such as Emmanuel Okoye show, the novel seems to get the ethnographic details of a traditional Igbo culture largely right.

Yet as many critics have argued, we should not read the novel simply in ethnographic, anthropological terms, for that would miss its significance as literature.[3] On the eve of Nigerian independence, as people grappled with what a postcolonial Nigerian identity might look like (Wole Soyinka wrote his well-known play *The Lion and the Jewel* around the same time), Achebe confronted complex forces through fiction. He was of Igbo heritage, but he was also the son of a Christian missionary (his father was among the first to convert to Christianity in his village) and attended a missionary school, which led him to state that he grew up "at the crossroads of cultures" (*Morning* 119). Like many postcolonial authors, he wrote from a position of in-betweenness and hybridity. We need to attend to the novel's narrative strategies and symbolism and interrogate the assumptions on which they are based fully to apprehend his vision.

Later in the novel, Achebe powerfully shows terrible effects of British colonial incursion, including a massacre of Igbo civilians in the nearby village of Abame (in response to their killing of a white stranger who rides a bicycle into their midst) and the inexorable suppression of a meaningful culture, but he does not present the British as uniformly malevolent or the Igbo as uniformly good. Diana Ackers Rhoads notes that "both the Igbo and the British cultures are for Achebe a mixture of types of human beings" (69). In a 1964 essay, "The Role of the Writer in a New Nation," Achebe addresses the question of how writers in newly independent countries should present the time before colonization:

> Quite clearly there is a strong temptation to idealize it—to extol its good points and pretend that the bad never existed. . . . This is where the writer's integrity comes in. Will he be strong enough to overcome the temptation to select only those facts which flatter him? If he succumbs he will have branded himself as an untrustworthy witness. But it is not only his personal integrity as an artist which is involved.

The credibility of the world he is attempting to re-create will be called into question and he will defeat his own purpose if he is suspected of glossing over inconvenient facts. We cannot pretend that our past was one long, technicolour idyll. We have to admit that like other people's past ours had its good as well as its bad sides. (9)

Achebe does not idealize the past or traditional Igbo society, presenting a way of life that has value and beauty but nevertheless contains problems that could be corrected and conflicting views even before the colonizers arrive.

In depicting such matters, Achebe presents the precolonial Igbo as having a living culture that is not perfect and sometimes subtly critiques their beliefs and practices, as David Hoegberg has pointed out. Early in the novel, Hoegberg notes, we learn that violators of the clan's Week of Peace used to be put to death, but the Umoufians changed the policy. "After a while this custom was stopped because it spoiled the peace which it was meant to preserve," the narrator tells us (31). When they conflict with other values, indigenous cultural traditions can thus be internally altered and corrected, but such changes have not been made in all Umoufian cultural practices. For example, Hoegberg notes that the shocking killing of Ikemefuna, the boy taken from another clan because his father had killed an Umoufian woman, breaks the clan's principle, introduced near the start of the novel, of not judging a person's worth by the worth of his father. Some Umoufians are disturbed by the killing, but the practice itself—which results from a decree from one of the clan's deities, the Oracle of the Hills and the Caves—remains unchanged. In this way, Achebe imbues his narrative with depth and opens up some precolonial practices to critique. After discussing similar cases, such as with the *osu*, or outcasts, Hoegberg concludes that the Umoufian clan fears instability and victimizes those perceived as hybrids. Within the normative culture of the clan, ambiguity is ominous.

Disability can make people seem ambiguous, too, so unsurprisingly in precolonial Umoufia, disability is often stigmatized: disabled people are frequently perceived as inferior, threatening, or foreign. From the opening of the novel, we see that the people of Umoufia esteem physical vigor. The first paragraph tells of the founder of the village wrestling with "a spirit of the wild for seven days and seven nights" (3). Even the mythic beginnings of the community celebrate bodily strength. Wrestling continues to be an important sport in the community; the narrator relates that, years before, the "tall and huge" Okonkwo had brought honor to his village through his wrestling skill (3). As the first chapter unfolds, it becomes increasingly apparent that the culture rewards accomplishment with one's muscles. Through prowess in war and success in yam farming, Okonkwo gains not only prosperity and fame but also two honorific titles and three wives. "A very strong man [who] rarely felt fatigue" (13), he embraces the clan's ideal of male physical vigor and becomes a leader at a relatively young age who is seen as "one of the greatest men of his time" (8). The narrator mentions that "achievement was revered" among Umoufians, which specifically seems to mean achievement that results from men's physical power (8). When Umoufia needs an emissary of war to the neighboring clan of Mbaino, Okonkwo is chosen. His wrestling success and prosperity attract women, too; they cause Ekwefi to leave her husband and marry Okonkwo. Meanwhile, those title-less men who are not successful farmers or warriors are sometimes dismissed as *agbala* (women).

This privileging of physical capability makes a certain amount of sense, given that Umoufians live in a warrior-agricultural community where life is precarious. Fertile land and food are evidently a bit scarce. When Unoka goes to consult the Oracle of the Hills and the Caves about why he has a poor harvest, the Oracle's priestess rebukes him for lazily sowing on exhausted farmland while his neighbors "cross seven rivers" and "cut down virgin forests" to make their farms (17). As Rhoads points out, this passage implies that the people of Umoufia have to venture ever farther from their village to grow crops, increasing the likelihood that they will have conflicts with other clans over land. Robert Wren backs up this impression when he notes that, historically at this time in Nigeria, increasing population reduced not just the amount of fresh land available for cultivation, but also the forests that had sheltered wild game, which were an important source of protein. No surprise, then, that the clan values physical capability: able-bodied men are more likely to protect the village in wars with neighboring clans and to be successful farmers and providers.

Against this celebration of capacity, disabled people have a transgressive nature that is sometimes inflected by the clan's supernatural interpretations of their difference. Occasionally, figures of disability assume powerful and intimidating roles in the Umoufian social order. Near the beginning of the book, the narrator tells of the clan's potent war medicine, which surrounding villages fear and is as old as the clan itself. According to the narrator, people agree that the "active principle" in the medicine "had been an old woman with one leg. In fact, the medicine itself was called *agadi-nwayi*, or old woman" (11). The past tense suggests that the one-legged old woman is no longer alive. Still, she remains a ghostly presence in Umoufia. The narrator states that if "anybody was so foolhardy as to pass by the shrine [at the center of the village] after dusk he was sure to see the old woman hopping about" (12). Together,

her potent abilities and distinctive hopping cause anxiety: one must keep one's distance. Aside from this brief description, the mysterious and powerful disabled woman disappears from the narrative. In the same way, disability adds uncanniness to a frightening figure when it comes to the most dreaded *egwugwu*, the masked spirit who seems to represent death. He has a coffin shape, sickly odor, and only one hand. "Even the greatest medicine man took shelter when he was near," the narrator tells us (122). Disability in these brief cases emphasizes terrifying and unfathomable power. It serves as warning that others should stay away.

We see more clearly how the Igbo in the novel hold disability at a distance when we contrast the one-legged woman with another female character who assumes authority through supernatural means: Chielo, the priestess of the Oracle of the Hills and the Caves. As critics have noted, women normally have subservient positions within the clan, but as a powerful priestess Chielo can berate a man such as Unoka and take Okonkwo's daughter in the middle of the night, despite his pleading with her to come back in the morning. With both the one-legged woman and Chielo, supernatural beliefs give the women power. Significantly, however, the nondisabled Chielo is named while the one-legged woman remains a mysterious presence. Moreover, Achebe presents Chielo in ordinary life outside of her priestess role as a woman at one of the clan's wrestling matches; we learn she is a widow who has two children and shares a shed in the market with Okonkwo's second wife, Ekwefi. Unlike the one-legged woman, Chielo is given a regular identity apart from being a priestess. The one-legged woman remains cryptic and unsettling in her intimidating power and ghostly hopping in the darkness, mentioned in just a few sentences and then left behind.

Unsurprisingly to anyone familiar with Mary Douglas's classic *Purity and Danger*, because Umoufians perceive certain kinds of disabled people as threatening, they treat them as taboo or even malicious, leading to abuses of their human right to dignity. Douglas shows that every culture has concepts of purity and danger that it tries to regulate. Such notions often intersect with disability, and one obstacle disability rights activists the world over routinely must confront is the belief that disability is shameful, a form of pollution, or just wrong. Early in *Things Fall Apart*, the narrator says that when a child is born with some aberration, such as "a missing finger or a dark line" (77), Umoufians commonly see him or her as being an *ogbanje*, "one of those wicked children" who repeatedly dies and returns to his mother's womb to be reborn and die again (79). We cannot tell whether the society perceives all babies born with physical anomalies as wicked or just those born to mothers who have had infants die and their corpses mutilated by a medicine man (to prevent the *ogbanje*'s return) in the past. Once more we can discern the basis of such beliefs: like parents everywhere, Umoufians understandably fear infant death. But what stands out is that, in at least some cases, the culture believes that babies born with disabilities are malignant.

The Umoufians' privileging of normality causes them to cast out those with objectionable physical differences even if those individuals are not usually thought of in other cultures as disabled. The most blatant example is baby twins, whom they consider abnormal and abandon to die in the clan's Evil Forest, which they believe is "alive with sinister forces and powers of darkness" (148). Death in the Evil Forest apparently prevents one from continuing as an ancestor and remaining part of the spiritual life of the clan in that way. Such infanticide disturbs Okonkwo's son Nwoye and likely most readers, too. Similarly, when Unoka experiences swelling in the stomach and limbs, Umoufians consider it an "abomination against the earth goddess" Ani, and "he was carried to the Evil Forest and left there to die" (18). Such abrupt ostracism seems rooted not just in spiritual beliefs, but also in a fear of the spread of disease. We learn that, among the Igbo, when people die of "really evil diseases," such as smallpox and leprosy, they are buried in the Evil Forest (148). The practice perhaps has a certain logic since these diseases are contagious, yet the medical conditions that cause swelling limbs, such as congestive heart failure, are typically not infectious. The narrator manages subtly to suggest the inhumanity of this practice, telling us about a man with swollen limbs who, after being taken to the Evil Forest, staggered back to his house "and had to be carried back to the forest and tied to a tree" (18). An ill person being tied to a tree to starve and die, like the abandonment of twin newborns, is hardly admirable. We are left with the poignant image of Unoka taking his flute with him to the Evil Forest, where presumably he will play as he awaits his death. In such cases the Umoufians treat those who differ from the norm ruthlessly, presumably to protect their own spiritual purity and physical well-being, and that attitude spills over to perceptions of disability.

In addition to these normative or metaphysical understandings of disability, members of the clan occasionally associate physical difference with foreignness. For example, the Umoufians believe that a "race of stunted men" guards caves containing locusts in a distant land (54). According to the elders, these men determine when locusts, which the Igbo savor as delicious food, come to the region. In the Igbo imaginary, the men's small size is bound up with their capability and exotic outsider status. Along the same lines, the first rumors of white people contain images of disability. Okonkwo's friend Obierika reports that "these white men, they say, have no toes" (74). While modern readers might understand this comment as indicating that white people wear shoes, the Igbo appear to comprehend it literally, in terms of disability. Alongside other instances of how the villagers typically interpret missing fingers and the like, the no toes rumor, while humorous, also contains a vague threat, a suggestion of mysterious power, incomprehensibility, and wickedness. Machi responds by jokingly likening white people to a man they know with leprosy (which causes the skin to be white). Again, this is witty—the men laugh—but when we remember that leprosy is considered an evil disease, the association is a bit unsettling. Later, Uchendu, the esteemed oldest member of Okonkwo's mother's family, carries the theme further. "We have albinos among us," he says. "Do you not think that they came to our clan by mistake, that they have strayed from their way to a land where everybody is like them?" (141). These instances not only suggest how Umoufians think of racial difference in terms of disability, but also how they cast disabled people as not belonging and foreign. The men's comments reinforce the normalcy and physical vigor of nondisabled members of the clan and the community they share.

All of this may be rather unsurprising, but we should note that it complicates the emphasis of some disability scholars (such as Marta Russell and Ravi Malhotra) on disability as an adverse product of capitalism. Before colonists and capitalism show up in Umoufia, we can see disabled people's human rights being abused, which underscores how achieving disability justice requires a comprehensive approach. We need to examine the effects not just of the global economic system, but of local beliefs and social practices, too.

In this way, in *Things Fall Apart* disabled people help to shore up able-bodied identity in precolonial Umoufia. Eve Kosofsky Sedgwick's theory of oppositional categories is relevant here. In a well-known analysis, Sedgwick explains how oppositional categories that seem natural and equivalent (heterosexual and homosexual in her case, but also, by extension, male and female, white and Black, and similar dichotomies) exist in a dominant-subordinate relationship, in which the first group is valued and the second group is degraded. However, the first group realizes its superiority only by repeatedly shunning the second group, so paradoxically the first group depends on the second group for its power and identity (9). We can discern this dynamic in the able-bodied–disabled relationship in Okonkwo's clan. The abjected disabled bodies that exist on the perimeter of Umoufian life serve to buttress and define the clan's ideal of physical accomplishment.

Even as he depicts many admirable aspects of precolonial Igbo culture and conveys distinct identities of different people in the clan, Achebe offers a subtle critique of the clan's consistent privileging of able-bodiedness. One element of this critique is the narrative itself, which sometimes contains implicit reservations or features Igbo characters with misgivings about what it describes. However, the most overt part of this critique comes through the story of Achebe's imposing lead character, Okonkwo. Despite his impressive achievements and bravery, Okonkwo's tragic flaw, paradoxically enough, is not his minor disability but the way he takes the clan's ideology of able-bodiedness to uncompromising extremes. He completely rejects disability and vulnerability in others and in himself, which ironically weakens him.

Okonkwo's Insistent Ableism

Readers may forget that Okonkwo has a small speech impediment because it disappears from view for most of the novel, but his attempts to suppress it and pass as normal epitomize his violent rejection of disability and of any appearance of weakness in general. At the start of the narrative, in the midst of describing Okonkwo's striking physical presence, Achebe deliberately mentions his impairment. "He had a slight stammer," the narrator says, "and whenever he was angry and could not get his words out quickly enough, he would use his fists" (4). Okonkwo—the accomplished wrestler, warrior, and farmer, the paragon of Umoufian physical capability—has a disability. When he is upset and speaks falteringly, he turns to fighting to cover up his difference from the norm. "He did pounce on people quite often" that narrator adds (4).

In this way, Okonkwo's minor impediment and the desire to escape stigma and achieve the prestigious social value of able-bodiedness in Umoufia shape his actions. While his disability may seem small, it implicitly sets him apart in a culture that prizes not just physical competency, but also the ability to speak well. "Among the Ibo the art of conversation is regarded very highly," the narrator tells us (7). As disabled people the world over often feel compelled to do, Okonkwo attempts to pass as normal and fit in with the able-bodied values of his surrounding culture, lest he be seen as wanting or inferior. Scholars have recognized such coercion around the world. Erving Goffman wrote about the often invisible but nevertheless powerful social pressure to conform in *Stigma*. More recently, Robert McRuer has termed this kind emphasis on being normal in relation to disability "compulsory able-bodiedness" (*Crip Theory* 2). Because his "great passion" is "to become one of the lords of the clan," Okonkwo internalizes the Umoufian ideal of able-bodied manhood (131). Significantly, we see no disabled elders in the clan, so seemingly no models of disability achievement exist. Okonkwo has risen in Umoufia through his will and physical strength and tries to cover up his stammer in the same way.

Okonkwo's impulsive turns to violence to avoid even the appearance of weakness prove a defining characteristic. While one explanation for his fear of looking vulnerable lies in his desire to pass as normal and fulfill the able-bodied values of Umoufia, another, related cause is his fierce determination to avoid his father's lack of success. As noted earlier, Unoka is indolent; he does play the flute with skill, but this musical talent apparently does not earn much respect in Umoufia. He lazily plants on exhausted soil, unlike others. "People laughed at him because he was a loafer," the narrator says, and such popular derision must have hurt the proud Okonkwo when he was growing up (5). As a boy he was evidently on the brink of starvation; we learn that Unoka's "wife and children had barely enough to eat" (5). The adult Okonkwo is understandably fixated on escaping this unhappy past. Unlike Unoka, he works assiduously and achieves a prosperous life. Whatever his shortcomings, he is a good provider, as the plentiful food and wine at his feasts attest. Yet despite the prestige he attains, he lives in terror of repeating his father's inadequacies. "His whole life was dominated by fear, the fear of failure and of weakness," the narrator observes early on. "It was fear of himself, lest he should be found to resemble his father" (13). No surprise, then, that Okonkwo does not express sadness when Unoka gets swollen limbs and the Igbo abandon him in the Evil Forest to die. He views his father as having lived a "contemptible life," and his undignified manner of death is "shameful" to him, a sign of weakness that borders on the immoral (18). Wren suggests that the title-less Unoka who has died in this disgraceful way will never join the community of the clan's spiritual ancestors. When Okonkwo later builds himself an *obi* and inscribes "the symbols of his departed fathers," we can presume that Unoka is not represented there (130). Okonkwo's aversion to Unoka seems in harmony with the values of the clan. "Fortunately," the narrator tells us, "among these people a man was judged according to his worth and not according to the worth of his father" (8). The clan does not appear to think that Unoka has much worth. Okonkwo's feelings appear sanctioned as correct; no one expresses any concern about them.

But elsewhere Okonkwo's deep desire to appear able-bodied and to distinguish himself from his unsuccessful father lead to violence that exceeds Umoufian mores, causing other Igbo to reprimand him. While his physicality leads to his achieving great stature in the clan, it also causes him to be cruel to those close to him. His wives and children live "in perpetual fear of his fiery temper" (13). He beats his third wife "very heavily" during the Week of Peace for the small infraction of not returning to cook a meal, causing Ezeani, the priest of the earth goddess Ani, to chastise him (29). "The evil you have done can ruin the whole clan," he says (30). Okonkwo dutifully takes a sacrifice to the goddess's shrine, but he is outwardly unrepentant. A few pages later he beats his second wife, Ekwefi, for cutting a few leaves off a banana tree; he also beats his son Nwoye for crying and threatens to break his jaw or even to hang him to make him conform to his notions of male toughness. Despite all of his accomplishments, Okonkwo emerges as a heavy-handed, misogynistic, imperious husband and father who sometimes goes beyond the clan's moral boundaries in his insistence on obedience.

The most disturbing example of this behavior is his stubborn participation, despite warnings from others, in the killing of Ikemefuna, the pleasant boy from another clan who lives with Okonkwo's family for three years and calls him father. He takes part in the murder because "he was afraid of being thought weak," yet again reminding us of his desire to appear able-bodied and to escape his father's fate (61). Afterward, his friend Obierika condemns his choice. "What you have done will not please the Earth," he tells Okonk-wo. "It is the kind of action for which the goddess wipes out whole families" (67). In both cases, important members of the clan censure Okonkwo's actions, which they see as violating the clan's moral code and offending the gods. Okonkwo's violence also alienates him from his likable, sensitive son Nwoye (who must on some level wonder whether, if his father could kill an appealing boy such as Ikemefuna, Okonkwo could not also kill him). Nevertheless, he prefers to appear strong rather than admit a mistake, even if his actions harm his family or village. In this way, the opening description of his behavior with regard to his stammer introduces how, throughout the novel, Okonkwo almost instinctively responds to the possibility of appearing vulnerable with ferocity. Through admonitions by respected fellow Igbo, Achebe offers a not-so-subtle critique of Okonkwo's impulsive proclivity for violence: readers are invited to see it as often wrong, which implicitly opens the clan's ideology of able-bodiedness elsewhere to question.

Despite what Isidore Okpewho aptly calls Okonkwo's "masculinist paranoia" (35), Okonkwo does have tender emotions, but he suppresses these feelings to fit his desire always to appear strong. Achebe skillfully makes him seem a complex figure. For example, he secretly regrets disturbing the Week of Peace, but he does not want others to see this. Similarly, we learn that he becomes fond of the boy Ikemefuna—"inwardly of course," since "Okonkwo never showed any emotion openly, unless it be the emotion of anger" (28). To uphold his masculine code of strength, he believes he must push all tender emotions away. After Okonkwo participates in Ikemefuna's killing, he berates himself for feeling upset and being unable to sleep. "When did you become a shivering old woman," he asks himself, showing again how he links humane feelings with femininity and weakness (65). We see him having loving feelings for his daughter Enzima, whom he repeatedly wishes was a boy so she would have more opportunities. When the priestess Chielo takes his daughter away in the middle of the night, he is so anxious that he returns repeatedly to the Oracle's shrine. Such moments suggest that in a different context, Okonkwo might have been more willing to express tender feelings. But in Umoufia, in a culture that rewards male physical capacity, and with a father who embarrassed him with his lack of success and caused him to go hungry, Okonkwo represses such tendencies toward compassion. He never realizes the power of gentleness and care.

In these ways, even before the colonizers arrive, Umoufian culture frequently victimizes those who are disabled or otherwise thought different, as Okonkwo makes especially clear through his extreme example. It may well be, as with the Week of Peace, that with more time Umoufians would internally alter some of their traditions to make them more humane and just. This social evolution could certainly happen: thoughtful Igbo such as Nwoye and Obierika express misgivings about some harsh Umoufian traditions, and world history has many examples of internal dissent and cultural changes for the better. But the arrival of the British in the last third of the book abruptly prevents any chance of Umoufian self-correction. Attitudes toward disability play a key role in this transformation.

Colonization and the Meanings of Disability

While the British exert military violence elsewhere, such as in their horrific massacre of the people at the Abame market in retaliation for the killing of one of their own, in Umoufia they employ softer methods, including welcoming those Igbo who are stigmatized. Christian missionaries show up first and diplomatically but firmly contest the whole Umoufian belief system, including their rejection of people with disabilities and other differences, gradually winning converts with their humanitarianism. They rescue twin babies abandoned in the Evil Forest, causing a mother who had had twins repeatedly taken away to convert to Christianity. By welcoming the long-haired *osu* outcasts who previously had to live at the edges of Umoufian society, they also increase their number. The missionary Mr. Smith expresses horror at the Igbo belief in *ogbanje* children—that infants born with scars are evil—questioning another basic notion about disability in Umoufian culture and, although we do not get direct evidence of this, potentially making parents of scarred newborns feel less stigmatized. Through their benevolence toward oppressed others, the missionaries gain converts to their religion and gradually divide the clan. In this way, the Igbo's strict enforcement of normalcy in the novel actually weakens them, making them more vulnerable to colonial incursion and rupture.

The most personal account of such fissure in the clan occurs when Okonkwo's son Nwoye chooses to join the missionaries because he is distressed by the values around him. Nwoye has long been unhappy with his father's harsh tactics. The killing of Ikemefuna, to whom he was close, and the clan's throwing away twin infants leaves him with a "vague chill," a grief and discomfort at the clan's actions in general and his father's terrifying role in particular (62). Nwoye joins the Christian missionaries because their hymns "seemed to answer a vague and persistent question that haunted his young soul—the question of the twins crying in the bush and the question of Ikemefuna who was killed." They give "relief" from such doubts and hope for a more humane way of life (147). For his part, Okonkwo sees his son's act as "despicable" and beats him, causing Nwoye to leave his father's family for good. This break signifies to Okonkwo that Nwoye will not honor his ancestors' shrine according to Igbo custom and makes Okonkwo disavow him as a son. The family splinters over ethical questions about the treatment of others, the essence of human rights.

The colonial presence causes Igbo converts and clan leaders to spiral toward confrontation, but Achebe clearly upholds a peaceful sensibility; his narrator tells this violent story while never endorsing violence, as postcolonial theorists such as Frantz Fanon would do. Converts make the separation in the clan even clearer when they assault some of its hallowed symbols, raising the possibility of a violent clash. One overzealous *osu* convert precipitates a conflict in the clan by killing the Igbo's sacred python, a revered representative of the god of water, while later Enoch commits the serious crime of unmasking an *egwugwu* in public and, according to Igbo belief, killing an ancestral spirit. Such actions ratchet up tensions, with extremists on both sides in the clan advocating violence. Okonkwo characteristically favors driving off or assaulting the Christians, while after the *egwugwu* unmasking Enoch and other converts hope for "a holy war" (188). "But wisdom prevailed," the narrator says, clearly disapproving of radical calls for violence, again espousing a compassionate view, "and many lives were thus saved" (188). The Umoufians collectively respond by first ostracizing the Christians and, after the assault on the *egwugwu*, destroying Enoch's compound and the Christians' church, which causes the British to use deception to capture, imprison, and physically humiliate Umoufian leaders.

As these tensions rise between the groups, colonization upends the traditional social order in Umoufia. The effect seems all the more sudden to readers because, as changes first take place in the clan, we do not see them. Instead, we follow Okonkwo as he goes away into seven-year exile for inadvertently shooting a boy. When he returns, he finds stunning transformation. The British have set up a government; now a District Commissioner Court presides over cases rather than the traditional Igbo *egwugwu* spirits. Administering justice according to "the white man's law," the commissioner has little care for or understanding of Umoufian mores (174). Moreover, the colonizers transform the balance of power among African clans. While at the beginning of the book we learn that Umoufia is feared throughout the region for its proficiency at war, now power comes to Africans who most closely align with the white occupiers, as we see when a few British officers use Black Africans ("like us," Obierika sadly notes [139]) to massacre people at Abame, or when the British employ corrupt Black court messengers from other regions who gleefully abuse Umoufian leaders under arrest, beating and starving them, and adding to the fine for their own gain. The narrator briefly refers to other new institutions: mission schools that teach literacy, presumably in English; a hospital; and a trading store that changes the local economy, purchasing palm oil and kernels with all the repercussions of people in the Global North profiting off of those in the South (which was, of course, the main driver of colonialism and prefigures the contemporary moment of vast global inequity). "Much money flowed into Umoufia," the narrator says, and one could reasonably conjecture that the Umoufians' relative poverty makes them more vulnerable to colonial incursion (178). All of these developments work as soft colonialism, causing more Igbo to embrace the colonial presence. The changes cause Obierika poignantly to observe that the white man "has put a knife on the things that held us together and we have fallen apart" (176). Attitudes toward disabled people play a small but crucial role in sparking these seismic cultural changes, as the colonizers' welcoming attitude toward outcasts is one of the first ways they gain traction.

As the novel rushes to its conclusion, Okonkwo's fierce desire to uphold the clan and its traditional value of masculine physical toughness shapes his turn to violence at the end. As soon as he returns from his seven-year time away, he laments that Umoufians tolerate the British presence. He "mourned for the clan, which he saw breaking up and falling apart, and he mourned for the warlike men of Umoufia, who had so unaccountably become soft like women," the narrator says (183). Okonkwo deeply regrets how the colonizers change the village's ideals of physical strength. In the penultimate scene, as Umoufian men assemble and begin to discuss what to do about the "sacrilege" of their gods and "abomination" that have come into their midst (203), they are interrupted by five court messengers. We should remember that it is Black court messengers employed by the British who beat and starve Okonkwo and the other Igbo leaders after the District Commissioner tricks and imprisons them.

> [Okonkwo] sprang to his feet as soon as he saw who it was. He confronted the head messenger, trembling with hate, *unable to utter a word*. The man was fearless and stood his ground, his four-man line up behind him.
>
> In the brief moment the world seemed to stand still, waiting. There was utter silence. . . .
>
> "What do you want here?"
>
> "The white man whose power you know too well has ordered this meeting to stop."
>
> In a flash. . . . Okonkwo's machete descended twice and the man's head lay beside his uniformed body. (204, emphasis added)

Okonkwo's anger, impatience, and desire for action against injustice prompt him to kill the messenger. Notably, the scene contains a hint of his stammer: as the narrator says at the beginning, "Whenever he was angry and could not get his words out quickly enough, he would use his fists" (4). In this case, Okonkwo is so enraged that at first he is "unable to utter a word," and though he does speak eventually, he quickly winds up resorting to his machete. He appears to try to control vulnerability with active violence once again, which is a tendency that the novel consistently presents as a weakness. Okonkwo's rapid turn to physical action seems to be censured by both his clansmen and the narrative. When nobody follows his lead after the murder, "he knew that Umoufia would not go to war" and leaves by himself (205). Okonkwo acts before the community has agreed on a plan of action and, equally important, before the warriors have received the Oracle's sanction for a just war. As we learn in the beginning, Umoufia "never went to war unless its case was clear and just and was accepted as such by its Oracle" (12). He again impulsively goes beyond the clan's traditional mores for physical violence. Although the narrator does not often mention Okonkwo's stammer, it shapes his memorable character.

In the final chapter we learn that Okonkwo has perished by hanging, although ambiguities remain. In the novel, his friend Obierika interprets this as a suicide, and Achebe in his comments on the book has also treated Okonkwo's death as self-inflicted, as have critics. Obierika explains to the British District Commissioner that in Umoufia "it is an abomination for a man to take his own life" and charges that "you drove him to kill himself," blaming the death on the British occupation (207–208). If Okonkwo does commit suicide, he joins his father, Unoka, in dying in a shameful way, and like Unoka, he presumably will not be honored as an ancestor. In this reading, his suicide belies all of his earlier strength and bravery and, ironically, drives home how strength taken to excess is a weakness—again, a lesson for those wanting to enforce human rights and dignity for all. However, the ending could be read another way, for Okonkwo could have been forcibly hung, perhaps by court messengers eager for vengeance for their slain comrade. Would not the ultimate revenge be to kill him in a way that is seen as a shameful abomination in his clan and that effectively nullifies his previous heroic acts? That ambiguous possibility lurks over the end of the novel, challenging readers on how exactly to interpret Okonkwo's death. Achebe creates uncertainty with his quick ending. As Quayson points out, we do not get to see his wife Ekwefi's or daughter Enzima's reactions to Okonkwo's death ("Realism" 247). Would they see it as a suicide, too?

For that matter, we do not get to see any disabled Umoufians other than Okonkwo after the colonizers arrive, which makes the fate of disabled people under British rule unclear. The narrator does refer to the missionaries' rescuing abandoned twin infants, but do they intervene when those with swollen limbs are taken to the Evil Forest to die? Are those born with missing fingers or marks seen differently after Mr. Smith challenges belief in *ogbanje*? Achebe chooses not to answer such questions in the novel, and the answers are not easy to infer. If we return to Agboola's bleak testimony that disabled people at mid-century were routinely ignored, with which I started the chapter, it appears that British colonization did not do much to empower disabled people in Nigeria. In Agboola's case, he credits his education and rise (he became a dean at Gallaudet University in Washington, DC, in the early twenty-first century) to a deaf African American, Andrew Foster, which adds another twist to the global disability dynamic. Foster was the first deaf African American student to graduate from Gallaudet, in 1954; he overcame racist obstacles to become a missionary and eventually founded thirty-two schools for deaf students in Africa, including the one Agboola attended. Despite some familiar trappings of imperialism—missionaries from wealthier places in the North, founding schools in the South—the story provides evidence that in some instances, transnational connections, especially those forged by common race and disability, can be mutually empowering.

But we do not see anything like that in *Things Fall Apart*. Instead, we find an ironic ending that opens outward, leaving much unsaid. The British District Commissioner imagines the "reasonable paragraph" he will write about Okonkwo in his planned book project, condescendingly titled *The Pacification of the Primitive Tribes of the Lower Niger*. As *Things Fall Apart* definitely shows, Okonkwo's story abundantly deserves an entire book, and the Igbo of Umoufia are not primitive before colonization, although, like societies everywhere, they have injustices, too.

Obierika's charge that the British drove Okonkwo to suicide is the closest Achebe comes explicitly to blaming the colonizers, leaving another ambiguity. Clearly, the British are themselves flagrant human rights abusers in the novel. They massacre the Igbo at the Abame market; they impose laws that work to their own benefit; and they deceitfully arrest and condone the torture of Umoufian leaders. Still, Achebe refuses to trade in simplicities, showing respectful British such as the first missionary, Mr. Brown, and gesturing to the potential good that the colonizers do—for example, by offering Igbo education and medical care, although even that could be called a form of soft colonialism designed to give the colonizers more power and control. (In colonial situations, colonizers could withhold medical help to get their way.) The complicated legacy of colonialism is something that, unlike in the North, many nations in the Global South must contend with on an ongoing basis. As *Things Fall Apart* suggests, the experience of colonialism was often traumatic, dividing families and people.

Achebe's novel makes us witness a disabled protagonist and the endangered culture he inhabits, but it probably stops short of producing strong feelings of kinship to disabled people. In Okonkwo's case, his violence and obvious character flaws likely prevent feelings of connection, however much his efforts to pass as normal resonate with disabled readers who often feel similar pressure. We do not encounter other disabled characters in much depth. Instead, while the novel contains many diverse perspectives and shows the complexities surrounding colonization, the book finally seems to uphold more moderate and thoughtful characters, such as Nwoye, Obierika, and the respectful British missionary Mr. Brown, all of whom seem tacitly to endorse humanity and compassion, values behind the ethics of disability justice. Notably, Nwoye resembles Achebe's own father, who was among the first Igbo in his village to convert to Christianity, lending weight to the sense that he is close to the ethical core of the book. The narrative forces readers to attempt to answer such questions, part of the reason it is so rewarding to read and teach.

In these ways, the 1958 novel introduces many central concerns that regularly appear across later depictions of disability in Anglophone postcolonial literature, including the imbricated and dominant power of colonialism, poverty, and indigenous metaphysical beliefs that surround disabled identity. Writing on the eve of Nigerian independence, Achebe presents the dignity and intelligence of precolonial Igbo culture in *Things Fall Apart*, but he is not afraid to include problems of that society. He implicitly critiques Umoufian celebration of physical power and able-bodiedness that leaves it vulnerable to outside incursion, most explicitly in his depiction of Okonkwo's characteristic devotion to strength, even as he shows the Igbo capacity for self-correction before colonization. Furthermore, we should remember that some able-bodied Igbo violate the human rights of disabled Igbo in the story. The novel illustrates the paradox that surrounds human rights: even victims of human rights abuses can perpetuate them on others.

This critique exists alongside the novel's quiet recognition of the power of storytelling, especially women's storytelling, and of women, who typically have a subservient role in the clan. Achebe seems intent not just on restoring a sense of dignity to his people who have been subjected by colonial rule, but also on warning them of the importance of being mindful and inclusive of all members of society. Through its attention to race, gender, economics, and culture, *Things Fall Apart* contributes to the consciousness that led to the subsequent adoption of core human rights instruments, including the United Nations' 1965 Convention on the Elimination of All Forms of Racial Discrimination; the 1966 Covenant on Economic, Social, and Cultural Rights; and the 1979 Convention on the Elimination of All Forms of Discrimination against Women. By showing the importance of including everyone, no matter what their physical ability, it also supports a movement that very gradually—and especially after 1981—led to more global recognition of the human rights of disabled people.

3

Extraordinary Bodies

Magic Realism, Disability, and Rushdie's Midnight's Children

A major lesson of the [1981 International Year of Disabled Persons]
was that the image of persons with disabilities depends to an
important extent on social attitudes; these were a major barrier
to the realization of the goal of full participation and equality in
society by persons with disabilities.

—UNITED NATIONS,
"The International Year of Disabled Persons, 1981"

When Salman Rushdie's novel *Midnight's Children* was published in
1981, it serendipitously appeared during the United Nations' first-
ever International Year of Disabled Persons, which stressed full participation of disabled people and their right to equal opportunity. The year
showed how disability human rights were gaining worldwide notice and directed attention especially toward the pivotal importance of social attitudes
toward disability. The novel not only quickly won international acclaim, receiving, among other awards, the Booker Prize for 1981 (it would later gain
the Best of the Bookers special award in 2008), but also contributed to notions
of disabled people's worth.

By making disabled characters the center of the narrative, the novel advances disability human rights in at least three ways, each of which I explore
in this chapter. First, depictions of disability proliferate in the narrative, both
reflecting and adding to the emerging global attention to disability. Rushdie
extends the transnational tradition of putting disability at the heart of magic
realist fiction. As I show, sometimes his disabled characters have surprising,
even extraordinary, capability that collectively testifies to disabled people's
value. Second, through its disabled narrator, Saleem Sinai, *Midnight's Children*
adds a revolutionary new element to the elusive kinship I have been tracing
between readers and disabled characters. A first-person disabled narrator is
seemingly easier for readers to feel a connection with, although Saleem's pro-
fessed supernatural powers might make it harder to identify with him. Finally,

despite their special abilities, Saleem and other disabled characters are always simultaneously disempowered, made passive and vulnerable by a society that frequently discriminates against and makes decisions for them. They cannot achieve self-determination, which is a key to human rights after 1960.[1]

Saleem is one of many disabled or physically anomalous characters in the novel, and together these extraordinary figures help to shape Rushdie's critique of normalcy, authoritarianism, and cultural rigidity. In depicting the lead-up to, and consequences of, India's independence from Britain in 1947 and simultaneous partition to form Pakistan, Rushdie repeatedly deploys extraordinary figures of physical difference. From Saleem's physical anomalies to the unusual forms of some other midnight's children to beggars and others with disabilities, the novel regularly returns to exceptional bodies. While the majority of critics have not seen the novel through the lens of disability, scholars such as Sanjeev Uprety and Clare Barker offer a corrective, resolutely identifying *Midnight's Children* as a disability narrative.[2] Barker argues that Saleem's disabled self and his claims of magical powers are not contradictory but part of a sustained critique. As she puts it, referring to Saleem and the other "midnight's children" born with extraordinary abilities near the moment of Indian independence: "On the one hand, the children (Saleem included) are larger-than-life beings whose superhuman powers" give a sense of hope for the newly independent nation-state. "At the same time," she continues, "they are vulnerable citizens marked by their extreme difference from the norm." Materiality and metaphor exist together. She concludes that "the magical and the real offer an interwoven attack on exclusionary discourses and practices" (132).

Such "exclusionary discourses and practices" raise implicitly the topic of disability rights; Barker sees Rushdie as using both magic and realism to denounce discrimination and injustice. Barker's framework helps us to see how these characters often have unexpected and seemingly magical powers and express vulnerability. Saleem and some other disabled figures emerge as having transgressive potential to upend the political hierarchy, a subversiveness that the government finally seeks to control through medical intervention in their bodies. Even as he shows disability to involve vulnerability, he consistently upholds the intrinsic value of disabled people. *Midnight's Children* implicitly but consistently points to disability as a basic element of human society and, by extension, of the need for disability human rights in India and elsewhere.

Before continuing, we should remember that this novel, which is unique in so many ways, belongs to the transnational literary genre of magic realism, which typically commingles the fantastic and the real in a matter-of-fact manner. The form emerged during the twentieth century and often implicitly critiques Euro-American scientific rationalism. Prominent practitioners include Jorge Luis Borges (Argentina) in the 1940s and Gabriel García Márquez (Colombia) and others associated with the Latin American literary Boom of the 1960s. Writers across the world have since employed elements of the technique. By using such factors as the supernatural, dreams, traditional cultural views, and fairy tales to express the seemingly fantastic as quotidian and unremarkable, such works regularly confound the dominance of Euro-American logic. As Michael Bell puts it, the common understanding of magic realism is that it "draws on pre-scientific folk belief to subvert the 'Western' commitment to scientific reason, itself associated with both imperialism and a history of realistic representation so that the genre is intrinsically oppositional and progressive" (179). Through its imaginative elements, magic realist fiction often defies the rationalism of Euro-American imperial powers, resists the verisimilitude of traditional literary realism, and asserts the value and uniqueness of its own culture even as it sometimes critiques it.

In *Midnight's Children* Rushdie extends this characteristic while giving the genre his own distinctive stamp. For instance, he applies magic realist techniques to India in a way that not only regularly shows India's distinctiveness from Euro-American scientific rationality but also seems to uphold hybridity. Saleem presents himself as an allegory for the postcolonial Indian nation. Because he turns out, biologically, to have a British father and Indian mother, Rushdie implicitly suggests that modern India itself has mixed parentage of traditional Indian and colonial British influences.[3] In his person, Saleem embodies the two. At other points in the narrative Rushdie parodies both British and Indian cultural traditions, moving between them; hybridity and in-betweenness seem the rule, as is characteristic in Rushdie's oeuvre.[4] Notably, though born and raised in India, Rushdie gained high school and college education in England, became a British citizen in 1964, and lived mostly in Britain during the 1970s when he was writing the novel.

Disability often lies at the core of magic realist narratives, which present it in fantastic or surprising ways. Here, too, *Midnight's Children* extends the genre. To be sure, this tendency is not unique. Northern narratives, especially before the Age of Reason in the eighteenth century, have a history of linking disability with the supernatural. In Greek mythology the blind Tiresias has gifts of prophecy, while several books reveal that in early eighteenth-century London, many people believed that the ostensibly deaf Duncan Campbell had clairvoyant knowledge.[5] Such associations contain the idea of compensation for disability, as if in losing a limb or sense disabled people gain some preternatural ability. Magic realist fiction functions similarly but often takes things further. For instance, Borges's story "Funes el memorioso" (Funes the Memorius [1942]), published in translation in his collection *Ficciones*, tells of Ireneo Funes, a Uruguayan farmworker who is thrown from a wild horse and becomes "hopelessly crippled" (109). Yet somehow through the accident he attains a perfect memory that allows him to recall things in precise detail. The story upends traditional notions of disability and ability and expresses ambivalence at easy correlations of disability and inferiority.[6] Moreover, García Márquez deploys disability on multiple levels in his masterpiece *Cien años de soledad* (*One Hundred Years of Solitude* [1967]), from José Arcadio Buendía apparently losing his reason (yet independently deducing that the world is round) to Úrsula achieving new insights once she becomes physically blind.[7] The pre–*Midnight's Children* list could also include influential Northern works such as Günter Grass's *The Tin Drum* (1959) and Toni Morrison's *Sula* (1973).[8] With Saleem's first-person narration and purported extraordinary abilities in *Midnight's Children*, Rushdie continues, and markedly increases, this tradition of centering magic realism on figures of disability.

Some readers might reasonably charge that such a linkage of disability to extraordinary powers amounts to representing "supercrips" who raise false expectations of actual disabled people. A supercrip describes a disabled person whom the public sees as excelling in surprising ways that may isolate "regular" disabled people still more. One could imagine depictions of disabled people with unusual powers as adding to public perceptions that disabled people are otherworldly, preternatural, and different, which could work against seeing disabled people as *people* and achieving disability human rights. But one could perhaps counter that such depictions are uncommon and challenge expectations of disabled people, contesting widespread notions of inferiority and making them worthy of attention while adding surprise, even humor, to accounts of them in a way that relates to the more prosaic but nonetheless real talents and verve that disabled people may possess. Magic realist deployments of disability frequently hover between progressive and regressive, complicating the meanings of physical, cognitive, and sensory difference in society.

Another of *Midnight's Children*'s signal contributions to elusive kinship and disability rights is that it features a disabled first-person narrator, which prompts a stronger connection in most readers' imaginations to disability. By identifying himself as a person with an exceptional body (with facial birthmarks and no sense of smell when he's born, and, adventitiously, deafness in one ear, a missing part of a finger, and more), Rushdie's irrepressible narrator, Saleem, introduces a change in point of view that is as subtle as it is momentous. Most, if not all, previous well-known Anglophone fiction of the Global

South, even if it forcefully dramatizes disabled people's lives in ways that make them vivid in readers' imaginations, presents disabled figures as separate bodies, as a *they* set apart. The arrival of a disabled *I* through Saleem compels readers even more to inhabit the life and consciousness of a disabled other in their imaginations and potentially to feel a stronger connection with them, providing a model that some subsequent authors from the Global South, from Chris Abani to Indra Sinha and Petina Gappah, would follow.[9]

Yet while the novel immediately adds a new element to the elusive, occasional kinship between readers and disabled figures in the literature, it also introduces a dilemma, for *Midnight's Children*'s exuberant style and Saleem's claims of supernatural powers and exceptional significance may actually make it *harder* for some readers (especially readers in the North) to identify with him. As we will see, Saleem asserts that he has singular telepathic capabilities and claims that he serves as a living allegory for modern India. According to Michael Gorra, "Both the fantasy and rhetorical extravagance of *Midnight's Children* can numb its readers to anything but its own exhilaration" (200). Along the same lines, Elizabeth Anker notes that Rushdie's pervasive irony, satire, and postmodern antics "seem to divert attention from [his fictions'] depictions of abuses of human rights" ("Narrating" 149). Paradoxically, we therefore could say the novel positions its disabled narrator as both startlingly close (through Saleem's narration) and distant and unfamiliar (through the playful style and his assertions of special powers and allegorical significance). Such contradictory features make this intricate epic novel and its relation to disability rights even more complex.

Tellingly, many critics have approached Saleem not as a figure of disability but as a grotesque, a literary creation whose physical aberrations satirically reflect postcolonial Indian history. The concept of the grotesque has traditionally been ambiguous; Geoffrey Galt Harpham calls it "the slipperiest of aesthetic categories" (461). Still, Mikhail Bakhtin and others have presented the grotesque as being connected to common people and having a life-affirming, transgressive quality that is an inversion of the existing political hierarchy. As we will see, Saleem and the novel's other disabled characters do have subversive potential, the possible ability to unsettle hegemonic order and assumptions. In this sense, they are grotesque figures. But to reduce them to an aesthetic category, or to focus only on the magical aspects of their representation, is to miss out on the *real* in magic realism and to elide the relationship of such depictions to actual Indians with disabilities.

Like Barker, other commentators also point to the difficulty of separating the fantastic from the "real." Some readers in India apparently have even received the magical in the narrative as a part of its verisimilitude. While critics such as Harish Trivedi have charged that Rushdie's use of the fantastic and excess to depict India amounts to Orientalism and accounts for the novel's popularity in Europe and America, in the novel itself, Saleem notes that the Indian popular press often contains accounts of "magic children and assorted freaks" (226). To him, the magical elements convey a reality of Indian identity and tradition. Twenty-five years after the novel was published, Rushdie confirmed this sense, writing, "In the West people tended to read *Midnight's Children* as a fantasy, while in India people thought of it as pretty realistic, almost a history book" ("Introduction" xiii). To many readers in India, his connecting disability to magic evidently did not seem surprising. Like the most effective magic realist stories, *Midnight's Children* makes it difficult, if not impossible, to distinguish the supernatural from the pedestrian. They seem bound up in each other.

Finally, all of these representations relate to the notion of self-determination, which has been central to third-generation human rights. In *Midnight's Children*, especially with Saleem's forced sinus surgery and final involuntary sterilization, we see how denial of disabled people's ability to make decisions for themselves is in effect a denial of dignity, a portrayal that maps well onto global disability activists' later slogan, "Nothing About Us Without Us."[10] Article 19 of the 2006 Convention on the Rights of Persons with Disabilities recognizes "the equal rights of all persons with disabilities to live in the community, with choices equal to others." In all of these ways, *Midnight's Children* is a revolutionary, if complex, literary work that advances disability human rights.

Representing Disability as Potent before Independence

The novel employs disability even before Saleem and the other midnight's children are born, establishing physical aberration as a common part of human experience and as something frequently connected to both tradition and supernatural powers. We learn early on that Saleem's grandfather Aadam Aziz in Kashmir has a gigantic nose, which the old boatman Tai admonishes him to cherish. "A nose like that, little idiot, is a great gift," Tai tells the boy. "I say: trust it. When it warns you, look out or you'll be finished. Follow your nose and you'll go far" (13). Tai somewhat comically introduces the idea that exceptional bodies can be an asset if one accepts them; he links them to the intuitive knowledge of Eastern tradition. When Aadam later returns from medical training in Germany with a stethoscope, Tai responds with disgust, noting that Aadam will "use such a machine now, instead of your own big nose" (17). Tai sees Aadam's reliance on modern Western technology as a rejection of the mystical tradition represented by his unusual nose and stops bathing in protest. Since Tai himself is called an "old half-wit" and talks in a "fantastic, grandiloquent and ceaseless" way, we could question his reliability (9). His fanciful monologues do connect him to the narrator, Saleem, whose own tale, he admits, contains some inaccuracies. Yet as the novel continues Aadam's nose does in fact warn him of danger, such as during the Amritsar massacre when it itches, causing him to sneeze and fall forward just before the British guns open fire, saving his life. For all his strangeness, Tai emerges as an insightful observer, showing that even cognitively eccentric people have value and anticipating the eventual importance of Saleem's own exceptional nose.

As Saleem goes on to introduce the "multitudes" who have helped to shape his life, we meet other minor characters with disabilities who occasionally have distinctive powers, suggesting that all people with physical differences in the narrative have unusual potential (4). For example, early on we learn that Aadam's father had a stroke that left him cognitively disabled; he spends his time sitting in a chair in a dark room making bird whistles. His situation is both tragic and funny. Even though he has lost the capacity to talk to other people and to work, when thirty different species of birds come sit on the sill outside his shuttered window and converse with him, it appears as if he has gained a rare skill. Like Borges's Funes, who somehow gets a perfect memory after falling from a horse, Aadam's father gains a talent with a major disability; the authors show these characters as happy even if they no longer pursue many life activities, which contradicts the trauma and deprivation society commonly associates with strokes and physical disablement.

Sometimes we cannot be sure whether a disabled character's power is magical or not, such as when Ghani, the blind landowner, engineers the marriage between his daughter Naseem and Aadam. Saying that his daughter suffers from a series of trivial medical complaints, Ghani arranges for the young doctor Aadam to examine her through a seven-inch hole in a sheet. After several years, having only seen parts of the mysterious woman on the other side, Aadam falls in love and proposes to Naseem, which appears to have been Ghani's design all along. Saleem says that the sheet works its "sorcerer's spell" (21), causing Aadam to "think of the perforated sheet as something sacred and magical" (23); Saleem himself refers to it as "my talisman" (4). The bemused sorcerer behind the spell here is the blind Ghani, although one could debate how magical his abilities actually are. He presumably draws on his personal experience with the power of limited vision to bring about what he desires: the marriage of his daughter to an eligible bachelor.

This linkage between disability and special power appears on a larger and potentially more threatening level when Saleem's mother, Amina, goes to a ghetto-like space in Bombay and is horrified by the destitute disabled people she sees.

> Look, my God, those beautiful children have black teeth! . . . And, Allah-tobah, heaven forfend, sweeper women with—no!—how *dreadful!*—collapsed spines . . . and cripples everywhere, mutilated by loving parents to ensure them of a lifelong income from begging. . . . [Y]es, beggars in boxcars, grown men with babies' legs, in crates on wheels. (89)

Some readers have criticized Rushdie for presenting too idealistic and romantic a picture of Bombay in *Midnight's Children*, and Rushdie does focus on relatively wealthy people in the novel, but passages such as this one realistically show the majority of disabled people in India living in conditions of deprivation.[11] The reference to "cripples . . . mutilated by loving parents" points to the irony that some parents disabled their children intentionally to make them more effective beggars. This resonates throughout the narrative and apparently reflects a true state of affairs; one might recall other representations of intentional disabling, such as the character of Zaita, who cripples people who come to him in the Egyptian novelist Naguib Mahfouz's *Midaq Alley*, written in the 1940s, or, more recently, the scene of an Indian beggar child being blinded in the Oscar-winning film *Slumdog Millionaire* (2008).[12] Later in the novel, we learn of "beggars . . . pretending to be blind," showing again how, in the economics of poverty here, becoming or appearing disabled can be an advantage that makes one into a more effective earner (310).

At any rate, in confronting the masses of impoverished disabled people, Amina is deeply unsettled not just by their physical aberrations, but also by the sense of their untapped power. As Saleem narrates:

> Children tugging at the pallu of her sari, heads everywhere staring at my mother, who thinks, It's like being surrounded by some terrible monster, a creature with heads and heads and heads; but she corrects herself, no, of course not a monster, these poor poor people—what then? *A power of some sort, a force which does not know its strength,* which has perhaps decayed into impotence through never having been used. . . . "I'm frightened," my mother finds herself thinking. (89, emphasis added)

Amina's complicated reaction reflects the confusing mélange of thoughts and emotions nondisabled people often have when they unexpectedly encounter disability. She initially feels so repulsed by the unfamiliar human shapes crowding around her that she imagines them as an alarming many-headed creature, in a way that resembles Ato Quayson's notion of aesthetic nervousness, in which disability makes other characters, and readers, anxious (*Aesthetic* 15). But she quickly tries to convert her uneasiness into a more acceptable and manageable pity. Just as rapidly, however, she fears the unrealized "power of some sort" that she senses the people have. This strength seems to be something beyond the usual cliché about the unrealized power of unorganized masses, although that element is present, too. It appears more directly connected to extraordinary bodies, to the special ability that the narrative often assigns to people with physical differences. Just as Saleem later discovers his own magical capabilities, so these disabled denizens of the slum appear to have a dormant potency that scares Amina.

From the start of the novel, Rushdie therefore makes characters with physical differences have potentially supernatural abilities and disruptive power even if they themselves do not know it. To be sure, not all, or even most, of the disabled people in the novel have remarkable traits. Later, one of Mian Abdullah's killers has a glass eye while Amina hobbles because of corns on her feet, and neither of them seems to have any exceptional skills. At the minimum, such examples remind us of the material reality of disability, of how it is an ordinary part of everyday human experience, cutting across class, gender, and race, quotidian, the seeming opposite of wondrous. But after the subtle powers associated with other characters with physical and sensory differences, we have to wonder whether these disabilities cannot lead to special abilities, too. The effect is to make it more difficult for readers to bypass disability, since every seemingly pedestrian physical difference might have magical properties.

In another twist, the novel early on sometimes connects unusual bodies with the fantastic by presenting some outward appearances as dramatic products and symbols of mental conditions. For instance, during the Amritsar massacre, when wounded people fall on Aadam, the clasp of his European doctor's bag digs into his chest, leaving a bruise that mysteriously does not fade for the rest of his life. The permanent bruise seems to signify his lingering trauma after the mass killing; it also suggests how he is marked by his experience abroad. Shortly thereafter, we learn that Rani of Cooch Naheen "was going white in blotches," which, she says, is the "outward expression of the internationalism of my spirit," the physical product of her transnational mentality (45). Her condition anticipates how later, after India gains independence, many businessmen grow progressively whiter, suggesting how they, too, follow Euro-American thinking and capitalist practices that are not traditional in India. Similarly, when Aadam's wife, Naseem (who becomes known as the Reverend Mother), gives her husband the silent treatment for three years, she gains substantial weight because, as Saleem explains, the "unspoken words inside her were blowing her up" (62). In these cases, the narrative attributes mysterious changes in appearance not to biological conditions (we do not get the kind of scientific diagnosis that Aadam learns in medical school in Europe) but, instead, to cognitive states. How one thinks and behaves can, of course, affect health, as anyone who studies psychosomatic medicine knows, but Rushdie converts this into something fantastic, humorous, and whimsically exaggerated. Physical differences function here as symbolic of something larger about the characters' selves.

As we can see, in the early chapters of *Midnight's Children* Rushdie treats physical differences in a manner that often eludes rational explanation. Bodily anomalies can serve as a harbinger of supernatural powers, insight, or strange manifestations of inner psychology. He further complicates matters by presenting some conditions that do not even seem to be physically real but are, instead, metaphors for cognitive states. When Aadam, recently returned from Europe, bumps his nose on the ground while attempting to pray at the beginning of the novel and resolves never to prostrate himself to a god or human again, "this decision," we are told, "made a hole in him, a vacancy in a vital inner chamber" (4). Although Saleem presents the hole as real, it does not seem literal: when Aadam subsequently asks his mother whether she can see the "hole in the middle of me the size of a melon," she cannot (18). No one, including Aadam, ever reports seeing it. Instead, it seems to signify the gap and loss that Aadam feels when he renounces the religion traditional to his family and Kashmiri culture. By declaring himself independent and agnostic, he loses part of his past identity, part of the belief system that makes sense of the world. We learn that the hole makes him "vulnerable to women and history" (4). Rushdie uses the metaphor of the hole to suggest what is lost through internationalism, how Aadam comes to question and reject parts of his traditional cultural identity without anything to replace them except his newly acquired scientific knowledge and European friends, who are far away. When Saleem later says that he has inherited a "hole in the center of me" from his grandfather, a hole "caused by his (which is also my) failure to believe or disbelieve in God," it epitomizes not just how he is estranged from traditional Muslim beliefs, but also how all the supernatural and allegorical meanings of disability, real and imagined, cohere and are magnified in his own extraordinary body (220, 315).

Saleem Sinai's Exceptional Body and Indian Independence

More than those of just about any other disabled character in literature, Saleem Sinai's physical differences seem overdetermined. More than Shakespeare's hunchbacked Richard III, more than Melville's one-legged Captain Ahab, Faulkner's cognitively disabled Benjy Compson, McCullers's deaf John Singer, or García Márquez's blind Úrsula Buendía, Saleem's abnormal body is freighted with meaning from the very first page. Part of this is due to the fact that he is the narrator, and we should question how seriously we should take his energetic, if also narcissistic, pronouncements. Saleem is born at the stroke of midnight on August 15, 1947, at the precise instant that India becomes independent from Great Britain, which makes him see himself as an instant allegory. "I have been mysteriously handcuffed to history," he famously says, "my destinies indissolubly chained to those of my country" (3). He presents himself as fundamentally connected to modern India. Even the fact that he turns out to be switched at birth and his biological father is British corresponds to the identity of postindependence India, which is profoundly hybrid, diverse, and partially shaped by the centuries-long history of British colonization. His physical aberrations, too, prove central to his relationship with the nation. In addition to being born with a large, congested nose, bulbous temples, and facial birthmarks, Saleem grows up incapable of smelling, becomes bowlegged due to typhoid, is deafened in one ear when his father hits him, loses part of one finger, and, late in the novel, becomes an amnesiac devoid of memory. Most significantly, he discovers his ungainly, perpetually dripping nose is the conduit for magical telepathic powers within India and, at the moment of the novel's composition, believes his thirty-two-year-old body is cracking and will soon crumble into millions of bits. A complex allegory, a vulnerable disabled character, and someone who says he has fantastic powers all at once, Saleem reveals the history of modern India and of disabled Indians through his corporeal differences.

From the opening of the narrative, Saleem associates himself both with the new nation born at the same moment and with disability, which has provocative but ambiguous implications. "I was not a beautiful baby," he says, going on to describe the birthmarks on his face and his "monstrous" nose (140–141). In contrast to the fireworks, newspaper story, and presidential letter at his birth, this self-professed allegory for India calls himself "ugly" and seems decidedly common (229). Read one way, Saleem's ugliness could represent his biological father's Britishness; he apparently gets his gargantuan nose from a French grandmother on that side of the family. As we explore more in the next chapter, many postcolonial authors deploy disability as a convenient metaphor for the scarring damage brought about on a nation by colonialism, and Rushdie may be following suit. Yet matters are not simple, for Saleem's adoptive grandfather, Aadam Sinai, also has a gigantic nose. Furthermore, we learn that Toxy Catrack, the cognitively disabled girl who lives near young Saleem in Bombay, is "the product of years of inbreeding," suggesting the dangers of being too insular in India or elsewhere (148). From another view, we could interpret Saleem's abnormalities as a potential product of the poverty of his biological mother, Vanita, who probably could not eat well or receive prenatal care while she was pregnant, a situation common to many indigent mothers around the world. (Tellingly, Vanita dies from hemorrhaging after childbirth while the doctors in another room absurdly focus on the broken toe of a prosperous man, Saleem's adoptive father, Ahmed Sinai.) Given Saleem's allegorical claims, his disabilities seem to ask for interpretation, for significance, but exactly what they mean at his birth remains elusive.

What becomes clear is that, from his birth, Saleem's physical differences stigmatize him, putting him, like many disabled people, outside of society's conceptions of normal and consequential. When the infant Saleem is slow to speak, his mother and ayah keep their fear that he cannot talk from his father, for, as Saleem ruefully tells us, "No father wants a damaged child" (141). Against the magical elements associated with disability elsewhere, we get a stark reminder of the rejection disabled children frequently encounter and their vulnerability; it is no accident that a significant number of children available for adoption internationally have special needs and have been given up by their parents. Although Saleem does eventually talk, his father interprets his gargantuan nose as the shameful result of masturbation while it causes his mother to feel guilt at her perceived failures, and both of them quarrel over it. Like many disabled children, Saleem internalizes others' views of him as inferior. As he grows, he worries that his own existence will turn out to be "utterly useless, void, and without a shred of a purpose" and, given his allegorical claims—Saleem *is* India—implicitly suggests that India's existence may be similarly pointless (173).

Things begin to change with the aid of Toxy Catrack, the cognitively disabled neighbor who apparently has preternatural powers. Introduced as an "idiot daughter . . . who had to be locked up with her nurse," Toxy is twenty-one, apparently does not speak at all, and is a figure of sexuality; at one point she masturbates naked behind the bars in her window. Her character in some ways alludes to Bertha Mason, the madwoman in the attic and a figure of passion in Charlotte Brontë's *Jane Eyre*, but Toxy takes on more explicitly positive qualities. Saleem finds her admirable. "Inside my head she was beautiful, because she had not lost the gifts with which every baby is born and which life proceeds to erode," he says (148). To him, she embodies something pure, unsullied by civilization, while the American girl Evie feels no such romantic appreciation, asserting that Toxy "oughta be put down like rats" (210). Toxy herself appears to have special awareness, making her another of the novel's disabled characters with supernatural skills. When her father starts an affair, she says, she somehow "knew what was going on" and cries and writhes at his departures (297). Moreover, Saleem credits her with first helping him to find his telepathic powers, saying she "gave a door in my mind a little nudge, so that when an accident took place in a washing-chest it was probably Toxy who made it possible" (148). Much later he refers again to "Toxy Catrack, nudging open the door which would later lead in the children of midnight," indicating that this easy-to-overlook disabled character plays a central role in shaping his fate (466). Coming after the "half-wit" Tai's influence on Aadam two generations before, Rushdie implicitly suggests that cognitively disabled people can help others find their gifts. They empower people who take them seriously.

If Toxy provides the first opening, Saleem's full epiphany comes when he is almost nine years old and discovers that the meaning of disability depends not only on context, but also on the fantastic, unexpected extrasensory abilities that optimistically reflect new national unity across cultural differences. While hiding in a container filled with smelly laundry, he realizes that having a perpetually congested nose becomes an asset. "A disability in the world outside washing-chests can be a positive advantage once you're in," Saleem observes, pointing out that the significance of disability is often not constant but shifts with the situation (176). After inhaling a pajama cord, young Saleem gives a colossal sniff, painfully pulling it up his nostril, and suddenly, astoundingly, his sinuses have fantastic telepathic powers that let Saleem hear others' thoughts in his head. While earlier Aadam's large nose warns him of danger, Saleem's goes further. "My nose began to sing," he declares, adding that he had "a headful of gabbling tongues" (184–185). He soon finds that he can control the voices, select what he wants to hear, and even go beyond the many different languages to understand the "universally intelligible thought-forms" that lie beneath, what psycholinguists today might refer to as "mentalese," the thoughts in the mind without words (192). Saleem's magical ability goes beyond that of any other character to this point; it lives up to the fanfare of his birth and adds another level to his allegorical meaning. His abnormal nose, which evidently comes from his British biological father, somewhat ironically unites and makes understandable the thoughts of diverse citizens throughout the nation, but only in India, causing him jubilantly to see his skill as "better than All-India Radio" (186). His newfound powers express the hope of a new postcolonial Indian unity and identity.

Although Saleem's magical abilities elevate him to special status, the realities of disability and stigma in India, at least in his social class, soon prompt him to hide his gift. When he tells his family that he is hearing archangels talking to him in his head, his father strikes him. "I could never hear properly in my left ear after that," Saleem says, adding to the litany of impairments in his body (187). He soon resolves to keep his clairvoyant powers from his parents for fear that "they would see his gift as a kind of shameful deformity" (190). His nation, he goes on to explain, is "a country where any physical or mental peculiarity in a child is a source of deep family shame" (193). Disability is highly stigmatized in India, Saleem says, a statement that could describe the condition of disabled people throughout the world.[13] Still, this assertion may apply only to the more prosperous classes. As we have seen, the novel refers to some impoverished but loving Indian parents intentionally disabling their children so they have a livelihood based on begging; they appear to use the very pity and shame that disability evokes to their advantage to make money. Disability again paradoxically becomes an asset; context again inflects the meaning of physical difference. By saying that a disabled child embarrasses a family in India, Saleem points to how, in his culture, disability is apparently often understood as indicating something wrong with the parents' morality. Anita Ghai, for example, refers to a "common perception" in India that "views disability as a retribution for past karmas (actions) from which there can be no reprieve" (89). This stigma causes Saleem to keep his special powers secret from his parents, who, to their credit, despite his "cucumber-nose stainface chinlessness horn-temples bandy-legs finger-loss monk's-tonsure and . . . (admittedly unknown to them) bad left ear" do love him (345).

Even as Saleem relates his secret and amazing mental journeys into other people's minds around India, we cannot quickly bypass the possibility that he is imagining things. As the Canadian critic Neil ten Kortenaar asks, "Is the magic of the novel a function of India's spiritual nature or of Saleem's madness?" (230). Kortenaar points out that "as a psychological case study, the novel is unconvincing" (10). Like other magic realist fiction, *Midnight's Children* asks us to accept the fantastic alongside everyday verisimilitude. Saleem himself seems acutely aware that readers might find him insane. He admits that he himself has considered the possibility, just as the Prophet Muhammad, on first hearing voices, believed himself insane. But Saleem insists his account is the literal truth. "Don't make the mistake of dismissing what I've unveiled as mere delirium," he says, "or even as the insanely exaggerated fantasies of a lonely, ugly child" (229). Although he admits being an unreliable narrator elsewhere, such as when he forgets the date of Gandhi's assassination, he asserts that his account, written for his son, is accurate. It would seem that Rushdie associates the magic in the novel with India (and often with Indian people with disabilities) rather than with any madness in Saleem. In response to Kortenaar's question, to try to read the *Midnight's Children* as the product of a "diseased mind" would be to go against the novel's sustained subtle critique of Western rationality, starting with Tai's disdain for Aadam's stethoscope and extending, as I show, to Saleem's fateful relationship with modern medicine (230).

While he secretly explores his magical telepathic powers, Saleem continues to present his unusual body as an allegory for India, insisting on its metaphorical significance. For example, he relates that a teacher at school, Zagallo, pulls him by his hair to the front of the classroom and explicitly compares the face of "thees ugly ape" to "the whole map of *India*" (265). Drawing attention to the birthmarks on each side of Saleem's face, the teacher compares them to eastern and western Pakistan. "Remember, stupid boys," he dramatically tells the class, "Pakistan ees a stain on the face of India!" (265). According to Zagallo, Saleem's nose is the shape of the subcontinent; taking up the idea, a student facetiously compares a glob of snot from Saleem's nose to Ceylon. This episode takes Saleem's connection to India to further exaggerated extremes. He not only was born at the same time as the nation and has telepathic powers only in the country, but he also literally looks like India. As the novel unfolds, Saleem's impaired body takes on ever greater significance.

Alongside the way, Rushdie conveys the real stigma and vulnerability that disabled people often experience in everyday life. Like many other disabled children, Saleem endures "a whole set of . . . taunts" at school (266). He is sometimes the target of bullies and is unable to fight back effectively. Zagallo's mocking of Saleem before the class ends with the enraged teacher pulling out a tuft of Saleem's hair. A short time later, several bullies confront Saleem during a school dance, which results in part of one his fingers being severed when a doorway slams on it. His bald spot, truncated finger, and deafness in one ear, rather than signifying anything magical, seem to represent the violent rejection he encounters in a society that privileges normalcy and able-bodiedness. As a self-described ugly boy, young Saleem also has little success in the area of romance. His crush on the American Evie Burns, for example, leads nowhere. "Whynt'cha tell him to jus' go blow his nose?" she says to one of Saleem's friends who acts as an intermediary (212). One could justifiably point out that bullying and frustrated romantic interests are a common rite of passage during adolescence, but in Saleem's case his disabilities magnify the rejection, making it all the more acute. However, the intertextual *Midnight's Children* not only draws on classic literature and Bollywood but also riffs on comic books. Just as the comic book heroes Clark Kent (Superman) and Peter Parker (Spider-Man) have hidden superpowers that allow them to transcend their rather meek everyday identities, so Saleem turns to his magical telepathic nose for a sense of power and reassurance.

Midnight's Children, Hope, and Denial

The most striking aspect of Saleem's extrasensory gifts is his eventual discovery of the so-called midnight's children, the fabulous figures with magical talents who, like Saleem, were born in India during the first hour of its independence and come to represent the freedom and potential of the new nation. Originally numbering 1,001 children—the number, with its echo of *Arabian Nights*, is another literary allusion in a novel full of intertextuality—Saleem finds through his telepathic journeys that 581 remain. Saleem tells us of midnight's children who can fly, travel in time, and perform a variety of other magical feats. Only the children born within the borders of the nation have these miraculous talents, showing again how the formation of modern independent India itself creates the miracle. As Barker has noted, many have exceptional bodies, including Siamese twins who can speak every language and dialect of the subcontinent, underscoring how they relate to the identity of the whole nation. The midnight's children, Saleem tells us, can be viewed as "the last throw of everything antiquated and retrogressive in our myth-ridden nation, whose defeat was entirely desirable in the context of a modernizing, twentieth-century economy; or as the true hope of freedom" (230). We do not have to pause long to determine that Saleem's view is the latter: he sees the children as the potential for liberation for a nation that is new but contains authentic supernatural traditions that predate colonialism. In Saleem's world, the midnight's children are tantamount to a team of superheroes, each with a special power and collectively with the possible ability to help the new nation achieve its potential and resist the challenges pulling it apart if they just work together. Such collaboration becomes more feasible when Saleem forms the Midnight's Children Conference (MCC), the nightly colloquium where the children converse through his mind, but almost immediately he must deal with conflict, especially in the person of his archrival, Shiva.

Switched at birth with Saleem, Shiva also is born at the stroke of midnight on India's first day of independence and has special abilities associated with a physical difference, but unlike Saleem, his extraordinary skill is physical power. Named for the Hindu god of destruction, he proves similarly potent and dangerous. He serves as Saleem's opposite in many regards. Shiva is the biological son of Amina and Ahmed Sinai, but due to the switch, he grows up in abject poverty; he apparently has little education; his name suggests he's Hindu; and while meek Saleem has a large nose, birthmarks, and assorted disabilities, Shiva has prominent knobby knees that prove to be tremendously strong. Through Saleem's telepathic nasal passages he tells of how, like some other poor parents, his father tried intentionally to disable him when he was a young child: "He blindfolded me, man! . . . Bastard was going to smash my legs up, man—it happens, you know. . . . [T]hey do it to kids so they can always earn money begging" (253). Through muscular strength, Shiva resists intentional disablement. He breaks his father's wrist using his knees as a vice and grows up as a tough on the streets, filled with anger and ressentiment at his fate. He also resists bullying. When Saleem's friend teases him about his knees early on, Shiva blinds him in one eye with a sharp stone. He becomes the leader of a street gang that is associated with murder and emerges as a figure of resistance to Saleem in the Midnight's Children Conference, with a resolutely individualist, amoral, rise-at-any-cost perspective. When Saleem makes an idealistic appeal for transcending dualisms, Shiva disagrees. "No, little rich boy," he says. "There is only money-and-poverty, and have-and-lack, and right-and-left; there is only me-against-the-world! . . . When you have things, then there is time to dream; when you don't, you fight" (292–293). We could ask how much his impoverished environment shapes Shiva's fierce character; like Achebe's Okonkwo, another character prone to violence, he could be read as a product of his destitute childhood. If he had been given a more prosperous and loving home, if he had stayed with his biological parents, would he have been less malicious? At any rate, Shiva serves as Saleem's opponent throughout the novel, embodying not just impoverished deprivation but also brute will and physical strength.

Shiva is only one obstacle in Saleem's MCC. The conference soon devolves into many competing individual voices that parallel the nation's actual All-India Congress, which, Saleem reports, has become more contentious with the rise of the Communist Party as opposition. Although Saleem initially hopes to have a "loose federation of equals" in the MCC, debates soon arise about hierarchy and leadership as different children claim superiority (252). Dissension also arises about the purpose of the MCC, with suggestions running from fantasies of taking over or invading Pakistan to declarations of women's rights, business greed, religious piety, and submission or revolution against parents. "I won't deny I was disappointed," says Saleem (261). It becomes evident that the children contain the prejudices of their parents and other adults. "I found children from Maharashtra loathing Gujaratis, and fair-skinned northerners reviling Dravidian 'blackies'; there were religious rivalries; and class entered our councils" (292). In this way the MCC really does serve as a microcosm for the nation, mirroring the internal divisions that block collective identity. When the children squabble like "half-grown brats," we see how difficult it is to achieve any meaningful unity in the diverse new nation and how, by implication, all such bickering in the All-India Congress is similarly childish (292). Like Jawaharlal Nehru, the first prime minister of India, Saleem calls for unity, but with limited success.

Saleem's grand hopes for himself and the children come to an end first through the gradual disintegration of the MCC and then, more finally, through medical intervention that unclogs his nose and takes away his magical telepathic powers altogether. Shiva is among the first to dismiss the conference. "Cucumber-nose, I'm fed up with your Conference," he says. "It's got nothing to do with one single thing" (293). Fraught with competing interests, the MCC begins to disband: "There was selfishness and snobbishness and hate. . . . Suspicions growing, dissension breeding, departures in twenties and tens" (348). Saleem stops convening it nightly, although he optimistically asserts that "what-we-had-in-common retained the possibility of overpowering what-forced-us-apart" (347). That possibility appears to close, however, when his parents deceive him into going to an ear, nose, and throat surgeon for a medical procedure on his nose. "Remembering how nasal passages had started everything in my head," Saleem resists the doctors, "kicking yelling so that they had to hold me down" (347). He is forcibly placed on an operating table and put under anesthesia; when he awakens, he learns that he no longer has his telepathic abilities: "Silence inside me. A connection broken (for ever)" (348). Earlier, Saleem loses his telepathic power when he leaves India and goes to Pakistan, but, significantly, the operation on his nose has the final effect of "depriving me of nose-given telepathy [and] banishing me from the possibility of midnight children" (348). Corrective surgery takes away his magical power and the children's collective potential for freedom, magical rebellion, and subversiveness. Being normalized, in this case, is disempowering. Yet the operation does succeed on a basic level, showing potential value in Western medicine: while the surgery takes away his nasal telepathy, it succeeds in giving Saleem an exquisite sense of smell for the first time.

That ability to smell, along with brain trauma that results from war, eventually plays a role in Saleem's becoming an agent of a corrupt state. When his parents die in a bombing in 1965 during the first Indo-Pakistani War, Saleem is struck in the head by a spittoon and loses his memory and sense of identity: he becomes "not-Saleem," a submissive buddha (414). Rushdie has Saleem claim that his brain injury allows him to become "purified" (398), a satirical poke at the so-called Land of the Pure (which "Pakistan" means in Urdu and Persian). He does become a citizen of Pakistan. Further irony appears as he serves the Pakistani army as a human dog tracker during the 1971 civil war between the West Wing of Pakistan and the East Wing. "Numb as ice, anesthetized against feelings as well as memories," he follows orders and enables brutal massacres, rapes, and other atrocities, using his exceptional sense of smell dutifully to track down leaders and officials (411). Through Saleem's head trauma, Rushdie conveys the barbarities that can result from submitting to a corrupt government, although again this horror is mitigated by the novel's playful, comical tone. We see Rushdie prizing individual autonomy over unthinking compliance, a value of human rights, which are directed to individuals regardless of the nation-state they are in.

While Saleem eventually escapes this predicament in a way that suggests the consciousness of even severely cognitively disabled people, oppressive government forces of regulation and control ultimately succeed in wiping out most of the midnight's children's magical potential for freedom. It turns out the buddha, the not-Saleem, in fact "knew what he was doing," again pointing to the value of ostensibly cognitively disabled people. He leads his group of three boy soldiers south into the jungle Sundarbans to escape the madness (414). When a snake bites him shortly thereafter, Saleem magically has his memory and identity return. Although Saleem temporarily finds a measure of peace with another midnight's child, Parvati-the-witch, Shiva, now a major and a war hero for India—specifically, for Indira Gandhi—captures him during the crackdown of the 1970s Emergency. The Emergency is about the arrest of "subversive elements," as Saleem speculates that Indira Gandhi might have read and felt threatened by the congratulatory letter her father, Nehru, wrote to him when he was born (481). Saleem concludes: "The truest, deepest motive behind the declaration of a State of Emergency was the smashing, the pulverizing, the irreversible discombobulation of the children of midnight" (492). Under duress, Saleem gives the names and identities of the other midnight's children, who are then rounded up and finally castrated and hysterectomized. When they awaken, the magical powers are gone and "now we were nothing" (505). The excessive force of the regulatory state and medical intervention crush the children of midnight, leaving them with a sense of broken promise and dreams. In his unmistakable critique of the Emergency and suspension of civil liberties, Rushdie, through Saleem and disability, denounces authoritarian regimes, as well as the insistence on homogeneity, on a standard of normalization and sameness that eradicates the promise of liberation.

Yet he does offer seeds of hope in the narrative through the offspring of Shiva, especially through baby Aadam, born of Shiva and Parvati-the-witch. Aadam is raised by Saleem and is probably the only offspring with two biological parents who are midnight's children. In a repetition of Saleem's own birth, Aadam is born "at the precise instant of India's arrival at Emergency" (482). And like Saleem, he has an anomalous body part: "colossally huge" ears that resemble those of the Hindu elephant-headed god Ganesh (482). After our experience with Saleem and other characters with exceptional bodies, Aadam's comical ears hold a latent promise. But here the promise is magical and the potential is unlimited, as neither Saleem nor we can predict what will happen with Aadam. (He does reappear in Rushdie's novel *The Moor's Last Sigh* [1995] as a corrupt businessman, but at the end of *Midnight's Children* he holds unlimited potential.) And Saleem tells us he's writing the book for Aadam so he will know his own history (as well as for an "amnesiac nation," a phrase that, coming after Saleem's own difficult experiences when he endures amnesia, contains a not-so-subtle critique of a forgetful and submissive Indian populace [530]).

As for Saleem himself, he expects his "helpless, pulverized body" to disintegrate at the conclusion, adding to the complex, multifaceted use of disability in the book (531). From the first page of the novel, Saleem has been writing against time, trying to get all of his—and the nation's—history down the best he can for his adoptive son before he expires. "I'm racing the cracks [and] my decay," he says halfway through (310). While the novel celebrates the potential power of unruly bodies, Saleem seems prepared to surrender to bodily pressures and die at the relatively young age of thirty-one. As he describes himself near the end as he looks at himself in a mirror:

> I saw myself transformed into a big-headed, top-heavy dwarf. . . .
> [T]he hair on my head was now as grey as rainclouds. . . . [N]ine-
> fingered, horn-templed, monk's-tonsured, stained-faced, bow-legged,
> cucumber-nosed, castrated, and now prematurely aged . . . a grotesque
> creature who had been released from the pre-ordained destiny which

had battered him until he was half-senseless; with one good ear and
one bad ear I heard the soft footfalls of the Black Angel of death. (515)

Notably, Saleem seems to attribute his physical differences to a fate, to a "des-
tiny which had battered him," seemingly overlooking that some anomalies,
such as his magical nose and his birthmarks, have been part of him from
birth. But others have pulled out his hair, injured his finger and hearing, and
castrated him, making his "grotesque" body into a symbolic progression, a
physical representation of others' mistreatment of him. If Saleem is an allegory for the newly independent nation of India, such attributes could be read
to represent the fate of India itself, which Rushdie seems to see as damaged by
war, intolerance, division, and authoritarian insistence on conformity.

Throughout the book Saleem maintains that he is slowly cracking; however, as no one else actually sees this, it appears that Saleem is following in
the tradition of using a bodily metaphor to describe a cognitive state, as his
grandfather Aadam did with his inner hole, although the end leaves this
uncertain. Early on he notices a "thin crack" on his wrist and says he is "falling apart" (35–36). When his girlfriend, Padma, alarmed by such references,
calls in a doctor, the physician examines Saleem and pronounces him whole,
which causes Saleem to mock the "medical profession [which has] sunk so
low," adding to the novel's critique of Euro-American medicine (70). He
alludes to the cracks throughout his story. "I feel the cracks widening down
the length of my body," he states (170). Allegorically, one can easily see how
the cracks correspond to the figures in the nation of India, which is beset by
competing tensions and groups—religious, ethnic, linguistic, and political—
much as the Midnight's Children Conference is pulled apart by competing
agendas. As Barker reminds us, Prime Minister Nehru embraced a philoso-
phy of "unity in diversity," but modern India has sorely tested such pluralist
principals, especially through the enforced homogeneity of the Emergency
(127). We could see Saleem's claims of his body cracking as a material symbol
of the cracks in the Indian body politic. He claims that the cracks are waiting for August 15, which is both Independence Day and his birthday, and
imagines that the cracks will then widen and pieces of his body will fall off,
"rip tear crunch," and he will disintegrate into "four hundred million five
hundred six" specks of dust, which corresponds to the six million people in
India when the novel was written (532–533). It is a poetic, suggestive ending,
but Saleem's imagined future does perhaps undercut the material reality of
his person. As with Aadam's hole, we cannot read Saleem's anticipated disintegration literally without sacrificing the realistic depictions of his identity
for more allegorical, figurative meanings.

In these ways, even as it criticizes postcolonial oppression and division, *Midnight's Children* offers a sustained critique of the forces that deny disabled people dignity and the right to self-determination. We see a critique of parents who do not accept their disabled children, of peers and teachers who bully disabled youth, of society's view that cognitively disabled people have little worth, and of society's incessant insistence on normality, even if it requires medical surgery. Through the fantastic elements of the narrative, Rushdie underscores the value and power of disabled people themselves even as he uses them as metaphors to critique oppression, authoritarianism, dogma, and pressure to assimilate. By making Saleem the narrator, he compels readers to identify with a disabled person even more (even if they do not quite realize they are doing so).

Perhaps the most poignant part of the novel is that Saleem fears his story will have no meaning or impact. "Above all things, I fear absurdity," he says at the outset (4). The novel presents a challenge to India to find a way to have a coherent national identity, and to all readers to have compassion and respect for disabled people, however marginal and powerless they may appear. Perhaps not surprisingly, given the views in the novel, the ensuing 1980s proved a time of disability rights advances in India, culminating in 1995 in the Persons with Disabilities (Equal Opportunities, Protection of Rights and Full Participation) Act, which reserved 3 percent of all government positions for disabled Indians. One is tempted to think that Saleem would be pleased.

How Metaphor Can Also Be Realism

Disability and Rights in Coetzee's Fiction

[The] wounded body of the colonized is a pervasive figure in
colonial and postcolonial discourses.

—ELLEKE BOEHMER, "Transfiguring"

[Disability] representations may be at once allegorical and
materially grounded, symbolic and politicized.

—CLARE BARKER, *Postcolonial Fiction and Disability*

Saleem Sinai's insistence that he and his disabilities have larger allegorical meaning throughout *Midnight's Children* introduces a prominent aspect of disability in postcolonial literature that I consider in this chapter: its frequent metaphorical significance. As stated in the Introduction, this metaphorical aspect has often caused critics outside of disability studies to skip over the realistic, material side of disability representation, but, as Clare Barker indicates, the two often happen simultaneously. To explore how such material-metaphorical depictions can work, I turn to the South African author J. M. Coetzee, who features disability in many of his best-known novels in provocative ways that lead to challenging questions of ethics and human rights for disabled and nondisabled people alike.

In his 1987 Jerusalem Prize acceptance speech, Coetzee denounced colonialism and its successor in South Africa, the racist system of apartheid, as inherently disabling. They lead to a "deformed and stunted inner life" among all people who live under such systems, he charged:

> The deformed and stunted relations between human beings that were
> created under colonialism and exacerbated under what is loosely called
> apartheid have their psychic representation in a deformed and stunted
> inner life. All expressions of that inner life, no matter how intense, no
> matter how pierced with exultation or despair, suffer from the same

stuntedness and deformity. I make this observation with due delibera-
tion, and in the fullest awareness that it applies to myself and my own
writing as much as to anyone else. (*Doubling* 98)

Speaking a few years before the South African apartheid system finally came
to an end in 1990, Coetzee was more direct than in his distinctly spare fiction. He used rhetoric of disability to assert that colonialism and apartheid
impair not only relationships between people but also their inner conscious-
nesses, a denunciation in support of equal rights that world media promptly
publicized. Several years later, he further developed the theme in an autobiographical essay, describing himself in the third person as impaired by apartheid. "The realization he is disabled comes early," Coetzee writes. "As a white
South African in the latter half of the twentieth century, [he is] disabled, dis-
qualified" (*Doubling* 392). Even though he is white and able-bodied, he avers
that state-sponsored persecution based on race, which was an outgrowth of
European colonialism, disables him.

With these claims, Coetzee participates in a marked trend in postcolonial discourse of using rhetoric of disability to depict the harmful results of
colonialism and its afterlives. To be sure, people in a wide variety of contexts
have employed disability metaphors to describe something weak, inferior, or
wrong. In the North, disability has served, in the words of Sharon Snyder and
David Mitchell, as "the master trope of human disqualification in modernity"
(*Cultural* 127). Language and images of disability especially permeate postcolonial writing. In his remarks, Coetzee may well have been channeling Frantz
Fanon, who in his influential works in the mid-twentieth century describes
the destructive effect of colonialism and its attendant racism on the psyches
of colonized people. In *Black Skin, White Masks* (1952), for instance, Fanon
contends that "the juxtaposition of the black and white races [through colo-
nialism] has created a massive psychoexistential complex," a cognitive disorder that he seeks to rectify through anticolonialism (12). Later he says that the
white racist gaze in a colonized setting causes him to make himself into an
object, which he calls "an amputation," suggesting how it metaphorically disables him (112). Such imagery of physical harm and psychic trauma became
prominent throughout the Anglophone literature of the Global South in the
second half of the twentieth century. As Elleke Boehmer confirmed in 1993,
the "wounded body of the colonized is a pervasive figure in colonial and
postcolonial discourses" ("Transfiguring" 268).[1] In this chapter I first survey
theory about disability as a metaphor before focusing in on Coetzee's deploy-
ment of disability, especially cognitive disability, in his two most recognized

novels, *Life & Times of Michael K* (1983) and *Disgrace* (1999). Challenging readers and steadfastly avoiding sentimentality, he uses disability simultaneously as metaphor and realism, depicting disability in ways that subtly communicate both the ravages of colonialism or apartheid and the real material need for disability justice.

Disability as Metaphor

Even as it flourished, detractors have sometimes expressed misgivings about the figurative employment of disability to describe colonialism and its effects. For example, among postcolonial writers, the Caribbean poet Derek Walcott chastised Afro-Caribbean artists in the 1960s and 1970s for being preoccupied with past trauma, although he later came to employ disability imaginatively himself in *Omeros* (1990), as Jahan Ramazani has shown.[2] For their part, early literary disability studies scholars such as Mitchell and Snyder were typically wary of disability metaphors, seeing them as almost invariably negative and as having little to do with the actual lives of disabled people (*Narrative* 48). While perhaps initially evocative, such metaphors have repercussions for the social meaning of disability. Writing about figurative language in general, Margaret Gibbon observes that "metaphor is always significant" because "when we use language, we make choices and choices are not always innocent, but determined by belief systems which underlie them" (3, 24). Because metaphors of disability usually have unfavorable connotations (the "belief systems that underlie them"), they likely increase the stigma of disability and make it harder for disabled people to achieve positive conceptions of self. Especially relevant here is Mark Sherry's firm directive to contemporary critics: "Neither disability nor postcolonialism should be understood as simply a metaphor for the other experience; nor should they be rhetorically employed as a symbol of the oppression involved in a completely different experience," he declares ("(Post)colonizing" 10). While the two conditions have some traits in common, he asserts, they have "vast differences," are "quite distinct" and should not be easily conflated ("(Post)colonizing" 18–19). Notably, Sherry is not writing specifically about fiction, but is calling for more precise thinking among writers and other commentators who, he feels, too carelessly recycle and expand on the trope.

However, some disability studies scholars have recently begun calling for a reappraisal of disability metaphor in general. In 2005, Michael Bérubé acknowledged the value of objecting to simplistic representations but argued that rejecting disability tropes because they are not realistic seems "incompatible with the enterprise of professional literary study" (570). Instead, he advocated a more rigorous approach that raises awareness of how many familiar metaphors and narrative devices are based on corporeal difference and analyzes how they function. Similarly, Amy Vidali argues against simply policing metaphors, urging artists and scholars to find ways to work "critically, ethically, transgressively, and creatively at the edges of disability metaphor" (51). Such arguments have opened the way to more nuanced considerations that are especially helpful in considering postcolonial narratives.

We can see these competing views of the figurative use of disability in two recent and seemingly contradictory appraisals of Fanon's disability language in *Black Skins, White Masks*. While acknowledging the incisiveness of Fanon's work, Rosemarie Garland-Thomson faults him for rhetorically treating "disability as the true mark of physical inadequacy from which he wishes to differentiate racial marking," as if racial difference does not make him inferior, but disability does (*Staring* 42). She persuasively points to how oppressed nondisabled people, in seeking to remove associations with disability, can actually reinforce the oppression of disabled people. By contrast, Tanya Titchkosky asserts that rhetoric of disability can potentially be productive. Noting Fanon's final prayer ("O my body, make of me always a man who questions!" [*Black* 232]), she argues that, rather than simply calling for a return to the ordinary, Fanon engages with his difference to describe both limits and possibilities. Metaphors are "a form of social action," she states, where words refer to common meanings but in relation to something different, "potentially releasing new meanings" (10). Titchkosky's claim implies that disability metaphor can aid the cause of a variety of liberation movements, including disability human rights. The differing views of Garland-Thomson and Titchkosky on Fanon's figurative language could demonstrate how the use of disability tropes remains controversial and unsettled among disability studies scholars.

Yet their interpretations are not necessarily contradictory; here is one place this study seeks to advance these theoretical debates. Together Garland-Thomson and Titchkosky suggest that the same text can contain both regressive and progressive uses of disability in intricate, overlapping fashion to argue for human rights, an idea I will bring to bear on the works I consider. How are representations of disability simultaneously progressive and regressive, positive and negative? This multisided aspect often characterizes representations of disability in the literature of the Global South, especially Coetzee's.

Adding to the sense of the varied meanings of disability imagery, scholars have increasingly recognized that disability in literature can be material and metaphorical at the same time. One need not go so far as Frederic Jameson,

who famously insisted that "all third-world texts are necessarily . . . allegorical," to see the potential slippage between realistic and metaphorical in the
case of disability (69). Ato Quayson observes that representations of disability rapidly oscillate "between a pure process of abstraction and a set of material conditions that ensures that the ethical core of its representation is never
allowed to be completely assimilated to the literary-aesthetic domain as such"
(*Aesthetic* 24). Because they always relate to reality, Quayson maintains, disability representations' real-world implications never disappear, even if they
are figurative. As shown at the outset of this chapter, Barker asserts that disability "representations may be at once allegorical and materially grounded,
symbolic and politicized" (20). She points out that such meanings may coex-
ist. Along the same lines, Julia Avril Minich writes of disability in Junot
Díaz's fiction as reflecting "an embodied experience" and having "discursive
function in both the subjugation and the liberation of colonized people"
("Decolonizer's" 49). Such comments show how scholars have recently recognized how disability can resonate on many levels in texts in the quest for
rights and dignity.

In some of the best postcolonial literature, authors do employ the trope
creatively, making it something fresh and new and creating connections
between readers and disability in the process.[3] Instead of just producing a
predictable victim's literature of passive suffering or anger, authors often use
figures of disability to create something that both testifies to the harmful
effects initiated by past colonial incursion and shows people's (and society's)
activity and resilience.[4] We need to remain on guard for ways that disability representation can be negative or have downsides, as Garland-Thomson
and others have astutely warned, but that does not obscure the productive
work some representations do. Perhaps authors depict this energetic, proactive nature most clearly in cases when the first-person narrator is disabled, as
when Rushdie has the multi-disabled Saleem narrate *Midnight's Children* or
as Chris Abani, Indra Sinha, and Petina Gappah employ disabled narrators to
tell stories in works I discuss in the final chapter. Such instances make readers
share in disability experience. In the process, they have the increased potential directly to create understanding and connection between readers and
disabled people in the Global South, although such kinship remains slippery.

Even when the narrator is not disabled and disabled characters are minor
figures or almost entirely passive, we can regularly discern care for disabled
individuals in this literature, or a sense that they matter. For example, early
in Gabriel García Márquez's *One Hundred Year of Solitude*, the narrator, in
typical lighthearted fashion, briefly describes a Colombian woman in the

sixteenth century who is so unsettled by an attack by Francis Drake and European explorers that she accidentally burns herself on a stove and subsequently does not walk in public. Fearful of English invaders, she cannot sleep peacefully until her husband moves the family far from the ocean and builds her a house with a windowless bedroom. The novel uses disability negatively to suggest the severe harms of imperial incursion, but at the same time García Márquez uses it quietly to uphold the humanity of the woman and the understanding and care of her husband. Compassion for others, a sense of connection and kinship, emerges as a way to endure and transcend obstacles. Of course, not all postcolonial literature follows these trends. Not all representations of disability in the vast, diverse Anglophone literature of the Global South metaphorically relate to colonialism and its effects, and not all depictions follow a pattern as authors rework the trope to fulfill their own creative visions.

Because he regularly uses oppressed figures of disability to describe the effects of colonialism (and apartheid), Coetzee serves as a good test case for these ideas. In his Jerusalem Prize acceptance speech, he calls himself disabled by colonialism and apartheid. The assertion may startle, not just because it seems a rare moment of forthrightness for the famously impersonal Coetzee, not just because he takes a clear stand against apartheid in a way that Nadine Gordimer and other writers accused him of avoiding in his fiction, and not just because it goes against disability politics in the North that frowns on nondisabled people calling themselves disabled.[5] The statement is also remarkable because Coetzee is a white South African of Afrikaner heritage.[6] It is one thing for the Black South African antiapartheid leader Nelson Mandela to say, in a 1963 speech, that without "equal political rights . . . our disabilities will be permanent" (qtd. in Titchkosky 8). It seems quite another for Coetzee to call himself disabled. Although he consistently distanced himself from the white supremacist system of apartheid—in a draft of his fictional autobiography *Boyhood* (1997) he identifies his family as being "recusant Afrikaners," a group that nationalistic Afrikaners saw as traitors (Attwell 11, 15)—Coetzee is keenly aware that the white Afrikaner minority created and perpetuated apartheid and that he, just by virtue of being a white person growing up in South Africa, benefited from the manifestly unjust system. Rather than disability being a negative trait that some other people have, Coetzee makes it a condition shared by him and all people in apartheid South Africa.[7] With such solidarity, he contradicts apartheid's rigid institutionalized systems of racial hierarchy and segregation. What makes his words especially provocative is that he's imposing the disability label on a group who would presumably deny it: white South Africans of Afrikaner heritage like him. As an award-winning, internationally recognized author, he clearly is not incapable, unqualified, or weak, yet he still uses disability to signify the oppressive psychic effect of the apartheid system on himself and on everyone who lives under it. Metaphorically, disability goes from being a stigmatizing mark of difference to one of oppressed commonality.

Small surprise, then, that in his novels disability often prominently turns up as both a material reality reflecting the lived experience of disabled South Africans and a metaphor for the oppressive results of colonialism or apartheid, usually at the same time. When Coetzee won the Nobel Prize for Literature in 2003, the Nobel Committee praised him for portraying "in innumerable guises . . . the surprising involvement of the outsider" ("Nobel"). He often marks these outsiders with disability, as well as Blackness. In two of the acclaimed novels leading up to the prize, *Life & Times of Michael K* and *Disgrace*, at least initially impaired characters are people of color, seeming to set up a predictable allegorical dualism in which subjugated people in a variety of contexts are disabled and subjugators are not. (With the character of the blinded, limping barbarian girl who has undergone torture, *Waiting for the Barbarians* [1980] does this, too, as does *Foe* [1986], with the mute enigmatic Friday who may be tongueless or cognitively disabled, but in the interests of space I focus on the two best-known Coetzee novels.) In Coetzee's hands, matters are not simple. As Alice Hall has noted, in Coetzee's writing "metaphor and materiality are inextricably linked" (*Disability* 174). Because the disabled characters' impairments overlap with the unjust situations in which they live, they raise ethical dilemmas about colonialism or apartheid that profoundly trouble white, intellectual narrators, who reveal a driving passion to understand both the disabled individual and, by extension, the structural injustice that lies behind their impairment.

Whether white or Black, Coetzee's disabled characters undergo some kind of suffering, which may give them special magnetism. In an interview in *Doubling the Point* (1992), he connects suffering and power, writing, "Let me put it baldly: in South Africa it is not possible to deny the authority of suffering and therefore of the body. It is not possible, not for logical reasons, not for ethical reasons . . . but for political reasons, for reasons of power. And let me again be unambiguous: the suffering body takes this authority: that is its power. To use other words: its power is undeniable" (248). Coetzee's words help to clarify why he repeatedly writes about disabled characters: they add "undeniable" force to his narratives, making the novels more compelling, memorable, and troubling. While people with disabilities are often marginalized and overlooked in real life, they are not disregarded in this fiction, where they serve as the magnetic center of the stories, drive the plot, and invariably have metaphorical significance.

Still, solidarity or feelings of kinship with Coetzee's disabled characters of color remains unsettled. Perhaps the relationship between readers and disabled characters here is the most elusive in this study. Coetzee eschews sentimental representations for a more understated—and arguably more provocative and forceful—narrative approach. Shot through with ambiguity and ambivalence, these depictions force readers to read carefully. Coetzee published *Life & Times of Michael K* in 1983, when apartheid was still in force; it features a disabled protagonist who is marginalized in society but nonetheless the central figure in the book. The narrators (an omniscient narrator in Michael's consciousness and the medical officer who narrates part two) treat him attentively but leave it up to us to figure out his significance. Why are we reading a book about Michael K? The pattern changes in *Disgrace*, the potent, controversial novel that Coetzee published in 1999, five years after the end of apartheid; in it, a Black disabled figure, Pollux, is less prominent but much more aggressive and disturbing. Along with others he brutally violates another person, causing the novel's protagonist (and most of us readers) to respond with revulsion. How can one care about an oppressed person whose full story one does not know or comprehend, or who even, in the case of *Disgrace*, performs a horrifying crime that could be said to reflect the worst stereotypes about racial minorities and about cognitive disability as something threatening or dangerous?

Considering this fiction and racial justice may be instructive. According to one South African scholar, antiapartheid activists in South Africa generally found Coetzee's 1980s novels, including *Life & Times of Michael K*, helpful to their cause, despite ambiguities. *Disgrace*, however, was very controversial in South Africa when it appeared; the African National Congress, among others, denounced it for its portrayal of race and postapartheid society. Such reactions show that activists have not found all literary depictions, by Coetzee or others, to support rights (some may even be dangerous, as Chimamanda Ngozi Adichie reminds us in her TED talk), but often Coetzee's novels do raise awareness of the need for justice.

Although indisputably human and tangibly present, Coetzee's disabled characters of color remain mostly silent and cryptic, just as the large questions they embody are not explicitly answered, which perhaps makes these depictions both more effective and frustrating. Raising fundamental ethical questions that underlie human rights, disabled characters hold the narrators' attention but resist clear understanding, presenting a hermeneutical impasse that recalcitrantly refuses firm resolution.[8]

In these ways, Coetzee compels readers to take disabled people seriously. He makes us imagine the experiences of marginalized, often invisible people and shows their importance, which in itself helps us on the first step toward the cause of disability human rights. It is worth remembering the human rights scholar Samuel Moyn's words: "Human rights would have to win or lose on the terrain of the imagination, first and foremost" (*Last* 5). Can Coetzee's ambivalent representations of recalcitrant or even criminal disabled people of color support their political rights? They can, perhaps, if we remember that in Coetzee all disabled characters are both material and metaphorical. Coetzee's depiction of disabled characters of color reveals strong and contradictory feelings not just about disability, but also about colonialism and apartheid, about subjugation and the tensions surrounding its aftermath, for it is difficult to separate the disabled characters in his work from the oppressive systems within which they reside or from the feelings of narrators or main characters about them. Yet by making disabled people in South Africa *matter* much more in readers' minds, and connecting them to the oppressive systems in which they live, Coetzee prods us to think carefully about them and their situations. He makes disabled people not invisible, but consequential.

"The Obscurest of the Obscure": *Life & Times of Michael K*

Life & Times of Michael K takes place in apartheid South Africa in the late twentieth century, but race and ethnicity, which were so significant in the system of apartheid, dividing and subjugating people, go largely unnamed.[9] Starting and ending in Sea Point in Cape Town, the story occurs in the midst of a distant civil war, complete with passing military convoys. This conflict does not correspond to any particular historical event, but it does reflect the increasing tension and violence over apartheid around Coetzee near the onset of the 1980s. As Susan VanZanten Gallagher notes, more frequent guerrilla attacks and bombings by Black nationalist groups caused widespread anxiety and millions of dollars in damage; in response, compulsory military service for white South Africans began in 1978. The novel contains similar turmoil and militarization but does not make overt references to apartheid or race, leaving them unspoken factors. The only direct evidence we have of Michael's race comes midway through the book when a police report obscurely identifies him as "CM," which, David Attwell explains, in apartheid-era discourse denoted "colored male" (108). Other subtle clues of race appear when Michael encounters a deserter with a "pale" appearance, but racial markers usually go unsaid (*Life* 61). Instead, we have to infer from events what race characters are; the novel compels us to be close readers.

While race is largely a hidden factor in the narrative, *Life & Times* makes physical and cognitive difference highly visible in ways that underscore the destitute situation of Michael and his mother and make disability, not race, more the fulcrum of injustice as the novel reveals the inequity of the social order. Disability appears in the opening line: "The first thing the midwife noticed about Michael K when she helped him out of his mother into the world was that he had a hare lip" (3).[10] Much later, the medical officer points out to the adult Michael that his cleft lip could be easily corrected through simple surgery. The fact that Michael's harelip never receives medical attention, although, as we learn, it makes his speech slurred and has a negative visual impact on other characters throughout the novel ("How could I forget a face like that?" asks an officer from Jakkalsdrif work camp [124]), underscores his mother's poverty and lack of access to health care. (His father is never mentioned or present, one of many unexplained lacunas in the narrative.) Understood this way, K's untreated lip suggests how they live in a system that impoverishes them.

While the harelip underscores Michael's abjection, so does his intellectual disability, an invisible trait that underlies and shapes his experience in the narrative. Near the outset, the omniscient narrator tells us that "his mind was not quick" (4). Noting Michael's characteristic silence, Quayson in *Aesthetic Nervousness* concludes he has autism. Bérubé cautions against such a diagnosis of a literary character (he terms it "needlessly reductive"), urging readers to consider K's role in the text as a whole instead of simply labeling him (*Stories* 66). Bérubé seems to me on the mark here, but we could still read K's cognitive impairment in a way that flirts with the medical model—namely, Michael's intellectual disability could well be caused by poverty, which, in turn, is a consequence of a brutal apartheid system that subjugates and disenfranchises people of color. As noted in the Introduction, in Europe and the United States, scholars in disability studies typically eschew talking about causes of disability because that almost inevitably returns one to pathological thinking, which positions disability as a problem in need of fixing and obscures society's treatment of disabled people. That practice deserves great respect; it has been part of the ascendance of disability rights and disability studies in the North. But I take my cue from Helen Meekosha, who argues that disability studies scholars must consider such causes as "war, famine, and poverty" fully to grasp disability in the Global South (677). Notably, all three of Meekosha's factors show up in *Life & Times of Michael K*, but poverty is especially significant here. While cognitive impairments occur in all places among all classes, poverty (and the accompanying high risk of malnutrition, exposure to toxins, poor-quality housing, insecurity, and inadequate health care for the mother while the fetus is developing) can cause mental impairments. Read this way, both of Michael's disabilities are potentially connected with the harsh dispossession associated with apartheid. The possible link between an oppressive system and disability is subtle and ambiguous, yet part of the power of the novel is the way it evokes images while leaving their meaning uncertain. Michael's disabilities at birth might have nothing to do with social formations, or everything. His impaired body and mind potentially reflect apartheid's grievous harms both metaphorically and realistically.

The novel takes place when Michael is a thirty-one-year-old adult, but we obtain glimpses of his upbringing that show that, as he grows, his identity is formed by overlapping biological and social factors in a manner that supports biocultural notions of disability such as Tobin Siebers's theory of complex embodiment. Some aspects seem clearly essential. His harelip is physically, indisputably present, marking him as different, affecting his speech, and possibly even contributing to his struggles with food (cleft lips can cause difficulties with eating). For its part, although more elusive, his cognitive disability regularly shows up, too, as when he lies in his bed during a period of unemployment "looking at his hands" (4) or when he fails to understand others or even his own experiences. We read: "Always, when he tried to explain himself to himself, there remained a gap, a hole, a darkness before which his understanding baulked, into which it was useless to pour words. . . . His was always a story with a hole in it, a wrong story, always wrong" (110). Such passages make us experience his life through his intellectual disability, where even he is a bit lost, and reflect ironically on the subject of the whole book, which from its very title is relating his story.

Yet Michael's identity is determined not just by biological conditions but, perhaps even more so, by the repressive environment in which he grows. The meanings of both impairments are socially formed in a manner that points to the negative effects of the apartheid system in which he lives. They may not only result from the destitution under a system based on white supremacy, but also lead to stigmatization that shapes his identity, including his distinctive preference as an adult for solitude and silence. When he is small, his mother keeps him away from other children because they smile and whisper about him, instead taking him with her to her domestic cleaning jobs (almost certainly in white people's houses), where year after year he sits on a blanket "learning to be quiet" (4). Silence, the quote suggests, is not innate to him; it is something that he has to be taught. Eventually she enrolls him at a special school for "afflicted and unfortunate children" where older boys bully him, making him seek out a place behind a shed where he can be alone. At the school, which is almost certainly segregated and impoverished under apartheid, he is often compelled to go hungry; the famished children search the garbage cans for scraps. The school also instills silence in him. One teacher forces his students to sit through hot afternoons with their eyes closed, hands on their heads, and lips pursed, while the sleeping quarters has a sign that reads, "There will be silence in the dormitories at all times" (105). Michael is compelled to adopt strategies (silence, seeking isolation, and tolerance of hunger) that allow him to survive the abusive environment. When he is assaulted and robbed as he returns from a night job early in the novel, it reflects not only the increasing chaos around him, not only the reality that disabled people are more likely to be victims of crime and abuse, but also how Michael is made vulnerable by the system in which he lives. One cannot discuss K's disabled state without discussing the state that disempowers him.

The narrative shows that marginalization while also occasionally revealing Michael K's admirable qualities and unexpected areas of competence. When Michael is an adult, his mother, despite working as a domestic servant, lives in deplorable conditions: she has an unventilated room without electric lights beneath the stairs in an apartment block. The door has a sign that reads "DANGER—GEVAAR—INGOZI" ("danger" in the three main languages of the region [Attwell 112]) (6). In addition to this poverty, his mother is seriously ill, and as what seems to be a racial riot started by military brutality unfolds around them, she beseeches him to take her back to the place of her birth, Prince Albert, which is far away in the countryside of the Karoo. K agrees, showing admirable loyalty and filial obedience, especially since his mother does not seem to be a particularly loving parent. He quits his gardening job (he expects soon to be let go anyway) and attempts to obtain a travel permit, which the byzantine wartime government bureaucracy ("Fill in the forms and take them to E-5" [19]) does not provide.[11] Displaying quiet ingenuity, he fashions a wheelbarrow into a cart and pushes his ailing mother out of town. Evading roadblocks and convoys, they slowly make progress, but his mother falls gravely ill, and he takes her to an overcrowded hospital, where she dies. Resolving to take her ashes to her place of birth, he journeys on, even though the cart has been stolen and he has been robbed. When he arrives at what he thinks is the right place, he scatters the ashes and is not sure what to do next. The remainder of the novel has him alternately living alone on the abandoned property and eluding various people—the Visagie grandson, the police—and living in grim detention camps that try to discipline or rehabilitate him.[12] Along the way, he evinces skills—for example, as a gardener (the happiest moments in the book occur away from society when he quietly raises and eats pumpkins with tender pleasure) and, later, in conjunction with a work camp, as a fence builder ("You have a feel for wire," a farmer commends him [95]). Such moments deepen his character—the novel makes us care about his fate—even as he deteriorates in a war-torn nation. At the end of part one, he is living in a hole in the ground, sleeping much of the time, and apparently slowly starving to death when soldiers, thinking that he is aiding guerrilla fighters, arrest him.

Although it contains textual echoes of Euro-American literary works, the novel presents a vision that is radically new, especially with its South African context, distinctive narration, and attention to a disabled figure's perspective. Critics have noted literary influences that include Heinrich von Kleist's German Romantic novel of 1810, *Michael Kohlhaas*, which depicts the failure of government and was apparently an early inspiration; Franz Kafka's *The Trial*, with its Josef K. suffering under a remote, unjust authority, and "The Hunger Artist," with its themes of fasting and extreme social marginalization; and Herman Melville's Bartleby, who may have a cognitive disability and, like Michael, engages in seemingly passive resistance to the existing order (in his case, Wall Street capitalism) to the point of not eating. Such intertextuality is a regular feature of both Rushdie's and Coetzee's oeuvres, yet *Life & Times* is unique, including in how it employs multiple points of view. In parts one and three, the omniscient narrator seems located in K's consciousness, subtly shifting between K's thoughts and those of an observer Quayson calls an "implied interlocutor," who voices Judgment or Opinion based on school rules and other social sources (*Aesthetic* 167).[13] These ambiguous multiple voices add to Michael's elusiveness and relate to the crucial question of whether Coetzee gives a voice to a disabled figure. The answer seems to be both no and yes, somewhat: while the novel contains numerous gaps, moments when K cannot even express himself to himself, it gives a sense of his internal thoughts that we do not get in, say, Melville's *Bartleby*. For example, when he is in a camp, a young girl's baby dies and, grief-stricken, she refuses to eat: "Michael K spent hours standing against the fence where she could not see him, watching her. Is this my education? He wondered. . . . He had a presentiment of a single meaning upon which [the scenes of his life] were converging or threatening to converge, though he did not know yet what that might be" (89). The passage gives a sense of his perspective, but clear meaning lies, as it invariably seems to, beyond him and, perhaps, us readers.

By having a medical officer in a rehabilitation camp take over the narration in part two, Coetzee emphasizes K's essential elusiveness and returns to the pattern that he established in an earlier novel, *Waiting for the Barbarians*, in which a white narrator is drawn to a disabled and subjugated person of color who appears profoundly significant but defies comprehension. True, the medical officer is a more uniformly benevolent figure, pleading with K to eat and trying to keep him alive when no one else seems to care. Yet many parallels exist. Like the magistrate who narrates *Barbarians*, the medical officer is skeptical of the system of which he is a part. He is deeply disturbed by a society that persecutes a vulnerable person like Michael, leaving him malnourished, a "skeleton" who only weighs seventy-seven pounds and looks like an old man although he is only in his early thirties, and forcing him at the camp absurdly to run in place (129). Just as the magistrate never truly knows the barbarian girl, apparently not even learning her name, the medical officer tries but fails to understand K, whom he incorrectly believes is named "Michaels" and had a terrifying mother, errors that readers, through the different points of view, can readily perceive.

Finally, while the magistrate sees the girl as the recalcitrant key to understanding the dehumanizing colonial world he inhabits, the medical officer similarly comes to perceive Michael as having deep allegorical significance that escapes him. At first he merely views Michael as innocent or stupid, observing that K "barely knows there is a war on" (130). Yet as the weakened Michael stays for two weeks in the clinic, the medical officer comes to look at him with a certain searching admiration. "Michaels means something, and the meaning he has is not private to me," he says (165). He sees K's stubborn refusal to eat as passive resistance to the oppressive society around him. When he muses to a colleague that perhaps Michael "only eats the bread of freedom" (146), he is only half-joking. Michael's very abjection comes to make him appear extraordinary to the medical officer, as he calls K "so obscure as to be a prodigy" (142), a "soul blessedly untouched by doctrine," and "precious" (151). "We ought to value and celebrate you," he asserts (152). He demands that Michael share his story, which he does not do. When Michael escapes the camp one night, the medical officer regrets not following him. He imagines chasing him and calling out what Michael means to him:

> Your stay in the camp was merely an allegory, if you know that word.
> It was an allegory—speaking at the highest level—of how scandal-

ously, how outrageously a meaning can take up residence in a system without becoming a term in it. Did you not notice how, whenever I tried to pin you down, you slipped away? (166)

The medical officer's words take us toward metafiction and underscore Michael's indeterminacy. Just as it is reductive to diagnose Michael, so it is dangerous to try to allegorize him, as Gert Buelens and Dominick Hoens warn. He perpetually eludes the laws and norms of the society in which he lives. He cannot be contained, whether by the various camps that abuse and try to discipline him (including the special school early in his life) or by other characters' attempts to understand him.

The resolution of the novel leaves matters similarly ambiguous, but one can hardly doubt Coetzee's intention for readers to see K's life and times as meaningful and instructive. In the short final section, Michael returns to Sea Point, meets street people who both befriend and appear to try to rob him, and finally goes back to his mother's old room beneath the stairs. As he falls asleep, he thinks of returning to the distant farm with a little old man in his cart and getting water from the shaft of the blown-up pump with a teaspoon. The ending has a satisfying circularity; we get the repetition of the cart and taking an elderly person out of Cape Town to the farm, and the teaspoon reminds us how the novel began, with his mother feeding the infant K with a teaspoon because he could not suck from breast or bottle. The ending is inconclusive, as Michael could be about to die from starvation, a possibility the medical officer warned him against: "If you don't eat, you are truly going to die" (147).

Furthermore, we are left with questions of what it all means. Why does Coetzee choose to tell this story? As Bérubé notes, people continually ask Michael for his story, but he never gives it to them. In a real sense, he is not narratable.[14] Toward the end we learn that his goal is to escape the notice of others. "I have escaped the camps," he thinks. "Perhaps, if I lie low, I will escape the charity too" (182). In his effort to resist society in all its disciplining and pitying forms, to establish an original relationship with the earth as a solitary gardener, we see that the medical officer is right at least in Michael's rejection of society. Meanings seem perpetually in retreat, but with the novel, Coetzee clearly wants readers to see the life of Michael K, harelipped, intellectually disabled, destitute, and homeless as he is, as significant and meriting our attention. We should care about Michael's story, even while we recognize that the medical officer's quick allegorizing contains errors and is reductive. Through his disabilities, through his poverty and oppression and vulnerability in a manifestly unjust, violent system, Michael implicitly serves as a metaphor for the results of South African apartheid that critiques many things, including the dispossession of large numbers of people, including disabled people of color, under the system. If we cannot understand Michael, Coetzee nonetheless consistently goads readers to think and care about him, to see him as significant in ways that dovetail with both the campaign against apartheid and global disability human rights.

"Something Is Wrong with Him": The Difficulties of Disability and Race in *Disgrace*

Coetzee's almost painfully realistic masterpiece, *Disgrace*, appeared in 1999 after the end of apartheid in South Africa. The novel has received more scholarly and media attention than any other work of fiction in South Africa's history, including the previous holder of the top position, Alan Paton's *Cry, the Beloved Country*, not just because of its powerfully told story, but also because of its controversial, troubling subject matter (Attwell 192). It also paved the way to Coetzee's winning the Nobel Prize for Literature four years later. Set in contemporary South Africa, it follows David Lurie, a white professor at the fictional Cape Technical University, who is dismissed from his position for not expressing contrition for a sexual relationship with one of his students. David, who presumably grew up under apartheid, displays a blithe arrogance in his dealings with the student and with a prostitute, which we might connect to the mental "stuntedness" to which Coetzee referred in his 1987 Jerusalem Prize speech, where he contended that colonialism and apartheid impair everyone involved. After he goes to his adult daughter Lucy's farm in the Eastern Cape, two black African men and a teenage boy ruthlessly invade her home and rape her, set him on fire, steal belongings, and kill the dogs in her kennel. The attack leaves Lurie stunned and impaired with a burned scalp, bad eye, and misshapen ear, physical disabilities that recall, again, the Jerusalem Prize speech. The remainder of the novel has David anxiously pleading with Lucy to press charges for the rape (she refuses, apparently because she sees the assault as a sort of reparation for years of white oppression of Blacks in South Africa through apartheid), working on a minor opera about Byron and his mistress Teresa, helping to put unwanted dogs down at a shelter, and trying to come to terms with his own social downfall. In the midst of such explosive material, which has been accused of being racist, sexist, and contrary to the reality of postapartheid South Africa, it can be easy to miss disability again reappearing in a subtle but nonetheless forceful, even hurtful, way: one of the rapists, the teenager who we later learn has the unusual name of Pollux, apparently has an intellectual disability.

While Michael K and Coetzee's other disabled characters are mostly sympathetic and passive, inviting readers' compassion even as they remain largely inaccessible, in *Disgrace* Coetzee reworks the trope to present a figure of disability not just as a possible product of injustice, but also as unsettling and dangerous. Pollux, unlike his literary forerunners, is not powerless and docile but rather an active participant in the brazen, disturbing crime offstage. He appears in three scenes in the book: when he comes to Lucy's farm with the two other African men and participates in a gang rape, when he subsequently shows up at Lucy's neighbor Petrus's party, and when Lurie catches Pollux outside peeping in the bathroom window at Lucy. The other rapists are never named and never reappear. Pollux becomes the focus for the rape. The third-person narrator closely follows David's point of view; he sees Pollux as menacing and, after the rape, malevolent and unrepentant. In his understandable rage over his daughter's violation, we do not get any sympathy for the young man. The dynamic seems different, much more challenging than what we have seen in previous novels. Is Coetzee abandoning his humane portrayal of disabled others?

Pollux shows aggressive behavior the moment he appears, although he is not the leader in the assault against Lucy. When Lurie first sees him, Pollux is at Lucy's dog cages; he "hisses at the dogs and makes sudden, threatening gestures," enraging them (92). His actions perhaps become more understandable when we remember that the minority white population often used attack dogs (the dogs neighbors have boarded in Lucy's kennel include German shepherds and Dobermans) against their black counterparts in South Africa. David perceives Pollux as having "a flat, expressionless face and piggish eyes" (92), a depiction that, Ken Barris argues, fits the dehumanization of Black bodies in colonial racial discourse, which could reflect Lurie's mindset (both Lurie and Pollux presumably grew up under apartheid). Yet notably, the tall "strikingly handsome" man and his companion, not Pollux, go into the house after Lucy and lock the door, beginning the assault (92). Later, when Lurie is imprisoned in a bathroom and set afire by the second man, he glimpses Pollux behind him eating from an ice cream container. While he apparently participates in the gang rape offstage, in what we see of Pollux he is a childish if combative follower of the adult men, raising the question of how much of his behavior is shaped by others and the society around him.

When Pollux reappears later, Lurie's visceral loathing differs from the troubled but more accepting attitude of Lucy and the tolerant head of an animal shelter, Bev Shaw. When Pollux shows up at her Black neighbor Petrus's party, Lucy is anxious and distressed, but she wants to leave quietly so as not to cause a disruption. David, in contrast, makes a scene: he angrily confronts the boy ("I know you" [131]) and says he will call the police. He does not, though, because of Lucy's wishes; she never reports the rape out of conviction that keeping quiet is the best way for her to survive in postapartheid South Africa. Pollux's cognitive disability plays into this decision. She says, "I suspect there is something wrong with him" and "he is disturbed," seemingly holding Pollux less responsible for his actions because of his condition (200, 208). David sees things differently: "In the old days we had a word for people like him. Deficient. Mentally deficient. Morally deficient. He should be in an institution," he declares (208). The "old days," of course, refers to the days of apartheid. David, in spite of progressive leanings, seems nostalgic for the era that repressed and excluded disabled citizens of color. Understandably upset at Lucy's rape and his own failure to prevent it, he thinks of apartheid practices as a desirable way to maintain order. His reference to an institution recalls Michael K's awful stay at his special school and constant efforts to stay out of camps as an adult; David privileges his own safety and comfort over that of disabled people of color. For her part, while Bev Shaw agrees that "I don't like the look of [Pollux]," she is confident that Petrus, who apparently is related to Pollux (perhaps Pollux is the brother of Petrus's wife, Lucy speculates), will prevent any assault from happening again (210). Both women seem unsettled but more understanding than Lurie, who acknowledges that "something about Pollux sends him into a rage" (209).

What angers David may be not just the gang-rape of his daughter, not just Pollux's being unrepentant and getting off scot-free, but also his own implicit similarity to Pollux, for he is a sexual violator, too. In the first part of the novel, he pursues a sexual relationship with a vulnerable student less than half his age who could well be a person of color; David thinks of her as "the dark one" (18). He seduces her, and later, when she's unwilling, he forces himself on her, although at the time he exculpates himself, thinking, "not quite rape, not quite that, but undesired nevertheless" (25). In this way, the violent rape of his daughter has parallels in his own actions. The unusual name Pollux comes from Greek and Roman myth, where Pollux and his twin brother, Castor, are involved in rape. (Rubens depicted them in his painting *The Rape of the Daughters of Leucippus.*) Who in *Disgrace* is the African Pollux's twin? According to Sandra D. Shattuck, it could be Lurie; the two are joined together not just by being sexual predators, but also by their mutual hatred of the other race in a South Africa that has only recently moved past apartheid. When near the end of the book David sees Pollux peering in the window at Lucy, he is overcome with "elemental rage": *"You filthy swine!"* he says and kicks him (206). Pollux responds with his own anger. *"We will kill you all!"* he shouts (207). It seems clear that by "we" he means Black South Africans, and by "you all," South African whites. As Shattuck trenchantly puts it, "Lurie hates Pollux as the perpetrator of violence against himself and his daughter, while Pollux hates Lurie for being white and thus an oppressor" (143). In David and Pollux's mutual hatred, we can see the deep challenges of moving past anger and violence in postapartheid South Africa. Shattuck points to Lucy and Petrus's unlikely partnership—they will marry, but it seems more of a business relationship in which Petrus gets Lucy's land in exchange for his protection—as preventing more violence and hatred from Lurie and Pollux and as moving toward a pragmatic accommodation that will allow white and Black citizens to live together harmoniously in postapartheid South Africa.

Just as disability can have larger metaphorical significance, the disturbing presence of rape has metaphorical meaning in the novel and in human rights literature in general. David's assault of the "dark" Melani has racial overtones that neatly express the privilege and arrogance of a white male raised in apartheid South Africa, while the later Black gang rape of the white Lucy has clear correlations with Black aggression and revenge after the end of the apartheid system that brutalized Blacks for so long (18). As we will see, rape appears again in work by Edwidge Danticat and Abani; in their cases, male soldiers assault vulnerable female citizens. In all of these instances, the violence of rape not only expresses the genuine, reprehensible suffering that takes place in the world but also is always about power. Rape is a way for male characters to assert themselves, to try to achieve self-actualization at the expense of others. Not surprisingly, rape has been a dominant concern in human rights— for example, general recommendation 19 in the Convention on the Elimination of All Forms of Discrimination against Women (CEDAW) expressly forbids violence against women. In these ways, we can see how racial justice, gender justice, and disability justice are all related and deeply enmeshed.

Although he has a minor role, Pollux nevertheless plays a crucial if recalcitrant part in the story of *Disgrace*, driving home the challenges of reconciliation. As with Michael K, we cannot say for sure that Pollux's intellectual disability has roots in the poverty and oppressive environment of apartheid into which he was born, but the possibility exists, as does the probability he has received little education or other resources. (During apartheid, the government devoted far less money to the education of Black students than whites.) In a subtle sense his disability both literally and metaphorically suggests oppression. Disability critics could charge Coetzee with, as Eli Clare puts it in a different context, "conflat[ing] justice with the eradication of disability"

(56), a provocative claim worth pausing over in this instance, but the dynamic here often seems more complex than that. First, while Coetzee's novels typically have allegorical potential, they leave us uncertain about how far to go with such allegorical interpretations. With Michael K, we see the worth of the disabled characters, whom at least one white narrator, the medical officer, yearns to connect with and understand. We do not encounter any such yearning in *Disgrace*. At one point David asks himself whether he can imagine what it is like to be the woman who's raped. With his opera taking on the voice of Byron's Teresa, he begins to move toward understanding a woman's view. But he never asks whether he can imagine what it is like to be a disabled person of color in South Africa. Lucy, Bev Shaw, and Petrus offer some idea of a more compassionate stance, but even they do not offer insight into Pollux's character, which is perhaps one reason *Disgrace* is more distressing than Coetzee's earlier work. In *Lives of Animals* (1999), which Coetzee published the same year as *Disgrace*, he has the fictional author Elizabeth Costello confidently assert, "There is no limit to the extent to which we can think ourselves into the being of another. There are no bounds to the sympathetic imagination" (35). Yet the evidence of Coetzee's novels differs: even when there is a strong will to understand and empathize, it seems, barriers inevitably prevent meaningful connection.

As he worked on *Life & Times of Michael K*, Coetzee noted this difficulty in his journal: "There is a fundamental flaw in all my novels: I am unable to move from the side of the oppressors to the side of the oppressed" (qtd. in Attwell 110). Coetzee's privileged position as a white person in an apartheid environment limits his writing, which takes us back to his contention in his 1987 Jerusalem Prize speech that all writing in apartheid South Africa is stultified, like one would expect from a prison. But he tries to conquer limits and his own ambivalence, which makes his writing both moving and consequential.

Even as Michael K and Pollux remain elusive and beyond definite understanding, the novels consistently present white protagonists' downfall as a path to a certain redemptive insight that sees disabled people and others as worthy of dignity that is often denied them. Just as the medical officer sees his own work as meaningless and yearns to escape the camp as Michael has, so David Lurie loses his university teaching position and much of his initial arrogance. In the end, his daughter is pregnant by one of the rapists (possibly Pollux) and intends to marry her Black neighbor Petrus. David, despite deep misgivings, gradually comes to respect her wishes so he can maintain a relationship with her. She has resolved to start again "with nothing," and so in a sense is he, working with Bev Shaw at her clinic to euthanize dogs and tenderly deposit their bodies at an incinerator (205). "There may be things to learn," he acknowledges (218). Deploying disability as both a metaphor and a reality, Coetzee raises awareness of not just the formidable effects and lingering challenges of colonialism and apartheid, but also the difficult place disabled people often have in South Africa, and presents the newfound humility and respect of able-bodied characters as they lose their positions of power as a key to a better future for all.

5

A Sense of Care

*Women Writing Disabled Women
in the Global South*

Notwithstanding the possibilities for a common platform of
resistance, disability is conspicuously missing in third world
feminist analyses of difference.

—NIRMALA EREVELLES,
Disability and Difference in Global Contexts

Although the 1948 Universal Declaration of Human Rights states it
is for "all human beings," many oppressed groups felt overlooked by
its general principles, leading decades later to follow-up human rights
treaties focusing on more specific aspects of rights for racial minorities and women, not to mention disabled people.[1] (According to Maya Sabatello and Marianne Schultze, when human rights treaties have not specifically named disability, they have "consistently failed" to protect disabled people [4].) In the 1970s,
the United Nations turned its attention to women, declaring 1975–1985 the
UN Decade for Women and adopting the Convention on the Elimination
of All Forms of Discrimination against Women (CEDAW) in 1979. Enough
countries ratified it for it to enter into force two years later, in 1981. Samuel
Moyn says that while the treaty "has always wanted for state agreement and
enforcement," CEDAW "remains easily the most transformative human rights
treaty ever envisioned, demanding a reach into the 'private' realm and thus an
attack on patriarchal relations not just in employment and politics but also
in families and homes" (*Not Enough* 204). The treaty helped to foster needed
changes large and small with regard to gender equity, but, notably, it did not
mention disabled women, a group that is particularly subjugated. Aware of this
oversight, in 1991 general recommendation 18 to the CEDAW asked states, in
their regular reports to the CEDAW committee, to report on disabled women,
including on their access to education, employment, health services, and social
security.[2] Still, as Nirmala Erevelles says, for decades women with disabilities
were left off the women's rights agenda of almost every country in the Global

South. Once again, literature proved crucial, helping to raise awareness of a marginalized, largely invisible group and to provide initial steps for achieving equity.

Disabled women in the Global South embody a contradiction that makes them, as a group, seem almost endlessly just beyond comprehension. On one hand, as mentioned in the Introduction, influential international organizations based in the North offer grievous statements about the circumstances of disabled women in the South in general. They report that such women often live in poverty and experience more prejudice and barriers than disabled men. According to the World Health Organization and the World Bank, 60 percent of disabled people in low-income countries are female, which equals hundreds of millions of people. Facing multilayered gender and disability discrimination (not to mention, in some cases, racism or prejudice based on ethnicity, class, or caste), disabled women in low-income nations reportedly often struggle to obtain access to such essentials as housing, health care, education, and employment (UN "Women"). They also almost assuredly endure more gender-based violence, rape, abuse, malnutrition, and exploitation, which are likely underreported. As the United Nations summarizes, "girls and women of all ages with any form of disability are generally among the more vulnerable and marginalized of society" ("Women").

Yet even as they acknowledge that disabled people in the Global South commonly live in a state of precarity, some feminist disability studies scholars, including those from places such as India, criticize broad generalizations about Southern disabled women for obscuring their actual circumstances, which can vary enormously. Janet Price and Nidhi Goyal, for example, call images of utter deprivation surrounding women with disabilities in the Global South myths that, while containing elements of truth, lack contextual detail and produce gaps in understanding. Countering the perception that the vast majority of disabled women in the South are unemployed, they draw from anthropological and sociological research to point out that both disabled and nondisabled women in agricultural subsistence communities in Africa and South Asia have always worked to support their households, but their (unpaid) labor has usually been overlooked in development surveys. They also note that models from the North do not account for the effects of colonialism and postliberation conflict, for widely varying cultures, including indigenous cultures, or for how some disabled women in the South do not even conceive of themselves as disabled. Broad generalizations do not reflect such complicated realities.

Moreover, sweeping statements typically produce perceptions that disabled women in the South are invariably passive victims, missing out how in some places they have proactively formed networks and organizations to advance their interests. To give one instance: in her YouTube video on the African Youth with Disabilities Network, Ruth Nabasirye, a Ugandan woman who uses a wheelchair, notes that violence against women with disabilities in her country is very high, especially in war zones.[3] "So many women and young girls with disabilities have been raped," she says, adding that many are left pregnant and vulnerable to further abuse. Through a coalition in Uganda called the National Union of Women with Disabilities, she and others are working to build the confidence and unity of the nation's disabled women, an example of local activism in response to a pattern of violence and exploitation. Generalizations typically do not convey such proactivity and fail to give a sense of these alliances and mutual care.

More than just missing out on reality, broad claims lead to stereotypes that have serious consequences for disabled women in the South. According to Erevelles, by conveying a sense of "pathetic victimized femininity" that omits Southern women's proactivity, stereotypes "justify patriarchal, imperialist, ableist interventions," setting them up for misguided solutions (*Disability* 130). Erevelles contends that many groups are too complacent about the situation. Along with media in the North, Erevelles criticizes feminists in the Global South, noting that "notwithstanding the possibilities for a common platform of resistance, disability is conspicuously missing in third world feminist analyses of difference" (130). Similarly, writing about disability in the American war zones of Afghanistan and Iraq, she chastises American people of color and disabled communities for their "unemotional response" (132). By reminding us that disability affects not only disabled people, but also their families and caregivers (often themselves women), Erevelles adds to the sense of the enormity of the situation. A large percentage—perhaps even as high as 50 percent in some nations—of the population in the Global South is closely affected by disability, which means vast numbers of people confront a situation in which they are positioned as essentially disposable. The stakes are high, affecting hundreds of millions of people. Yet stereotyped as destitute and passive, and largely invisible to people in the North, disabled women in the South too often have been left on the margins of society.

In this context, authors of widely read fiction once again play a crucial role by offering a potent form of witnessing that can help to make tangible and personal in readers' minds the widely varying experiences of disabled women across the Global South. In the 1990s, after the United Nations Decade of Disabled Persons (1983–1992) had thrust disabled people onto the world's stage, but before the adoption in 2006 of the Convention on the Rights of People with Disabilities (CRPD) that specified their human rights, authors of Anglophone postcolonial literature depicted disabled characters, including disabled women, more frequently. Even if they are fictional, such representations break the anonymity and stereotypes of passivity and lack surrounding Southern disabled women. By provoking readers' engagement with disabled femininity, they raise awareness of actual local situations for disabled women in ways that, as I have been arguing, sometimes lay a crucial foundation in readers' minds for justice for disabled people, although such equity certainly is not easily or readily brought about.

This chapter focuses on portrayals of Southern disabled women by three contemporary female authors—Anita Desai, Jhumpa Lahiri, and Edwidge Danticat—who in the 1990s not only offered nuanced depictions, but also showed notable attention for the disabled female characters in their works. We might call this attention an ethic of care, related to the sense of interrelatedness and compassion that Northern feminist theorists have been remarking on for decades, but with an added twist as the dynamic concerns Southern disabled women in often oppressive situations. In the process, they point to the importance of care and interdependence in human rights.

The theory of a feminist ethic of care emerged in the North in the late twentieth century and, especially at first, served in many ways as the opposite of rights-based discourse. Scholars usually trace the ethic in part back to the work of the psychologist Carol Gilligan, who in 1982 published *In a Different Voice: Psychological Theory and Women's Development*, a book that criticized traditional models of moral development that prioritize a "morality of rights" and independence over a "morality of responsibility" and relationships with other people (19). Similarly, a few years later, in *Caring*, Nel Noddings contended that care in personal contexts is more desirable than distant universal rules. In 1993, Joan Tronto outlined some central differences between notions of care and of rights—namely, that an ethic of care is based on relationships, responsibilities, and material circumstances rather than abstract rules, and that the ethic of care relies on activity rather than principles. Other scholars, from Sara Ruddick (1989) to Virginia Held (1993), pointed to the importance of caring, personal responsibility, and maternal relationships as necessary to ensure the well-being of vulnerable people, including children, requiring care. Meanwhile, feminist philosophers such as Eva Feder Kittay criticized the social contractarian framework of justice developed by philosopher John Rawls in the 1970s, arguing instead for the necessity of care and compassion without regard to whether the other party can give back.[4]

Such work on care has clear implications for disability studies, as some disabled people rely on some kind of care, but the appeal of such a personal approach is not automatic for disabled people. In *Disability Rights and Wrongs*, Tom Shakespeare points out potential problems with the ethic of care from a Euro-American disability studies perspective. In the United States and Europe, the disability rights movement has stressed independent living, working for autonomy for disabled people. While the feminist ethic's celebration of interrelationships and interdependence may seem welcome in public, Shakespeare says that many disabled people in the North "may well have reasons to reject this [because] they may feel taken over, spoken for, undermined, disempowered or even neglected and abused by carers" in the private domain (145). Northern disability activists have sometimes seen an ethic of care as potentially more oppressive than rights that ensure independence.

Complicating such matters further, societies in the Global South often have different notions of care and of autonomy. In "Global Kinship," the anthropologist Michael Herzfeld points out that, while kinship in its familial sense is a "strong organizing principle" of relationships around the world, it takes "different forms and expressions" (314, 316). For example, societies may have contrasting values about treatment of the elderly, end-of-life care, and related matters. Moreover, different cultures may have different models for family structure. Attitudes are complex and shifting in an increasingly globalized world, though. As Herzfeld notes, kinship in the Global South is often marked by the aftershocks of colonialism, which promoted a Eurocentric idea of a nuclear family, but in the resulting mix the traditional and new can be hard to distinguish. "Much of what appears to be new is inflected with older ideas," he writes. "Much of what seems to be 'traditional' and 'local' actually represents an adaptation to intrusive and imperial values" (320).

Such concerns show up prominently in this fiction, where disabled women characters regularly confront issues of family, stigma, care, and independence. Both part one of Anita Desai's novel *Fasting, Feasting* (1999), a finalist for the Booker Prize in 1999, and Jhumpa Lahiri's short story, "The Treatment of Bibi Haldar," from her celebrated first collection *Interpreter of Maladies* (1999), take place in modern India and depict women who have mysterious seizures that may be caused by epilepsy. Yet Desai's Uma and Lahiri's Bibi Haldar have very different situations: Uma lives with her stern upper-class parents, while Bibi's parents have died and she lives near destitution, with just a cousin sometimes taking responsibility for her. Meanwhile, Edwidge Danticat's first novel, *Breath, Eyes, Memory* (1994), portrays the ongoing mental anguish of a woman who was raped in Haiti, raising difficult questions for the daughter born of that rape about how to best care for a traumatized parent, while her story "Caroline's Wedding" (1995) demonstrates the love of a Haitian American immigrant in New York for her sister, who is missing her forearm. In these disparate cases, Desai, Lahiri, and Danticat break the anonymity surrounding disabled women in the Global South and often implicitly critique patriarchal structures. These works engage in an ethic of care in two ways. First, the authors themselves demonstrate care by focusing on disabled female figures who might otherwise be overlooked and presenting them as worthy of attention. Second, the narratives present other characters who care about the disabled subjects—almost always women themselves—in a positive light. Through such strategies, these authors not only make individual disabled women visible in their local settings, but they also implicitly urge readers to care about disabled women like these characters, producing a subtle kinship between readers and disabled characters that advances the ethos of global disability rights.

Care in Desai's *Fasting, Feasting*

Part one of Desai's *Fasting, Feasting* concerns Uma, a seemingly unremarkable woman in India with impairments. (In addition to having occasional seizures, she is myopic, uncoordinated, and probably has a learning disability.) She deals with persistent neglect and misunderstanding, showing the stigma that can come with being a disabled woman in India even in the upper classes. Set between the 1960s and 1980, well after India achieved independence from Britain in 1947, in part one Uma is the protagonist; the third-person narrator closely follows her experiences in understated fashion, jumping around chronologically from chapter to chapter.

The novel depicts the kind of postcolonial cultural mixing of traditional and new that Herzfeld writes about. For example, Uma's father, a provincial attorney, has learned at his (presumably British) school to believe in the "benefits of meat along with that of cricket and the English language," all of which seem to him progress, even as we see ardent followers of Hinduism and vegetarians in other parts of the narrative (32). It can be difficult to distinguish traditional from new. Is the family's having a cook, driver, and gardener a sign of British influence or not? What about Papa's domineering attitude and persistent need to be in control? Such forces shape Uma's experience as a woman with a disability.

The greatest tension between older and more modern ideas in the novel shows up in societies' attitudes toward gender roles. As critics have noted, women in the narrative—whether single or married, able-bodied or disabled, or in India or the United States (in part two)—are in various ways regularly treated as subordinate. In part one, Papa consistently exerts a strict patriarchal role, such as when Uma's mother feels she has to slip off surreptitiously so she can play rummy without Papa's knowledge; when she ceremoniously peels an orange, carefully removing all the pith, and serves it to her imperious silent husband at a meal; or in Papa's evident disdain for unmarried women who have careers. When he meets Dr. Dutt, a single female doctor, toward the end of part one, we learn that "Papa was quite capable of putting on a progressive, Westernised front when called upon to do so—in public, in society, not within his family of course" (141), which indicates how he continues to subscribe to traditional notions of gender roles. His own wife did not attend school. Uma and her sister Aruna have the opportunity to be educated but also receive the message that arranged marriages are the only reputable way for them as women to leave the family home. Such attitudes extend beyond Papa. The most prominent and tragic example of the costs of demeaning women is the fate of Uma's brilliant, attractive, kind cousin Anamika, whose parents compel her to turn down a prestigious scholarship to Oxford and instead to marry an abusive older man. We learn that the new husband and his mother treat Anamika like a servant and beat her, so much so that she loses the ability to bear children. When she mysteriously burns to death at age forty-five, through either murder or suicide, no investigation takes place, underscoring her complete victimization in a patriarchal system. So even before we consider her as a disabled character, Uma as a woman already is deeply disadvantaged in her small-town society that perceives women as inferior.

Attitudes toward Uma's impairments disempower her further. To their credit, Uma's parents allow her to go to school and try to arrange a marriage for her, giving her the opportunity to be "normal" like her able-bodied sister, but when Uma does not succeed at those things she has few options and is seen as an embarrassment. Unlike her mother, Uma has the chance to gain an education, attending a Catholic convent run by nuns apparently from Europe. She is an enthusiastic student but fails miserably in every subject and has to repeat grades before her parents take her out of school as a teen, against her wishes, to care for her newborn brother. Similarly, she receives the chance to marry, but when her mother arranges marriages with two men, they prove corrupt (one turns out to be already married), pretending to be interested in the plain, clumsy Uma only so they can take her father's dowries. As a result, after his retirement, when financial resources evidently become more limited, Papa is especially tightfisted and parsimonious with regard to Uma, refusing to let her go to Bombay to see an expensive eye specialist ("Our optician is good enough"), leaving her in near-darkness when he and Mama go out, and even discouraging her from using the telephone (108). The women in the family are at times more explicit about their disgust. After the adult Uma goes without permission to a public restaurant with a cousin and drinks, Mama cannot contain her indignation: "You idiot child!" she says. "You disgrace to the family—nothing but disgrace, *ever!*" (53). Her words show how she sees her disabled daughter as humiliating, as something to conceal from public view to safeguard the family honor. Anita Ghai's words about a "common perception" in India that "views disability as a retribution for past karmas (actions) from which there can be no reprieve" may pertain here, although Mama and Papa never refer to this view (89). Similarly, after Uma has a seizure at her sister's cocktail party before her wedding, Aruna tearfully calls her an "idiot" who "should be put away, locked up" (102). Mama's and Aruna's powerful language speaks to the strong stigma attached to disability and their feelings of shame by family association, as if Uma's condition is something repugnant to be disavowed and hidden away.

Small surprise, then, that Uma chafes against the constrictions of home life and tries to escape them, sometimes with the aid of others who have compassion for her plight. Often, her trips away from home have not just liberating, but also religious, overtones, suggesting a sort of spiritual yearning. One reason that she enjoys the Catholic convent school as a girl is its freedom from home, a place that to her "seemed a denial, a negation of life as it ought to be" (21). The religious atmosphere at the school also appeals to her; she finds "golden promise" in it (20). After her parents take her out of the school, she makes a desperate effort to run away to the convent using her own savings, pleading with a nun before she has a seizure and is returned home in "ignominy" (29). A distant relative, Mira-masi, seems to have pity on her, apparently feigning an illness to convince Mama and Papa to let Uma accompany her to a Hindu ashram. There Uma spends hours wandering by the river, where she "had never been more unsupervised or happier in her life" (57). The trip takes on a religious element when Mira-masi claims that Uma is "the Lord's child," and priests, after she has a major seizure, view her with extra respect. Later, Mrs. O'Henry, a Christian missionary who apparently sees Uma as a potential convert, takes interest in her, gives her Christmas cards that Uma collects, and invites her to a summer retreat in the mountains. While Uma is delighted, she is too nervous even to ask her father if she can go. These two latter cases show caring women inviting Uma away from the house. Both have a religious element, suggesting that Uma's longing for freedom has spiritual meaning. At one point, during a ritual bath where attendees are supposed to prove their Hindu belief with an excursion on the river, Uma, "thrilled by . . . license," jumps recklessly into the water, and after she is rescued she does not have a seizure again, hinting at some metaphysical transformation (110). Such religious nuances add spiritual weight to Uma's story, opening its significance to interpretation. One is reminded, for instance, of "the meek . . . shall inherit the Earth" (Matthew 5:5) in the Christian Bible, with its emphasis on the values of each person, and Hinduism's stress on kindness and charity to help build a good karma for believers' next life. Then again, perhaps liberation itself has curative effects. For Uma, freedom and happiness are most easily attained through spirituality—whether Christian or Hindu does not seem to matter to her—an area open to women in the society of the novel.

Another person who briefly empowers Uma is her cousin Ramu, the only other disabled person Uma has contact with in the novel. He has a clubfoot. Comparing Uma and Ramu suggests the differences gender can make. Ramu, like Uma, is stigmatized. Mama and Papa view him with tight-lipped disapproval; he is the "black sheep of the family" and is rumored to drink or use drugs (46). If that's true, one could hypothesize social opprobrium as a driving factor. While Uma remains subserviently at home, he travels about freely and responds to his displeased elders with mischievous insouciance; he clearly does not submit to authoritative control. He proves the only character who can make Uma laugh. "I want you to enjoy yourself," he tells Uma when he takes her out for dinner and drinks (51). Uma's delight points to how she never has access to other disabled people, organizations, or services throughout the novel. The Indian anthropologist Nilika Mehrotra says that sometimes in India disabled people marry other disabled people. While a medicalized view dominates, Mehrotra reports that occasionally Indian families can break stereotypes and "normalize disability" in their midst by bringing disabled men and women together. No such opportunity comes up for Uma. She remains isolated at home, increasingly working almost as a servant, fetching things and performing tasks for her demanding elderly parents. When she reads the words "You are wasting your life in that dull, dark room" in a poem, it encapsulates her situation (135). Yet Ramu does not escape, either. Despite his carefree air, Ramu eventually disappears from the narrative. Evidently, his parents have given him a farm to keep him from drink and drugs, so he, too, is a disabled character who is hidden away.

How much Uma's elderly parents come to depend on her appears near the end of part one, when Dr. Dutt offers the gray-haired, forty-three-year-old Uma a job and escape from home life. She wants a person to take care of the new nurses at her medical institute. "We really need Uma to come and help us," Dr. Dutt says, joining the ranks of Mira-masi, Mrs. O'Henry, and Ramu as a caring person seeking to offer Uma liberation (142). She calls Uma someone "who has been running the house for her parents for so long," qualifying her for the job (142). The tables have turned; now Uma is the caregiver whose elderly parents depend on her. Suddenly she has an opportunity to get out of the home. Although Uma pleads with her father to agree, he and Mama grimly refuse to let her go. At the end of the novel she remains isolated and unfulfilled.

To be sure, Uma is complicit in her own subordination. She seems to internalize the attitudes around her. When her sister says she should be locked up for having a seizure, Uma moans, "Lock me up, Mama, lock me up!" indicating how easily she takes others' views of her as objectionable (102). Yet Desai also vividly shows how the society around Uma disempowers her. She does not have access to special education, support services, or other disabled people. Her family devalues her and hides her away. Although caring women and a disabled male relative try to intervene, Uma remains constricted and devalued at the end, with no promise of liberation. *Fasting, Feasting* shows how families play a crucial role in India and much of the Global South (as opposed to notions of individualism and autonomy) and must be factored into conversations about disability rights. While Desai makes readers feel a certain connection with Uma, she also compels us to see how families and societies can be oppressive.

Lahiri's Bibi Haldar and Care

Lahiri's short story "The Treatment of Bibi Haldar" also presents a woman in contemporary India with unexplained seizures who has difficulty finding a husband. Unlike Uma, however, Bibi's parents are dead and she lives in poverty. With only an unsympathetic cousin to look after her, the twenty-nine-year-old Bibi has sudden unconscious fits and seems exceedingly vulnerable. But evincing genuine care and not a little interest in others' affairs, the married women in the apartment complex give her unstinting support. The story is apparently narrated by an anonymous woman who speaks on behalf of all the female neighbors in a collective first-person plural "we"; this technique is reminiscent of the distinctive "we" narrator (what some critics have referred to as a Greek chorus) of William Faulkner's classic story "A Rose for Emily." While Faulkner's townspeople follow the life of a mysterious lady in their midst, Emily Grierson, Lahiri's women track Bibi's experience, showing exceptional interest in what might seem an unremarkable existence. Faulkner's tale ends with gothic horror—Emily, we learn in the final lines, poisoned her former suitor and slept next to his corpse—but Bibi does not poison anyone, as Lahiri gives her an unexpectedly fortunate outcome. Lahiri's title refers not just to the myriad prescriptions Bibi has received from all manner of doctors, priests, and hypnotists, and not just to the treatment that ultimately apparently works, but also to the behavior of the people around her, including the neighbor women's care, that plays a significant role in shaping her experience.

Like Desai, Lahiri shows family as having crucial importance in a disabled person's life in India, and that family can sometimes be oppressive. When Bibi was young, her father apparently was a dedicated presence, even quitting his work as a teacher to focus on her and research her condition. He has died, though, and Bibi's only remaining relative is a disdainful cousin, Haldar, who runs a tiny cosmetics shop in the complex and does not seem to care when Bibi has attacks. After Bibi has a seizure, Haldar arrives ten minutes later looking "impassive apart from the red in his face" (161). His demeanor could indicate anger or embarrassment; both interpretations have evidence later when he accuses her of exaggerating her condition for attention and of driving customers away. Bibi has "sullied enough the family name," he says, words that echo Mama's similar sentiment about Uma disgracing the family in *Fasting, Feasting* (165). Such language shows that families sometimes feel compelled to hide disabled offspring or distance themselves from them. Under pressure from Bibi and the women, Haldar grudgingly agrees to advertise Bibi for marriage, but no takers appear. His wife shares his rancor, showing how, like Uma's mother and sister, a woman can participate in dismal treatment of a disabled relative. Seeing Bibi as a gender deviant, she points out that Bibi does not know how to cook and has never learned to be a woman. She thinks Bibi is possessed by the devil and might be contagious. When her newborn baby becomes ill, she blames Bibi and compels her to live in a cramped storage room on the roof. In the face of such strident rejection, Bibi is surprisingly unruffled. "Now I am free to discover life as I please," she assures the women, claiming a liberation that Uma never permanently finds (170).

Crucially, the female neighbors give Bibi, who otherwise would be isolated and alone, a supportive community while acknowledging the limits of their involvement. They follow her welfare closely, provide her with attention and companionship, go shopping with her, offer her advice about seeking a husband, and console her when a potential husband does not appear. Yet they are aware of their limits. "None of us were capable of understanding such desolation," the narrator admits. "But she was not our responsibility, and in our private moments we were thankful for it" (166–167). By making one anonymous woman narrate for all of the female neighbors, the story encourages readers to share their compassionate view of Bibi while also acknowledging the constraints on connection and perhaps gesturing toward the need for more formal, impersonal disability rights legislation that would offer Bibi more protection. In protest of Haldar's dismissive attitude to Bibi, the women boycott his cosmetics shop and eventually cause him to go out of business and leave. They repair the shutters of Bibi's storeroom, provide food, and, at every opportunity, "we reminded her that we surrounded her, that she could come to us if she ever needed advice or aid of any kind" (171). Even aware the limits of what they can do, they provide a caring web that nurtures Bibi on her own.

However empowering the women's care is, Bibi's own independence helps her to reach a positive, surprising fate. She retreats into silence and secrecy during the winter, to the point where some of the women wonder whether she is dying. In the spring, though, Bibi emerges about four months pregnant. Who is the father? Was Bibi raped? Did she voluntarily sleep with someone? Was there artificial insemination? She steadfastly refuses to say. The women eventually help her deliver a son and provide her with support: "We showed her how to feed him and bathe him, and lull him to sleep" (172). She not only raises the boy but also sells her cousin's leftover cosmetics at half-price and soon has a thriving business. The sudden fortunate turn of events may test readers' credulity or invite talk of magic realism. In contrast to Uma, who remains stifled by her parents, Bibi achieves autonomy and a career for herself and becomes a mother, a source of special status in the Indian context. (According to Mehrotra, in India a woman who is childless is typically perceived as more "disabled" than a disabled woman who has children.) The women soon give up on finding out the identity of the father, as Bibi is clearly flourishing. This upbeat resolution leads to the memorable final sentence: "She was, to the best of our knowledge, cured" (172).

Such an ending could well be controversial in a Euro-American disability studies frame as it positions disability as negative. As David Mitchell and Sharon Snyder point out with their influential theory of "narrative prosthesis," Western narratives traditionally have often used disability to advance plots only to kill, rehabilitate, remove, or cure the disability in the end in a way that buttresses a hegemony of normalcy. Bibi's cure could certainly be seen that way, although we should note that the cure is not absolute: The narrator qualifies it with "to the best of our knowledge," suggesting that Bibi herself never tells the women. We should remember that Uma also has a seemingly miraculous healing: she stops having seizures after she jumps in the river, which gives her cure spiritual overtones. For the impoverished Bibi, in a situation where she does not have resources or access to medication or support services, where she lives in a tiny storeroom and eats handouts, her apparent cure seems to empower her. One could even suggest it comes about because of the emotional uplift and control she achieves at the end, things that have eluded her for most of the story, when she was demeaned by her cousin as annoying and disposable. Her pleasant fate seems to come not only from her very autonomy and independence from family and others, but also from starting a separate family of her own, something Uma can never do.

At any rate, works such as these pieces bring disabled women in the Global South out of their invisibility and make them subjects of interest and concern. Both Lahiri and Desai show the importance of family in the lives of disabled people in India, the stigma of disability in their families and culture, the difficulty of finding a husband or becoming independent, and, most of all, the importance of other characters who care, who are compassionate and offer support. They suggest how disabled women may find supportive networks outside of the home. Such an ethic of care gently prods readers to care, as well.

Trauma and Care in Danticat's Fiction

In their incisive article "Disabling Postcolonialism," Clare Barker and Stuart Murray contend that, to account properly for disability in postcolonial contexts, we need to pay attention to the category of trauma. War, violence, and other acts frequently create not only disability, but also feelings of profound anxiety and loss. Barker and Murray assert that Euro-American theories of disability are insufficient in the Global South, where ideologies and the material context of disabled people differ and trauma and disability regularly occur together. As they put it, "Disability criticism should address . . . how 'loss' may be constituted within disability experiences" (231). As noted in the Introduction, James Berger has argued that in the North disability studies and trauma studies have had little connection: "Disability studies exhibits a significant degree of *denial* with regard to trauma and loss," he says (572). One does not have to look far to explain this state of affairs. As the Introduction explains, disability scholars in the North have typically turned attention away from the individual, medical model toward a social model that emphasizes how society and culture disempower those with impairments. Along the way, they have stressed the capabilities of disabled people and contested the assumption that a disability is tragic, even as it moves to embrace a biocultural definition of disability that acknowledges biological factors. The question remains for the field: How can we incorporate trauma into disability studies without confirming dominant beliefs that disability is invariably a misfortune, a grievous disadvantage that if at all possible needs to be cured?[5] As any disabled person knows, such views are often as automatic and widespread as they are problematic. Furthermore, trying to differentiate between disabilities that are not a loss and those that are seems precarious, at best, and could fragment the admirable unified advocacy now animating in the field.

The Haitian American author Edwidge Danticat's 1994 novel *Breath, Eyes, Memory* especially offers a way to explore these difficult issues while confronting vexing questions of care. Narrated by Sophie Caco, a girl who grows up in Haiti and then moves to New York City at age twelve (as Danticat did) to join her mother, the novel shows not only a caring bond between family members, even though they have been separated for years, but also how disability can intersect with trauma. The story seems to take place in the 1970s and '80s. Dealing with such painful but all-too-real subjects as rape, self-mutilation, and suicide, it also includes both disability and trauma in ways that reverberate across generations and national boundaries. The novel shows the rewards and perils of considering trauma part of disability and a difficulty that surrounds care.

Not all disability in the novel is traumatic, although Danticat makes us aware early on of how, in Haiti, thinking about physical difference can significantly differ from such thinking in North America and Europe. Sophie describes how other Haitians perceive an albino man, Chabin:

> He was thought to have certain gifts. . . . For example, if anyone was chasing him, he could turn into a snake with one flip of his tongue. Sometimes, he could see the future by looking into your eyes, unless you close your soul to him by thinking of a religious song and prayer while in his presence. (5)

The surrounding society, which in Haiti has powerful traditions of vodou that likely inflect matters, views Chabin as having extraordinary powers. Although the descriptor "gifts" may make his rumored abilities seem positive, such qualities are also threatening, something foreign and almost evil to be warded off—notably, with religious songs or prayers. As Chabin approaches, Sophie's aunt does appear to say a prayer to protect herself. Despite such stigmatizing treatment, Chabin himself, a cheerful lottery agent, does not seem affected. Danticat does not have her narrator, Sophie, comment, but one can imagine that Danticat expects at least some readers—the novel was selected for Oprah's Book Club—to see how this metaphysical tradition dehumanizes him and reduces him to a menace. Already we can perceive that, although Danticat cares about her home country's culture, she is not afraid subtly to critique it. (Here she is probably influenced by the fact that she is Haitian American and has lived in the United States throughout her adulthood.)

Disability does show up intertwined with trauma when Sophie arrives in New York City and discovers that her mother, Martine, is haunted by debilitating nightmares. Her first night she finds her mother "screaming as though someone was trying to kill her" and "thrashing against the sheets" (48). It gradually emerges that Martine was raped at sixteen by a strange soldier in a Haitian cane field. Because she had no chance to bring the perpetrator to justice and was beset by fears, Martine left her family and village, but she did not escape the trauma. Sophie, born of that rape, is a living reminder of the violation; no matter how much she cares about her mother, she embodies that ordeal. Martine says she did not see the rapist's face but believes Sophie looks like him. Readers may recognize Martine's nightmares, anxiety, and unwillingness to speak about the incident (she does not even tell her longtime boyfriend about the rape) as signs of post-traumatic stress disorder (PTSD), a cognitive disability. Martine serves as a stark reminder of how PTSD affects men and women equally and how countless women around the world are tragically traumatized as victims of rape, war, and domestic violence.

How does PTSD fit into a positive disability framework? By its very name, PTSD includes trauma, and it is hard to see anything redeeming about the condition. To turn to a pathological description for a moment, the psychologist Jonathan Haidt calls PTSD "a debilitating condition that leaves its victims anxious and overreactive. People who suffer from PTSD are changed, sometimes permanently: they panic or crumble more easily when faced with later adversity" (136). When Martine screams and inflicts bodily injury on herself in her sleep, most readers probably want her to get therapy, to confront her issues head-on, and try to break the cycle of torment, but she does not, and her anguish plagues her continuously. It seems an entirely negative experience.

Danticat connects Martine's rape to the history of Haiti, which serves as a reminder of how trauma associates with a past of occupation and, by extension, with the North. In a trenchant analysis, Donette Francis writes about how Martine and Sophie's last name, Caco, symbolically links them to the Cacos, Haitian peasant guerrillas who resisted the occupation by U.S. Marines from 1915 to 1934. Both the Caco fighters and American soldiers sometimes raped Haitian women, suggesting Martine's and Sophie's strangely vulnerable position years later as women in an impoverished postcolonial nation. Furthermore, it appears likely that Martine was raped by a Tonton Macoute, a soldier from a militia group that the U.S.-backed National Guard helped to train around 1960, when, in the novel's chronology, Martine was a teen. At one point Sophie explains how these Macoute soldiers often used rape as a tool of political oppression:

> The *Macoutes*, they did not hide. When they entered the house, they asked to be fed, demanded the woman of the house, and forced her into her own bedroom. Then all you heard was screams until it was her daughter's turn. If a mother refused, they would make her sleep with her son and brother or even her own father. (139)

Again, we see rape connected with the abuse of power. Such atrocities by Haitian men, who were originally trained partly by Americans, indicates how powerless Haitian women could be and how Northern intentions can be corrupted and have a lasting negative legacy in the Global South.[6] To this specific situation in Haiti we could add instances of politically motivated rape and torture around the world, especially in impoverished countries wracked by violence and warfare, which I consider more in the next chapter. It helps us to understand what Ato Quayson means when he calls for confronting "a traumatic history of disability at the personal as well as social level" ("Looking Awry" 228).

Like Martine's PTSD, Sophie's disability is bound up with trauma. Briefly, we learn that in Haiti women are expected to remain virgins until marriage (which is another reason that Martine's rape is traumatic for her—it reduced her marriage prospects and stigmatizes the family). Sophie's family in Haiti has a tradition of "testing," in which the mother inserts her pinky into the vagina to ensure that the hymen is still intact. Sophie's grandmother explains that she saw this as her duty: "The mother is responsible for [her daughter's] purity. If I give a soiled daughter to her husband, he can shame my family, speak evil of me, even bring her back to me" (156). Martine hated testing when she was a girl, but she nonetheless does it in the United States to Sophie, who despises it herself. The act reveals how sexual abuse can come not from just soldiers but also from one's own female relatives and in the name of love. The testing complicates the feminist ethic of caring by showing how caring can become damaging instead of supportive, which relates to Shakespeare's insight about why some Northern disability activists are uncomfortable with an ethic of care, seeing it as a mechanism for disempowerment and potentially abuse. Sophie hates the testing so much that she mutilates her own hymen with a pestle. The resulting damage allows her to find liberation from the testing, but she spends two days in the hospital and later experiences pain during sex with her husband, to the point where it drives her and her husband apart and she seeks therapy. Again, a physical difference is bound up with trauma and with gender, and Danticat depicts the negative effects showing up in different generations.

Sophie and her mother have markedly different results in dealing with their trauma. In a tragic sequence of events, when Martine finds that her boyfriend has made her pregnant, her PTSD becomes even more severe; she thinks that the fetus is talking to her and associates it with her rapist. One night she stabs herself in the stomach seventeen times with a rusty knife, bleeding to death. As Francis points out, her body is the only thing over which Martine has control. Sophie, who previously had vowed never to send her mother to a mental hospital, upbraids herself for not taking better care of Martine, raising the prospect that sometimes care requires submitting to institutional control (a controversial sentiment that goes against much Euro-American disability advocacy, which, especially in the second half of the twentieth century, was often critical of asylums and institutionalization). Yet in her grief, Sophie insists that her mother is liberated. "She's going to be a butterfly or a lark in a tree. She's going to be free," she tells her mother's Haitian American boyfriend, who doesn't quite seem to grasp that Sophie is interpreting her mother's death through Haitian folkloric and spiritual traditions (228).

For her part, Sophie appears to find a more hopeful path. She enters therapy and a sex therapy group with two other women from postcolonial nations who have suffered abuse. One woman from Ethiopia, for example, had her clitoris cut by her grandmother when she was a child, reminding us that such sexual abuse can be culturally sanctioned. Strengthened by this community, Sophie manages to recognize that "my hurt and [my mother's] were links in a long chain and if she hurt me, it was because she was hurt, too" (203). Sophie has the insight to see that the trauma of testing and rape goes beyond individuals to a larger patriarchal culture that consistently subjugates women. Here the ethic of care spills over into shared identity. She resolves never to test her own baby daughter, breaking the chain of trauma.

At her mother's burial in Haiti at the end of the novel, Sophie runs and attacks a cane field, striking the cane stalks with her shoes. The cane field is, of course, the site of her mother's rape, so she is confronting her mother's rape in a way that Martine never did. The field is also the site of her grandfather's death from heatstroke, as we learn at the beginning of the novel. Moreover, the cane field suggests the history of plantation slavery in Haiti, for slaves were imported from Africa by the French to work the fields in the seventeenth and eighteenth centuries. Sophie rejects all of this with her dramatic strikes. As she hits the cane she identifies with her mother. "Yes, my mother was like me," she says. Her grandmother calls to her, "Are you free?" (234). Before Sophie can reply, her grandmother presses her fingers over Sophie's lips and the novel ends. Is she free of all her trauma? One can find hope in her resolution never to test her own daughter and in her proactive attempts at therapy; her therapist is the one who first suggests that she confront the cane field. But there is much we do not know. Will her marriage survive? Can she escape harmful memories? As the novel shows, cycles of trauma—whether individual or, on a larger plane, cultural or political—can be hard to break.

Danticat's depiction suggests that disability studies and disability human rights should contend with trauma by always opposing actions in which people harm one another or themselves, physically or psychologically, as simple—

and as difficult to achieve—as that may be. Such destructive actions would include rape, war, self-mutilation, intentionally wounding others, and subjugation of others (including workers and other races or genders), sentiments with which most contemporary readers would probably agree. That would provide a similar rubric that the United Nations uses for human rights, saying that harming others is always a violation of rights, as discussed in Chapter 2. Such an ethical guide might be a way to contend with some of the challenges of bringing trauma into the field and might allow us to preserve the valuable strengths now in disability studies. The importance of the field is not just how it upholds individual dignity, but also how it frequently celebrates mutual respect and interdependence, values that dovetail with human rights. While we of course should advocate for disabled people, we must speak out against violations. As Danticat shows in her courageous novel, silence only allows trauma to grow.

Danticat's story "Caroline's Wedding" provides a final affirming instance of an ethic of care in fiction by women featuring disabled women. From the collection *Krik? Krak!* the story concerns a family originally from Haiti that has emigrated to New York. The narrator, Grace, expresses warm affection for her disabled sister, Caroline, who was born missing a forearm. Laughing together in their bedroom, talking, exchanging memories and dreams, they clearly share a close connection. They do not discuss disgrace or sullying the family name, although, of course, we are in New York, not Haiti. To be sure, some see Caroline's disability taking on metaphorical significance. Their Haitian mother thinks the disability happened because, while she was pregnant with Caroline in America, she was arrested as an illegal immigrant during a raid of a sweatshop; she blames a shot she was given in jail to calm her for the disability. In a reverse of the colonialism-as-disabling meme that we saw in Chapter 4, the mother conceives coming to the United States, to the North, as causing disability, and the narrator appears to half-believe this. Physical disability becomes the symbol of the hardships of immigration.

But the sister and mother mostly seem to see Caroline's disability as an integral part of her human identity. To Grace, Caroline, finally, is just her sister who has adapted to her condition. While sorting playing cards, she skillfully holds some in her mouth. She likes to have her stub stroked, even if that stub startles people on the street who see it. She is not an outcast but in the story gets married—notably, her fiancé is a man with a learning disability and "extremely slow" speech (183). The mother has critical reservations about the fiancé mainly not because of his disability, but because he has Bahamian, not Haitian, ethnicity. He does not even know the proper way to approach a potential Haitian mother-in-law. Yet when Caroline has qualms on the day of the wedding, her mother, remembering her own fears on her wedding day, is supportive and gives her a reassuring bath. Reversing her earlier interpretation of the disability, the mother says, "God made you this way" (199). The mother does not reject Caroline's disability; her primary concern is not wanting her to move out. Disabled or not, Caroline is clearly accepted and loved as family, in a way that Uma and Bibi Haldar are never embraced.

Coming Together: An Ethic of Care and an Ethic of Rights

Read together, Desai, Lahiri, and Danticat illustrate the widely varying experiences of disabled women in the Global South and the different forms care can take. While they are fiction and acts of the imagination, these stories help us to think about the real material life of disabled women in the Global South and what could be done to achieve more justice. The authors demonstrate their own compassion and respect for the characters, in effect modeling an ethic of care that aligns well with human rights and dignity. As relations among characters in these works show, care can turn oppressive, as in the case of Mama and Papa in Uma's life. At its best, though, a care ethic might be like what the collective female narrator expresses to Bibi Haldar or the warmth and acceptance shown toward Caroline.

Returning to the issue of the relationship between an ethic of care and of rights, since these works were published, more scholars have moved to see the two as compatible—indeed, almost necessary for each other. If care holds the potential for harm and abuse in some cases, rights counter that, while care adds an interpersonal element that abstract rights principles may lack. Building on the work of Kittay, the philosopher Martha Nussbaum puts forward a version of the capabilities approach that, as she acknowledges, strongly mirrors human rights conventions. "The capabilities approach is, in my view, one species of a human rights approach, and human rights have often been linked in a similar way to the idea of human dignity," she says (*Frontiers* 78). For her, capabilities are the necessary freedoms and opportunities that each and every person, including disabled people, should have for a dignified human life, including such things as being able to live to the end of a human life, to enjoy good health, to live with others, and to laugh and play. As did Kittay, Nussbaum differs from Rawls's social contractarian notions, arguing that people should take care of one another without regard to material benefits. Why would people form such a society? As Nussbaum puts it, "It can only be out of our attachment to justice and our love of others, our sense that our lives are intertwined with theirs" (222).

Emphasizing how rights and ethic of care have converged, Michael Ashley Stein identifies Nussbaum's version of the capabilities approach, along with the social model of disability and the human right to development, as influential in shaping the Convention on the Rights of Persons with Disabilities (CRPD), which was adopted by United Nations General Assembly in 2006 ("Disability" 75). An ethic of care and an ethic of rights have come together and, arguably, literary depictions such as those in this chapter have helped make that happen, pointing to the importance and relation of both.

The 2006 CRPD required states to guarantee that disabled women had "full and equal enjoyment" of rights and freedoms and to empower disabled women. Meanwhile, in 2018 Ana Peláez Narváez was elected to the CEDAW committee, becoming the first disabled expert on this important human rights board. Much work unquestionably remains to be done, but progress with disabled women's rights is occurring, and authors such as Desai, Lahiri, and Danticat have helped us get here.

The Limits of Human Rights

Twenty-First-Century Depictions of War, Poverty,
Global Capitalism, and Disability

Many of the everyday experiences of disabled people in the global
South lie outside of the reach of human rights instruments.

—HELEN MEEKOSHA AND KAREN SOLDATIC,
"Human Rights and the Global South"

Thus far I have been arguing that these works of the literature of the
Global South reflect and helped to bring about the gradual change in
how the public saw disabled people during the second half of the twentieth century, a shift that culminated in the ratification of the Convention on
the Rights of Persons with Disabilities (CRPD) in 2008 by the vast majority
of nations around the world. We can discern increasing attention to disabled
people in this fiction and, often, a sense that such marginalized people have
significance, a perspective the works invite readers to share even as authors use
disability to comment on any number of other topics, from colonialism and
apartheid to the chaos of Indian independence and feminist interdependence
and care. Recent novels that appeared at the beginning of the twenty-first
century before or after the CRPD both advance these trends and testify to the
potential inadequacy of human rights mechanisms alone to ensure dignity for
disabled people in the midst of formidable challenges.

As triumphant as many disabled people around the world felt at the ratification of the CRPD—finally they were getting international recognition
and moral support of their rights—questions about the efficacy of the convention soon appeared, questions that mirror reservations about human rights
more broadly. In 2011, just three years after ratification of the CRPD, Helen
Meekosha and Karen Soldatic argued that "many of the everyday experiences
of disabled people in the Global South lie outside of the reach of human rights
instruments," contending that the convention has limited ability to make a
difference (1383). Similarly, some prominent scholars have recently contended

that human rights in general often have not accomplished their objectives. The title of Samuel Moyn's *Not Enough: Human Rights in an Unequal World* (2018) indicates how some scholars increasingly feel that rights by themselves are inadequate in a world beset by appalling inequality. In "The Case against Human Rights," the law professor Eric Posner points out that a gap between idealistic human rights discourse and actual practice frequently exists. "It is hard to avoid the conclusion that governments continue to violate human rights with impunity," he says. As an example, Posner states that, although human rights law has as a core principle the abolition of torture, the majority of nations (stunningly, more than 75 percent of those in the United Nations, including the United States after September 11, 2001) around the world still employ it. Moreover, despite human rights treaties that seek to protect and empower women and children, women continue to have subordinate status in most countries while children still work in mines and factories in many places.

Posner identifies several fundamental reasons for this unsatisfactory state of affairs, from the ambiguity of human rights law to weak enforcement mechanisms to countries not having enough resources to make all human rights a priority. First, he refers to the "deliberate choice to overload the treaties with hundreds of poorly defined obligations," which creates vagueness and provides little guidance to governments, leading to sharply different interpretations of rights laws. Moreover, countries have given little power to international institutions that might otherwise compel them to recognize rights they reject, so governments have enormous discretion over which rights they implement and how, even though, paradoxically, human rights since 1948 have been devoted to empowering individuals rather than nation-states. Although rights treaties are supposed to benefit individual people, often governments get in the way. Finally, all governments have limited budgets, and poor ones especially do not have the resources to emphasize all rights (well over one hundred now) simultaneously, which has led some commentators to debate whether some rights should take precedence over others. Such factors have conspired to make human rights in general less successful in practice than advocates had hoped, and we can see such forces affecting the application of the CRPD, too.

Still, human rights can have great benefits. For example, as Posner acknowledges, they provide language and moral support for oppressed people everywhere and force governments to take their rights obligations more seriously. We see a specific example of empowerment of disabled people in the African Youth with Disabilities Network video series with which this book began. In similar fashion, the World Federation of the Deaf has used the passages on sign language in the CRPD to lobby governments in nations around the world for the linguistic rights of deaf children, who usually do not have access to sign. Furthermore, advocates for specific groups can use human rights treaties to buttress their cases, while nongovernmental organizations (NGOs) such as Amnesty International and Human Rights Watch can use rights to pressure governments for specific improvements. Rights have opened up the way for criticism of nations that are abusing or not ensuring the dignity of all of their citizens. In some cases, human rights have led to noticeable improvements. Posner notes that the political scientist Beth Simmons found positive impact in Japan and Colombia as a result of the ratification of the Convention on the Elimination of All Forms of Discrimination against Women (CEDAW). Along the same lines, one could plausibly argue that the United Nations' attention to disability spurred actions such as Kenya's adoption in 2003 of its Persons with Disabilities Act or the Bethlehem Arab Society for Rehabilitation Rights' saying that the definition of disability is "evolving," the same phrasing as in the CRPD (Puar *Right* 157). Even while arguing that human rights are not enough, Moyn maintains they are "essential" (*Not Enough* xii). Despite limitations, they have value even to the most dispossessed.

Further complicating matters, in recent years some disability studies scholars have pointed out that, despite human rights conventions that have achieved worldwide consensus such as the CRPD, some companies and organizations in the Global North continue actively to *produce* disability and debilitation in the South, even as other organizations in the North work to resist such violations. (We should remember that both "the North" and "the South" contain tremendous diversity.) That is, even as the CRPD seeks to protect and empower disabled people everywhere, some exploitative organizations in the North bypass human rights to create more precarious lives, most prominently through the system of global capitalism. Meekosha identifies other factors as war, pollution, nuclear testing, poor labor conditions, and a world system in which the North sells pharmaceutical medicine and assistive devices to people in the Global South for profit ("Decolonising"). Most of these elements are the aftereffects of colonialism, she says, which continue to play an influential role in twenty-first-century global inequity, exploitation, neoliberalism, and conflict. To this we might add other causes, such as the global trade in human organs that disproportionately go from the Global South to the North.[1]

Such realities have caused some scholars passionately to denounce the global systems that produce injustice. Denouncing "imperialist/neocolonial contexts [of] fundamentally unequal social relationships," Nirmala Erevelles decries "oppressive conditions of poverty, economic exploitation . . . , neocolonial violence, and lack of access to adequate health care and education" that mark some bodies (especially bodies of color) in the Global South as disposable (*Disability* 130). Advancing such criticisms, Jasbir Puar critiques how some Northern organizations consistently impair and wear down other populations to maintain their privilege. She faults how instruments such as the Americans with Disabilities Act and, by extension, the United Nations' CRPD, use "capitalist logic to solve a problem largely created by capitalism" (75). Moreover, she provocatively contends that rights and notions of disability pride actually serve as foils to "obscure the production of debilitation" around the world, further adding to a view of rights as inadequate or, in her analysis, flat out destructive (70).[2] Notably, Erevelles and Puar do not deny that some organizations in the North work to resist exploitative violations, something we see in literature, too. Rather, they denounce the underlying global *system* that often promotes inequality and injustice.

To be sure, some organizations in the North are not the only cause of acquired disability in the South. Corrupt leaders and interethnic or religious rivalries also play a large part in military conflicts, which are sometimes a great driver of disability, while exploitative factory and sweatshop owners in the Global South, often in partnership with companies in the Global North, perpetuate unsafe labor environments that help to disable and debilitate many people. Ableist actions and ideologies unfortunately continue to exist throughout the world, including in the Global South.

To what extent do human rights create possibilities and to what extent do they have limits? Four recent twenty-first-century novels that prominently feature disability in the Global South vividly illustrate such consequential matters as they relate to the present day. Chris Abani's works *Graceland* (2004) and *Song for Night* (2007) and Indra Sinha's *Animal's People* (2007) depict common causes of and influences on acquired disability in the Global South: war, transnational capitalism, endemic poverty, and environmental devastation. We have, of course, seen such factors in previous chapters, especially in J. M. Coetzee's *Life & Times of Michael K* and Salman Rushdie's *Midnight's Children*, but these novels put renewed focus on them through a twenty-first-century lens. Meanwhile, Petina Gappah's *The Book of Memory* (2015) adds a depiction of the complexities of implementing rights, especially in a culture with strong metaphysical traditions, and how medicine and wealth can help to destigmatize a congenitally disabled person. Furthermore, through their well-meaning white characters Lloyd and Elli, Gappah and Sinha, respectively, present a meditation on white saviorism and the productive role outsiders can play.

These literary works each show ways that organizations in the North affect the lives of disabled people in the Global South and add to the elusive kinship between readers and disabled characters. Building on the precedent of Rushdie's disabled narrator, Saleem, in *Midnight's Children*, three of these novels present first-person disabled narrators, inviting readers to identify with them and whose personal accounts create drama, add suspense, and move the stories along. Notably, all four of these works are set decades before the CRPD but still in the human rights era, and though they are fiction, they all relate to actual historical events (some more than others). In all of these cases, disability plays a central role in the plot as the authors offer readers a closeness to disabled people's lives in Nigeria, Zimbabwe, and India, an intimate form of kinship that seems a long way from the understated detachment of Chinua Achebe's narrator in *Things Fall Apart*. These works make readers experience along with disabled characters the continuing, formidable challenges to disability justice and offer insight into vexing questions about the usefulness of human rights.

"What You Hear Is Not My Voice": Disability and War in *Song for Night*

In her African Youth with Disabilities Network video, Victoria Davis, from Liberia, shares how she became disabled in 1990 when she was hit by a missile, which damaged her spinal cord and forced her to walk with crutches.[3] One does not typically encounter that kind of story in Europe and North America, although we could perhaps draw parallels with the impact of current gun violence and police shootings in the United States or with terrorist attacks in America and Western Europe. Such violence disables and debilitates people worldwide. Yet in the contemporary Global South, war plays an especially large role in the production of disability, helping to explain why four out of five disabled people live there. Meekosha cites an estimate that 85 percent of major military conflicts since World War II have taken place in low-income countries ("Decolonising" 675). The impact of war, like that of poverty, neoliberalism, and environmental disaster, can be so broad and immense, and statistics so faceless, that it can be difficult to see and understand. Literature again can make these factors more personal and graspable, as we perceive starting with the Nigerian American Abani's short novel *Song for Night*, which takes us into a horrific military conflict.

The narrator, a fifteen-year-old child soldier called My Luck, is in a war that is at first so dreamlike and ambiguous as to seem almost universal but gradually, through clues, proves to be the Biafra War (as the Nigerian civil war of 1967–1970 is known) during its end stages. My Luck shares his story with us readers in English, which somehow—he says that he does not have time to figure out how—is translated from the Igbo he says he thinks. That he speaks Igbo hints that he is a member of the ethnic group of the same name in southeastern Nigeria. Later, he refers to the Yoruba and Hausa, other ethnic groups in Nigeria; to a divided nation; to pogroms against Igbo living in northern parts of the country; and to murderous bloodshed between Muslims and Christians. Such ethnic and religious violence historically took place in the years after Nigerian independence from British colonization in 1960 and later in the decade caused Igbo in southeastern Nigeria to try to secede and form their own country of Biafra, resulting in a devastating civil war. At one point, My Luck remembers his platoon of mine diffusers encountering a group of starving old women who are eating what turns out to be a human baby, a gruesome scene that evokes the calamitous mass famine that happened as the result of a Nigerian federal government blockade. Experts variously estimate that between five hundred thousand and two million civilians perished during the conflict.[4] My Luck in horror shoots the women with his AK-47.

In this ghastly environment, My Luck seeks to come to terms with the brutality around him and his own acts of violence. When the novella begins, he wakes up alone after a mine blast, and much of the story concerns his search for his platoon. Along the way, through flashbacks, we not only see the corruption and depravity of a Nigerian Igbo commanding officer and desperate war-hardened people, but also learn that the Global North powerfully influences the conflict, from the agonizing effects of colonial incursion in the recent past to providing the guns and land mines that kill and wound so many people. Far from being uninvolved, as many American readers might expect, the United States has a subtle but distinct behind-the-scenes presence, showing its harmful effects on far-off people during the Cold War. (The events, we should remember, happen at the same time as the war in Vietnam, and the novella was written during the Iraq War, two examples of misguided American imperialism and disastrous military entanglements that negatively affected millions of people.) In *Song for Night*, we witness not only appalling violence, corruption, and poverty but also how the North shapes identity, including disabled identity, in postcolonial Nigeria and the paradoxes surrounding human rights in such situations.

My Luck himself has invisible disabilities that emphasize his disempowered situation and add power to his story. First, three years earlier, in boot camp, the training officer had a doctor intentionally sever My Luck's vocal cords along with those of the other child soldiers in his landmine-diffusing platoon, apparently so they would not scare others with "death screams" if a mine exploded on them (35). "What you hear is not my voice," My Luck memorably begins (19). In a setting that includes brutal killing, rape, and starving civilians, he and the other child soldiers communicate with one another silently through what he calls "a crude sort of sign language" (19).[5] His inability to speak vocally serves as an almost too obvious metaphor for the extreme vulnerability and voicelessness of child soldiers and disabled people everywhere, and it gives the narrative unusual poignancy. Each of the short chapters is titled with an evocative description of one of the child soldiers' improvised signs, such as "Night Is a Palm Pulled Down over the Eyes," which serves as a consistent reminder of My Luck's voiceless status (25). Moreover, Abani, who is also a poet, gives My Luck an eloquence in his thoughts that belies his age. "There is a lot to be said for silence, especially when it comes to you young," My Luck says, adding that it makes him more contemplative (21). In these ways, the structure and lyrical language add depth and feeling to the narrative that contrasts with the shocking brutality My Luck describes. (Despite all the horror, college students generally respond positively to the book.)

Disability extends beyond My Luck's severed vocal cords, for he endures traumas that lead to harrowing memories and a cognitive dissonance that initially seems to resemble post-traumatic stress disorder or another cognitive disability (although it is always tricky to attempt to diagnose literary characters). Both of My Luck's parents are brutally murdered before the war, leaving him an orphan at twelve. He recounts the murder of his gentle father, an Igbo who, unusually, was a Muslim cleric in northern Nigeria; My Luck fled just before the killing, which he refers to as "my sin," indicating his abiding sense of guilt and shame (157). He cannot even find words to describe the horror of seeing his mother killed from a hiding place in the ceiling. "I cannot name it, those things that happened while I watched," he says (43). Their deaths inspire My Luck to join the Biafran army; he and other child soldiers who had lost loved ones in the conflict, he says, "all wanted revenge" against the enemy (19). Those traumas are the first of many. *Song for Night* offers an unsparing account of rape, murder, and extreme violence and cruelty. Early on, My Luck tells us that the memory of the face of the dead baby the old women were eating "keeps me from rest," hinting at his understated anxiety and distress, and we regularly see how past traumas cause distress and anxiety that continue to haunt him (29).

While African characters perform these abhorrent acts themselves, governments and organizations in the North bear major responsibility, too. Frantz Fanon asserted a few years before the start of the Biafra War that "decolonization is always a violent phenomenon," adding that it is also a "programme of complete disorder" (*Wretched* 27). Drawing from his experience with the Algerian War of Independence against the French, Fanon presented violence as an inescapable part of the transition away from oppressive colonial rule. In the case of Nigeria, his words were prescient. We should recall that Nigeria itself was originally an artificial construct, devised by British colonizers to bring together many different religious, ethnic, and linguistic groups under one national identity. Tensions among the groups, largely hidden during British occupation, flared up in the years after Nigeria achieved independence in 1960 in a way that is reminiscent of the appalling strife between Hindus and Muslims when Britain left India in 1947. Just as the Hindu-Muslim conflict related to the formation of Pakistan, so the Biafra War started in 1967 with the Igbo southeast attempting to secede from Nigeria and form its own separate nation, Biafra. As has so often been the case, one of the frequent legacies of colonialism, with its artificial boundaries, oppression, and privileging of some groups over others, is violent unrest when independence arrives. One cannot understand the horror that *Song for Night* depicts or the experience of disabled people such as My Luck in the Global South without accounting for the history of colonialism in Nigeria.[6]

The North shapes the events not only through Britain's past colonial occupation, but also through its provision of the arms used. My Luck refers to the superior weapons, bags of ammunition, and grenades that "U.S.-armed enemy soldiers" possessed (28). While the Lyndon Johnson administration did hope that a diplomatic solution preserving one democratic Nigeria would be reached, the U.S. government officially remained neutral. Roy Melbourne points out that it was Britain and the Soviet Union that provided arms to the Nigerian federal forces, but as the Association for Diplomatic Studies and Training states, the illegal arms trade was active, and U.S.-produced arms may have made it to enemy soldiers that way, so it is difficult to say whether My Luck is correct. But clearly the weapons come from the North. My Luck also says that France had promised weapons to the rebels and that "since land mines are banned in civilized warfare, the West practically gives them away at cost" (47). Such comments suggest how Europe and the United States contribute to the destruction. By providing mines they themselves deem barbaric, companies in the North and traders on the black market demonstrate their disregard for African lives: the only thing that seems to matter to them is the bottom line. Hidden land mines are unmapped and have the cruel potential to kill and wound unwitting civilians for decades after hostilities end. In 2017, the Nigerian government agreed to pay $245 million to victims of the war, including those affected by land mines, and to clear former conflict zones of mines, showing the lasting aftereffects of the war fifty years later (Durosomo). In these ways, the narrative illustrates Puar's point that war and military occupations often serve as "circuitry" where "disability—or, rather, debility and debilitation—is an exported product of imperial aggression" (89).

The United States has a pervasive cultural influence in My Luck's narrative that extends beyond weapons. When he enters an abandoned restaurant and helps himself to a Coke, it shows the presence of American commercial products in Nigeria. He smokes American cigarettes inveterately, too. When he sees American public information films advising children to hide under their desks in the event of an attack, it underscores the vast gulf between the experience of children in the United States and those in Nigeria. And when the Nigerian commanding officer in boot camp claims to have been trained at West Point, he uses American prestige to get the children to follow his orders. Because he wears shiny cowboy boots, the children eventually nickname him John Wayne after the American film hero. Despite these trappings, the Nigerian John Wayne turns out to be hideously corrupt and sadistic. Without explanation or anesthesia, he has a doctor sever the children's vocal cords. In the war, he forces a man to butcher his children with a knife before shooting him and compels the twelve-year-old My Luck to commit rape, illustrating again the connection of rape to gross abuse of power. When John Wayne holds a seven-year-old girl and implies he will have sex with her—"I will enjoy her," he says (40)—My Luck almost automatically shoots him, and the other child soldiers make him the leader of the platoon. That such depravity could come in the name of a popular American film hero is more than a little ironic and encapsulates both the prestige and arrogant destructiveness of the North in My Luck's mind.

In his mind, My Luck repeatedly returns to the ethics of his actions, gesturing toward convoluted issues of human dignity and rights. Near the beginning of the novella he appears to be a hardened soldier: he calls enemy combatants "scum" and admits that "deep down somewhere I enjoy [killing them], revel in it almost" (12). He compares killing to the pleasure of having an orgasm. Yet we also see a sensitive boy whose mother was killed as he watched helplessly from an attic hideout; who cannot sleep because he sees the face of the dead baby the women were cooking; who fights tears on occasion; and who carves small crosses on his left forearm to remember the loved ones he has lost (there are twenty crosses). As the narrative progresses, he wonders about his own morality. "There are some sins too big for even God to forgive," he muses at one point, acknowledging his guilt (79). Later he asks, referring to child soldiers, "If we are the great innocents in this war, then where did we learn all the evil we practice?" (143). Feeling that he was denied his childhood and has no future, he gradually becomes more concerned with morality as the novella proceeds and comes to express fatigue at the hatred, conflict, and killing. "I have lost my taste for death" he avers (62), and states, "I am tired of all this hate" (91), effectively renouncing the violence in which he has participated. Eventually his search becomes one for home, for respite, rather than for his missing platoon.

Along the way, Abani makes readers see the humanity of the mute child soldier, his peers, and others with disabilities, depicting them as complex people who are not invisible or unimportant but have deep emotions and deserve respect. My Luck himself exhibits his feelings throughout his perceptive narration and seems at peace with not being able to speak, perhaps because the others in his platoon share the same fate. Other disabled people show their humanity, too. At one point, My Luck describes a group of disabled children dancing, a scene of unexpected happiness in the midst of the gruesomeness of the war. A young one-legged girl laughs at the dancers and, when challenged to do better, throws her stick aside and merrily joins the circle. My Luck says:

> Balanced on one leg, her waist began a fierce gyration and her upper body moved the opposite way. Then like a crazy heron she began to hop around, her waist and torso still shaking. She was an elemental force of nature. I couldn't take my eyes off her. I have never seen anything like it before or since—a small fire sprite shaking the world and reducing grown war-hardened onlookers to tears. (51)

In this episode, disability works on multiple levels. It serves as an undeniable material sign; the ravages and mass trauma of the brutal war are inscribed on the bodies of the disabled children. Yet simultaneously, and seemingly paradoxically, the girl is a life-affirming figure of irrepressible joy, provoking a sympathetic emotional response from spectators. Rather than summarily relegating physical difference to the margins, the novella presents it as an integral and often startling part of experience. Disabled people are indisputably human, which underpins how the novel invites readers to care about their dignity and fate.

My Luck embodies the enigmas and limitations surrounding human rights and military conflict. He is a child soldier, which is itself fraught with contradiction. On the one hand, he is clearly a victim of human rights abuses. The 1948 Universal Declaration of Human Rights (UDHR) proclaims childhood as a time of special care and assistance, while the 1989 Convention of the Rights of Child affirms that states should take steps to protect children (defined as those younger than eighteen), and Article 38 specifically states that children younger than fifteen should not take direct part in armed conflicts.[7] Meanwhile, Article 11 of the CRPD calls on states to ensure the safety of disabled people in situations of risk, including armed hostilities. Such human rights conventions fail to help My Luck, though, because first, historically, all but the UDHR came after the Biafra War of the 1960s, when the novel occurs, and second, his account shows the difficulty, or even futility, of trying to protect populations' rights during an all-out war in which civilians' well-being and dignity are often intentionally assaulted. At the same time, however, My Luck commits atrocities, such as killing and raping others, that mark him as a human rights violator, underscoring a central paradox surrounding human rights—one we also see with Okonkwo: how the same person can be both a victim of rights abuses and perpetrator of them. Abani shows how the norms of human rights and international law thus prove woefully insufficient at times of all-out warfare.

With a memorable *Wendepunkt*, a surprise turning point, Abani brings this unsettling story to a close. (Spoiler alert!) My Luck turns out to be dead and to have been narrating from beyond the grave, something even he did not realize at first. The mine blast just before he wakes up at the beginning apparently has killed him. We get small clues that he is not alive, such as that he is rarely hungry and seems to have an endless supply of cigarettes. When an elderly woman sees him, she says "*Tufia!*" an "old word for banishing spirits or bad things" (84). Still, there are confusing complications—for example, when he pinches himself at one point, it hurts. Abani may have been influenced here by the Bruce Willis film *The Sixth Sense* (1999), which has a similar surprise ending, but he gives the conceit a uniquely Nigerian twist. As My Luck says when he is slowly realizing he might no longer be alive:

> Here we believe that when a person dies in a sudden and hard way, their spirit wanders confused looking for its body. Confused, because they don't realize they are dead. I know this. Traditionally, a shaman would ease such a spirit across to the other world. Now, well, the land is crowded with confused spirits and all the shamans are soldiers. (109)

Without a shaman to provide help, My Luck's journey proves to be a revisiting of sites of past trauma to come to terms with them before moving to the next realm. He goes through a kind of therapy in which he gradually becomes disenchanted with the persistent hatred and killing around him, a seemingly necessary step before he can move on. In the final lines, he rides in a coffin across a mystical river to find his mother, young and smiling, sitting on a porch swing on the veranda of a house. She embraces him, calls him by name, and tells him he is home. My Luck concludes: "I am trying to make sense of it, to think, but I can't focus. 'Mother,' I say, and my voice has returned" (167).

So the novella ends. It could be called a sentimental ending, a too easy way to resolve My Luck's predicament happily and leave the dreadful, overwhelming reality of war behind, but after My Luck's harrowing experiences as a child soldier, the soothing ending works. It does conform to David Mitchell and Sharon Snyder's original notion of narrative prosthesis, the theory about how disability often not only moves narratives along but also is typically eradicated at the end of stories. As we have seen, it does not always hold in relation to Southern narratives, where disability often remains at the end, a realistic part of existence. Perhaps Abani arrived at this narrative strategy because he wrote the novella while living in the United States. We should also remember that, despite My Luck's fate as a spirit, his narrative indicates that many disabled people, like the disabled child dancers, remain in Nigeria to grapple with their place in society after the bloody conflict. They are not removed from the narrative. The novella reminds us of the pressing state of disabled people in many war zones around the world. In any case, at the end of My Luck's journey, he's both killed and cured and an orphan no longer. While he is honest about the evil he has committed, at the end he seems to achieve a certain redemption. Despite showing the unsparing violence and cruelty of the conflict, and despite My Luck's onetime conviction that his sins could never be pardoned, the novella offers a hopeful way out through traditional Igbo beliefs. At the same time, it shows the gross insufficiency of human rights treaties in settings of all-out war. As another Abani novel reveals, the challenges to human rights extend well beyond military conflict.

Beyond War: Disability, Poverty, and Neoliberalism in *GraceLand*

Although it was published three years before *Song for Night*, Abani's novel *GraceLand* is set just after the Biafra War, between 1972 and 1983, and shows how the legacy of the war overlaps with global capitalism and widespread poverty, additional factors that frequently limit human rights generally and for disabled people in particular. The novel's teenage protagonist, Elvis Oke, lives in a squalid slum in Lagos, Nigeria, and we see the perilous consequences of poverty for people in the fractured postcolonial nation.

Two characters with prominent disabilities from the recent war experience ongoing social suffering due to extreme poverty. The self-proclaimed King of the Beggars, an indigent who becomes something of a mentor for Elvis, has only one eye. "The other socket, empty, gaped red and watery," the narrator says, which, like the thick scar across the King's face, is a wound from the war (30). Like My Luck, the King has traumatic memories: during the conflict, an army officer executed his wife and children, causing him to seek the officer to take revenge (which the King does near the end, killing the officer with a knife before he is shot by soldiers). His present life is shaped by poverty; when he first meets Elvis, he asks for money because he's very hungry. At another point, a former child soldier (ironically named Innocent) appears, hungry, nervous, fearful, and haunted by memories of a bloody church massacre more than a decade before in the war. "Dat time na rough time," he says. "I was only a child, you know" (209). He also appears traumatized by war experiences. Eventually, he abruptly flees, spooked by something only he sees. He possibly has been hired to kill someone—a fact, if true, that hints at his similar need for money—but we never know for sure. Both the King and Innocent emerge as impoverished people disabled by the war who must struggle for daily existence in the postwar environment, matters on which human rights treaties have limited effect.

Corruption and a neoliberal economic system that produces a stark divide between the uber-rich and extremely poor shape both disabled characters' experiences. We learn that in 1983

> a newspaper editorial . . . stated, rather proudly, that Nigeria had a higher percentage of millionaires . . . than nearly any other country in the world. . . . The editorial failed to mention that their wealth had been made over the years with the help of crooked politicians, criminal soldiers, bent contractors, and greedy oil company executives. Or that Nigeria also had a higher percentage of poor people than nearly any other country in the world. (8)

This gaping socioeconomic divide shows up throughout the novel. Elvis and his father have come from a village and live in the infamous Maroko ghetto, a sordid shantytown built over a swamp with wooden walkways over water that is one of more than ten ghettos in Lagos. These slums exist in proximity to more affluent areas. For example, when Elvis and his friend Redemption sit at a bar and gaze across a lagoon at the lights of Ikoyi, a wealthy part of the city, Redemption comments, "Though dey hate us, de rich still have to look at us" (137). The divide is not as complete as the wealthy might desire— and, indeed, the affluent depend on poor people for labor that provides their luxuries.

Influencing these characters' lives are the realities of a global economic system that is both invisible in the narrative and all too apparent. To review the larger economic history, in the early 1970s Nigeria was able to expand its oil production dramatically and sharply increase economic growth, leading to an economic boom, although the ensuing prosperity was unevenly shared with citizens. American oil companies, as well as those from other nations, paid the Nigerian government to extract oil. By the mid-1970s, revenue began to wane as oil prices dropped. Nigeria had to pay increased interest on its International Monetary Fund loans. In the early 1980s, the time that Elvis is in Lagos, the nation experienced a severe economic depression, with no strong industries other than oil on which to rely (Omelsky 87).

Such realities make the lives of all lower-class citizens precarious, with disabled characters in the novel making such desperation especially visible. For example, Elvis's father connects deformed children begging in the streets to oppressive poverty. "Their parents know dey have no future," he says. "So at birth, before de child knows pain, dey deform it because it increases its earning power as a beggar" (188). The father, Sunday, presents the intentional disabling of children as an act of love in a world beset by crushing privation. Just as war increases disability, so does destitution. In some places where poverty is especially prohibitive, intentional disabling apparently happens. As we have seen, Rushdie alludes to it in India. This practice is another way that disability is a product of a global neoliberal system that benefits some people but leaves many others behind.

Abani offers another chilling glimpse at how the world economic system exploits, debilitates, and even kills impoverished people in the Global South. When Elvis cannot find a livelihood in the city, he begins to perform shady deals along with his friend Redemption to earn money. One such deal involves escorting two mysterious coolers to Togo, two countries over. Along the way, they discover the coolers' grisly secret: one contains six human heads and the other, hearts and livers packed with ice. They have stumbled onto an illegal global organ trade (the heads contain valuable eyes and stem cells, Redemption later explains) that reflects not just how some on the black market murder to make money, but also, again, how economic pressure disables and kills people in the Global South. According to Redemption, the organs are bought by certain people in Saudi Arabia, who in turn sell them to American hospitals and "rich white people so dey can save their children or wife or demselves" (242). Such a practice reflects the frequently vast economic disparities between parts of the Global North and South and shows how even an ostensibly neutral global economic system can cause violence and more disabled people, with some organizations in the North ultimately responsible.

The King of the Beggars offers a more vivid and direct critique of such a neoliberal system. This character is more than a beggar; he's a political activist and part of a troupe of performers who use drama to criticize the government (not unlike Abani in the late 1980s). At one point, the King calls for a return to traditional Igbo ways and decries American-style capitalism: "He spoke of the evils of capitalism that the United States of America practiced—a brand of capitalism, he said, that promoted the individual interest over the communal. It was a land of vice and depravity, infested with a perverse morality based on commercial value rather than a humanistic one" (155). The King critiques a global capitalist system that puts money ahead of people, and he advocates a return to traditional Igbo community living. Elvis recognizes that this solution is unworkable—the Igbo are only one of "nearly three hundred indigenous people in this populous country"—and wishes the King would talk instead about "how to cope with these new and confusing times" (155). The narrative powerfully dramatizes the deleterious effects of poverty but stops short of offering a clear prescription for how to give impoverished people justice and dignity.

Abani manages to humanize both Elvis and the King, despite the challenging circumstances. From its music and films to Bazooka bubblegum, Elvis esteems America and at the ambiguous ending of the book is poised to fly to the United States. The King, like My Luck, emerges as a complex, humane, and worthy disabled person, despite being impoverished, with something of value to testify about the cruel inequality of the world system, even if a solution eludes him. Abani manages to make both characters important to readers while deploring the circumstances that deny them dignity and, finally, life.

Abani shows how in Nigeria and, by extension, much of the Global South, any account of human rights that does not include warfare, colonial history, and neoliberal policies is incomplete. These things limit lives for his disabled characters. He illustrates not only how people can be very cruel to one another, but also how exploitative organizations in the Global North shape and have an ethical responsibility for conditions in the South. Along the way, he shows that disabled people are people who deserve attention, dignity, and a place in society.

Abani's works are, of course, about much more than disabled people. In his 2008 TED talk "On Humanity," Abani says that, as a writer, he tries to offer "stories that offer transformation, that lean into transcendence, but that are never sentimental, that never look away from the darkest things about us." By depicting some of the darkest things, such as brutal war and crushing poverty, both *Song for Night* and *GraceLand* help to illustrate the barriers that meaningful implementation of human rights around the world face.

"Black but Not Black": Disability and Justice
in Gappah's *The Book of Memory*

Disability and questions of justice also lie at the center of the Zimbabwean author Petina Gappah's debut novel, *The Book of Memory*, which offers a moving take on an impoverished disabled person's challenging position in another postcolonial African nation. Memory, or Mnemosyne, the narrator, is an albino woman imprisoned on death row in Zimbabwe for murder, but she maintains she's innocent. At her lawyer's suggestion, she writes a narrative of her life for an American journalist specializing in injustice. That account is the novel, an approach that allows Gappah to address an international readership about not only the details of Zimbabwean life that may be unfamiliar, but also specific challenges to human dignity there.

Memory's narrative is replete with matters of rights, which, as we see, are often difficult to achieve. It concerns not just her legal case, but also issues of crime, corruption, and uneven punishment in a country where magistrates give "stiffer sentences for stealing cows than for raping children" (23). Sometimes she testifies to gaps between formal laws and lived reality, such as when we learn that national laws "guarantee women equality" even as "a culture . . . ensures that they remain subservient," indicating how rights codified in law by themselves are seldom sufficient (80). A much greater and more difficult challenge is to change the popular culture, to weed out entrenched discrimination that people may habitually consider correct and normal (an insight that applies to all of the literary works discussed thus far). In addition, her account depicts the chasm between the desperately poor area where she grows up and the affluent white household she later joins, raising questions about equality, race, and fairness. After she is adopted at age nine by a wealthy white Zimbabwean professor, Lloyd, he proves to be gay and at one point is arrested and imprisoned for two weeks for suspected homosexuality, bringing up issues of the treatment of people with queer sexual orientations. Finally, because Memory is an albino who endures prejudice and stigma—and because at the very end her mother is revealed to be so mentally unstable that she kills two of her children—the book takes on intricate matters of disability justice. Set in a nation that did not achieve full independence from Britain until 1980, with references to farm seizures, rampant inflation, genocide, political unrest, ineffective Northern rights initiatives, and general chaos after independence, *The Book of Memory*, while in some respects uneven, provides vivid further demonstration of the paradoxes that can limit human rights, especially in the postcolonial Global South.

Through Memory's first-person narration we share the experiences of a smart, funny, and occasionally mean albino person (she is not a one-dimensional character) and see how social factors make her childhood especially difficult. She manifests Tobin Siebers's theory of complex embodiment. On the one hand, her disability clearly has biological aspects. She has unnaturally white skin, eyes without pigment, and white hair. Although she is a child in a Black family, Memory calls herself "like a ghost against the others" (35). Her biological impairments include blisters on her face, cracking skin, and an inability to be in the sun, which causes her to remain indoors as a young child. Yet social elements have even more influence on shaping her identity. Her family lives in the cramped township of Mufakose, a suburb of Harare, and does not have the means to give her sunscreen, creams to protect her vulnerable skin, or medical care. She endures taunting from other children, who regularly call her *murungu-dunhu*, a derogatory Shona word that roughly means "fake white person," and when she leaves the township with her family, they "danced around me and announced my presence to everyone" (54). Adults regularly do a double take, look at her with pity, or even spit when they encounter her because they perceive her as possessing occult powers. "A lot of people believe in the power of witchcraft and dark magic," Memory tells us (82). Her own mother views her as a curse, taking the girl to a variety of traditional healers in quest of a cure. In these ways, society makes Memory an outcast furtively wishing she was invisible, offering insight into the kind of challenges albino people may face.

Memory's fortunes change when Lloyd adopts her. Paradoxically, this kind, liberal, white descendant of Northern colonizers, with a modernity that eschews traditional beliefs, has an empowering influence. While the novel contains pointed critiques of colonialism and of organizations in the North's treatment of the South, it also indicates indigenous shortcomings and resists easy solutions. In Memory's case, we see that financial resources can dramatically change the nature of disability. Lloyd pays for medical care, creams that heal her skin, and a prestigious education that includes college at Cambridge, in England. Perhaps drawing on Northern disability activism, he also gives insightful counsel that she has a choice. "You can spend your life feelings sorry for yourself, or you can simply choose not to" he says (56). "You can invite people's pity or you can refuse to be an object." Biology may determine her skin color, but Memory learns she can help to determine what that means socially and what kind of identity she has. Subtly, Lloyd encourages Memory to disregard a Zimbabwean tradition that positions her as cursed. Even as we see the negative legacies of colonialism elsewhere—we learn that English is privileged, for example, because "the best-educated among us have sacrificed our languages at the altar of what the whites deem supreme"—a white person helps Memory achieve dignity and comfort within her own skin, even if she is strangely cut off from her own family (52). "More than anything else, I felt an incredible sense of freedom not from want but scrutiny," she remarks after Lloyd takes her in. "I had found a place where I could belong" (170). Yet she is an outsider in this new, affluent white world, too.

Withholding key details to create suspense, Gappah answers two central mysteries near the end of the book. First, Memory learns why she was given up for adoption at nine in a development that shows how disability can be intricately related to metaphysical beliefs. Her mother was mentally ill, and her madness led her father to give Memory up for her own safety. Early on we get clues that something is amiss: the mother excitedly plans a party and then suddenly throws a cake against a wall; she is never left alone with her children; and, strikingly in a communal culture that values family, we encounter no mention of extended family beyond Memory's immediate clan. Only near the conclusion do we get the full story. Memory's sister visits her in prison and tells her that Memory's mother (now dead) believed she was in the grip of a curse. When her mother was young, her parents pledged her to a much older man to atone for a murder that had happened generations before. She ran away from the unhappy arranged marriage, where she was the third wife, bringing an angry spirit, called *ngozi*, upon her (253). Worse, while she was gone, her three-year-old boy drowned, making her believe she had another vengeful *ngozi*. When she visited traditional healers about her situation, they all advised her that the only way to appease the *ngozi* was to return to her abusive first husband, something she could not do. Inspired by voices, she tragically killed two of her young children and saw Memory's albinism as further evidence that she was cursed, causing the father to give up Memory for adoption. "I now understand my mother's persistence in seeking out a cure for me," Memory reflects (254). While her father imagines that a supernatural force external to the mother is causing the deaths, Lloyd gently tells him, when they meet, that Memory's mother is not cursed but "dangerously ill" (260).

Traditional and modern ideas conflict, and Gappah leaves it unclear exactly how the mother's madness should be understood, just as she often critiques both Christian practices and those of indigenous metaphysical faiths while leaving it to readers to decide what is right. However, we cannot sufficiently understand the mother's situation with a Northern perspective; we need to situate it in a society where bonds are not only familial but also ancestral and spiritual. Representations of cognitive disability are somewhat unusual in African literature. It still seems somewhat taboo. The novel *Nervous Conditions* (1988), also by a Zimbabwean author, Tsitsi Dangarembga, serves as an important precedent, as does Coetzee's depiction of Michael K in *Life & Times* and of Pollux in *Disgrace*. Gappah calls attention to the importance and complexity of cognitive disability that does not receive enough attention in the Global South especially.

Near the end of the story, we also learn why Memory, who says she loved the gentle Lloyd, is now on death row for his murder. When she finds him dead, his body naked and a plastic bag around his face, in front of a laptop computer that presumably displays some kind of pornographic image, she decides to hide the circumstances. "I did not want anyone . . . to see him like that," she says (228). Attempting to make it look as if he has been attacked, she shoots the corpse and starts to drag it to the swimming pool, only to be discovered by Lloyd's sister. Memory is captured and condemned as the killer, presumed to be part of a larger pattern of attacks of Blacks on wealthy whites in postcolonial Zimbabwe.

At the end of the book, Memory remains in prison—in some sense, back where she started, but also with reason to hope. Without creams, her skin starts to crack. She finds among inmates "the usual fear-laced fascination and superstition around my condition" (28). A fellow inmate stares at her and thinks she is a witch. "It was as though I was going back to the child that I had once been," she writes (236). But she has causes for subtle optimism. A prison guard gives her creams and turns out to have an albino daughter. She learns of an Albino Society that now "gives out free sunscreen and advice" to people like her (245). Furthermore, she learns that a government commission is reviewing all prison sentences and finds restorative hope in the power of writing her story to an international journalist specializing in rights and justice.

The Book of Memory shows that even when rights are codified, more is often needed, since prejudice, harmful spiritual beliefs, intense poverty, and ingrained inequities can be difficult to address. When the new minister of justice visits Memory's prison, she talks about the United Nations' standards for treatment of prisoners. "We all wanted the same things," the minister tells the prisoners, "human rights and human dignity." Recounting this scene, Memory says, "I cannot say I have seen any human rights since her visit—or much human dignity, for that matter" (259). The recognition and acceptance of rights is an important start, but Memory's story gives more evidence that a tremendous amount of work is still required to implement them and to make them a reality for disabled and other vulnerable people across the globe.

"I Used to Be Human Once": Sinha's *Animal's People*

Turning to Indra Sinha's *Animal's People* is a fitting way to close both this chapter and this book. Based on a historical incident (the disastrous chemical leak at an American factory in Bhopal, India, in 1984), the novel powerfully depicts what Ato Quayson calls "a worrisome link between global capitalism and local disabilities" (*Aesthetic* 3). Sinha fictionalizes the accident to simplify the complex story of the leakage's aftermath and to write freely. Set in the imaginary town of Khaufpur, the book prominently deploys disability to tell its tale. The narrator is a nineteen-year-old Indian who is profoundly affected by the poisons the factory emitted "that night" shortly after he was born. His parents apparently died, leaving him an orphan; when he was six, the chemicals caused his spine to twist so badly that he now walks on all fours, and he is unsure of his identity, not knowing his name and defiantly adopting the moniker Animal after he is mocked with it by other children at school (1). Such a "species-bending identity," as Michael Davidson aptly calls it, raises questions about the definition of human, but the novel ends up showing the humanity of Animal and of other disabled people and, implicitly, their deserving human rights (*Invalid Modernism* 141). Feisty, funny, raunchy to the point of offensive, and smart, with at times a preternatural ability to hear voices, including the thoughts of others and even of unborn fetuses, Animal is a worthy heir to Rushdie's Saleem Sinai and the other extraordinary disabled narrators and characters we have encountered. Moreover, through his narration he adds an important new dimension to the elusive kinship between readers and literary characters: he periodically addresses readers directly, forging a more explicit bond with us and making us part of the tale. As it shows injustice, corruption, and transnational corporate crime through the voice of its disabled subaltern narrator, *Animal's People* reveals the inadequacy of rights alone to ensure dignity in the face of global capitalism.

The actual leak at a Union Carbide plant in Bhopal in 1984 illustrates the potential negative effects of not only neoliberalism, but also a history of colonialism and current neocolonialism. The accident instantly killed 3,787 people and resulted in more than 550,000 subsequent injuries, some of which led to permanent disabilities, and more than eight thousand deaths (Davidson *Invalid Modernism* 148). An estimated sixty thousand gas survivors still apparently experience depression and other cognitive trauma (Sinha "Life"). The disaster is ongoing. As one Indian news source pointed out in 2016, "Generations born after the incident are also marked by the poisons that leaked from the pesticide factory" (Aggarwal and Bera). Protestors note that underground

water is contaminated, but the company has not cleaned it up or made pay-
ment beyond $470 million in 1989, all of which illustrates Jasbir Puar's theory
about the right to maim.[8] It shows how global capitalism can lead to disability
and debility in the Global South, how disabled subaltern people's rights are
often not taken seriously, and how human rights instruments are not enough
in themselves to prevent such deplorable situations. Furthermore, Alexandra
Schultheis Moore points out that these violations are "deeply embedded in
past colonial and present neocolonial relations," suggesting the possible harms
of the world's current economic and political structure despite the existence of
human rights ("Disaster" 232).

Such matters can seem almost too big to fathom. To relate the story in a
way that will move readers, Sinha avoids polemic and instead turns to fiction,
inventing a place that is clearly based on Bhopal and using a vibrant figure
of disability as narrator. Tellingly, Sinha says that before conceiving Animal
he struggled for years to write the story, which remained "dark and lifeless"
(Sinha "Animal's"). Only through disability did he find an effective way to
relate the tale. With his twisted form, occasional mad mind, and orphan status, Animal serves as a living metaphor for the disaster; he represents all of the
thousands of people that the disaster disabled, debilitated, killed, or otherwise
harmed. Yet he is also a realistic individual who insists on his own singular-
ity. "*In all the world is none like me,*" he defiantly sings (366). Sinha says he got
the idea for the fictional character of Animal from a figure some friends told
him they met in India who went around on all fours, a "good-looking chap"
who "took no shit from anyone," as well as from a person, Sunil, who lost his
loving parents and five siblings in the Bhopal accident and apparently heard
voices (Sinha "Animal's," "Life").

That the witty, cynical, and ribald Animal addresses his account directly
to us readers makes his narrative even more effective and adds to the dynamic of elusive kinship between disabled characters and readers that this study
has traced. At the start of the novel, an Australian journalist visits Animal
and asks him to tell his story in Hindi to a tape recorder for a book. At first
Animal is resistant, skeptically saying of the journalist, "You were like all the
others, come to suck our stories from us, so strangers in far off countries can
marvel there's so much pain in the world" (5). He is wary of the dangers of
passive readerly voyeurism and imagines readers' curiosity feeling like acid on
his skin. Saying he does not want pity, he bitterly adds that to foreign readers
poison victims are "not really people," which makes his claim not to be human
all the more poignant (9). To most international individuals, he implies, *no*
impoverished poison victim in Khaufpur is human. But after getting the journalist to agree that the published version will include only his words, Animal

relents, saying the story "wants to come out" (11). The journalist encourages him to talk into a tape recorder straight to readers, to imagine their eyes reading his story, so Animal periodically refers to readers as Eyes and personalizes the entire narrative to each reader: "Now I am talking to you," he says (12). Still, he realizes the impossibility of knowing how readers will react, saying, "Never . . . can I ever know what pictures you see" (21). The approach shows the importance Sinha attaches to the connection between reader and character in winning readers' imaginations to causes of justice, as well as his awareness of potential pitfalls.

Animal's account resembles a bildungsroman, the literary form that Joseph Slaughter has especially linked to human rights narratives. In the course of the story Animal grows and changes in significant ways; he moves from relative isolation to being part of a warm community, from political ambivalence to activism, and from choosing to see himself as a nonhuman to all but explicitly embracing a human identity. At the start, he is an outcast whose words echo William Shakespeare's disabled Richard III, who in his opening soliloquy famously refers to not being made to court a looking glass and whose shadow reveals his deformity. In similar fashion, Animal says: "Mirrors I avoid but there's such a thing as casting a shadow—I'd feel raw disgust" (1–2). He largely lives on the street, scavenging for food and consumed with jealousy of people who can go about on two legs. His best friend is a dog; he cynically says that words such as *"rights, law, justice"* cause choking; and he does not even consider himself human (3). "I used to be human once," he memorably begins, seeing himself as deprived by the poison leak of not only his parents and able-bodiedness but also his very humanity, which, he implies, he does not want because of his moral disgust at how corrupt people can be (1).

But whereas Shakespeare's Richard III uses his isolation as reason for evil, Animal discovers a welcoming community that causes his perceptions gradually to evolve. He meets a kind young woman, Nisha, who introduces him to the activist leader Zafar and other people involved in a campaign for justice and reparations from the faceless transnational American corporation that Animal calls the Kampani. Zafar hires him as a spy to keep him informed. Through Animal, we encounter an array of people living close to the abandoned plant who were harmed by the accident, including Pandit Somraj, whose wife and infant son died because of the leak and who was a famous singer but can no longer sing due to damaged lungs; Shambhu, who says his "body was a sack of pain" (147); Hanif, who "hasn't seen a thing since that night" and coughs (178); and Aliya, an ill eight-year-old girl whose lungs are inflamed; as well as references to poisoned water, unborn fetuses, and more than a half-million claims from people injured by the disaster. Animal's account makes it easier for readers to relate to the grim effects of the chemical leak in Khaufpur decades after the disaster. The most prominent evidence of his belonging to a community comes near the end, when he runs away to a jungle because of unrequited love and a group of friends spend more than a week searching for him, hugging joyfully when they are reunited. Earlier, when an American doctor yells that she does not understand "ANIMAL'S PEOPLE," the novel's title, she is referring to all of the residents of Khaufpur (183). Rather than ostracized, Animal comes to be a central player in the neighborhood, even representative of all the diverse people in it.

The American doctor, Elli, and the Kampani illustrate how "the North" is heterogeneous, containing divergent views. The exploitative Kampani owns the plant that releases the poisons and refuses to pay more settlement. It causes Animal's and the community's disabilities and is part of the faceless cycle of neoliberalism around the globe. By contrast, Elli is a doctor who comes to Khaufpur and opens a free clinic, wanting to treat victims and counter the worst effects of the Kampani's violation, only to find that Khaufpuris boycott her office because they suspect she's an ally of the Kampani. "I hate the Kampani," she angrily tells Animal, and in the end she proves her independence, marrying a prominent resident of Khaufpur, Somraj, and probably scaring the Kampani lawyers who try to avoid responsibility with a stink bomb.

As Animal enters the community, he changes with regard to political activism, too, leaving his skepticism behind and slowly becoming engaged. Like citizens have actually done in Bhopal, those in Khaufpur campaign for justice, including for reparations and cleanup of the environmental waste by the Kampani, but without substantial progress. Efforts to build a court case against the Kampani's executives have failed twelve times, in part because of bribes that ally Indian politicians with the Kampani. Seeing passionate demonstrations, hunger strikes, and violent clashes with police, Animal grows more impatient for justice that is overdue.

Along the way, he comes closer to seeing himself as a human, even if he does not say so explicitly. Early on, Animal clarifies that his choice in names is not just about his appearance, but also about how others respond to him: "When I say I'm an animal it's not just what I look like but what I feel" (87). He later adds that he prefers Animal because "others . . . treated me like one" (209). He feels like he's an animal because in society he's denied the dignity supposedly due to all humans. Yet his claims of being an animal seem to be a ruse. "Cheap lying bastard, I'm," he thinks at one point, acknowledging how throughout the narrative he yearns for corrective surgery and to walk upright again, like other people, although he carefully hides that desire from others

(186). Notably, he is sexually attracted to human women, climbing trees to see them naked and to masturbate. He also falls in love with a human, Nisha, the first stranger in the story to show him kindness. His acquaintance Chunaram calls him a "beastly boy" early in the story, with "boy" acknowledging his humanity while "beastly" signifies both nasty and animal-like, showing how at that point, in some respects, Animal inhabits a border zone between humans and other animals (9). But humans *are* animals, and one could, like Davidson, read him as evidence of Mel Chen's idea of an "animacy spectrum," where no firm line exists between human and animal.

Yet Sinha clearly intends for us to see Animal as a person who deserves human rights. Other characters in the book never see him as an animal. "You look a lot like a human being to me," says his colleague Farouq. "You pretend to be an animal so you can escape the responsibility of being human" (209). The charismatic Zafar consistently asserts he's a person. "Animal, my brother, you are a human being," he confirms near the end (364). Perhaps the greatest evidence comes during his sojourn into a jungle. While searching for food, he captures a lizard that, with his unusual perception, he hears say (with not a little humor), "You are human, if you were an animal you would have eaten me" (346). Everyone around Animal, even other animals, regard him as human, and so, it seems, does he himself, because despite their disabled subaltern status, he comes to see himself and all Khaufpurians as deserving human rights and justice.

The conclusion of *Animal's People* provides a mix of the unusual and conventional endings while issuing a stark warning to readers about the ongoing need for justice. Enacting the first parts of Mitchell and Snyder's theory of narrative prosthesis, the novel uses Animal's disability to start the story, and as the narrative unfolds, it takes center stage. However, the end of the novel disrupts the theory as Animal renounces surgery—which he acknowledges will not fully help him—and stays proudly four-footed. Like that of other disabled characters in postcolonial literature, including Memory, Uma, and Caroline, Animal's disability does not disappear; it is not killed, cured, or rehabilitated but remains. Instead, he uses his savings to buy a female friend out of forced prostitution so she can live with him, in a way that echoes Jane Austen's and many other authors' convention of ending novels with marriages. He finds a human partner and embraces his disability, but Animal concludes by returning to the reader and giving an arresting caution: "Eyes, I'm done. . . . but the poor remain. We are the people of the Apokalis. Tomorrow there will be more of us" (366). Animal testifies to the existence of disabled poor people and their continuing fight for justice. Sinha has acknowledged how, although he says the novel must succeed first as fiction, "I hope that

Animal's People can make a difference to the Bhopalis and help them in their campaign" ("Conversation").

In these ways, *Animal's People* is perhaps the most prominent example of the elusive kinship between disabled characters and readers in promoting human rights. With its direct attention to the reader, the novel makes the potential rewards (testimony, raising awareness around world, connection, and perhaps moving to action) and potential problems (passive voyeurism, pity, condescension) of elusive kinship between the disabled narrator and readers apparent in the quest for dignity.

Taken together, the novels by Abani, Gappah, and Sinha show the contradictions and inconsistencies in how human rights are applied (or not) in the circumstances of all-out war, dire poverty, neoliberalism, traditional metaphysical beliefs, and environmental disaster. In such situations, the novels suggest, human rights are not enough by themselves, and injustice prevails. Along the way, they offer a powerful form of witnessing and remembering, letting readers experience these situations up close through our imaginations. With disabled characters, they not only offer us close literary kinship with the experiences of disabled humans, but also show the immense challenges to, as well as urgency for, contemporary global disability justice.

Epilogue

Human rights . . . are essential—but they are not enough.

—SAMUEL MOYN, *Not Enough*

In 1980, when the American disability rights leader Frank Bowe, who was deaf, became the first disabled person to represent a nation in planning the United Nations' landmark International Year of Disabled Persons, he was aghast to discover the dire circumstances of millions of disabled people around the world. Deciding that "mere words, statistics, and research reports" were not enough, he later wrote: "I came to believe [that] the abilities of disabled people had to be dramatized" (152). His words fit into the arguments that we saw in Chapter 1 by Chimamanda Ngozi Adichie and many others about the power of stories to move people and bring about real-world change. Bowe thought stories could help to begin reversing the common misconception around the world that disabled people were uninteresting and useless.

This book demonstrates that postcolonial fiction in English begins to fill the need Bowe noticed. By dramatizing disabled people and deploying disability to depict any number of pressing topics, including not only such issues as colonialism and racial oppression but also the lived experiences of disabled people in the Global South, it regularly shows disabled people's humanity and, in so doing, helps to advance disability justice. We have seen a remarkably diverse number of characters that together help disabled people in the Global South to break out of their invisibility. These representations serve as a powerful form of witnessing. They make it easier for readers to imagine and sometimes to feel a connection or kinship with disabled characters, a crucial first step toward disabled people achieving more equity and rights.

Perhaps the works with disabled narrators make this bond most possible, as Saleem Sinai, My Luck, Memory, and Animal compel readers to experience events through a disabled person's perspective. Third-person portrayals invite readers to care, too, as we have seen especially with the narratives of Uma, Bibi Haldar, Sophie and her mother, Caroline, the King of the Beggars, and, perhaps, the enigmatic Michael K. All of these depictions show forces that subjugate disabled people—from ableism, bullying, taunting, and ostracization to metaphysical beliefs that position them as evil or cursed; from poverty and environmental disaster to war, racism, sexism, colonialism, and transnational capitalism that leave many behind. Even the portrayal of largely unsympathetic or even offensive disabled characters such as Chinua Achebe's Okonkwo or J. M. Coetzee's Pollux reveal injustices, such as a culture insistently privileging able-bodiedness or the racist system of apartheid, pervasive forces that disempower disabled people even more. As this study argues, such deployments reflect and contributed to the marked increase in attention to disabled people in human rights events and treaties since World War II that culminated in the Convention on the Rights of Persons with Disabilities (CRPD), ratified in 2008, even as they show that human rights alone do not add up to equity for disabled people around the world. These representations implicitly challenge us: what more should be done to achieve true disability justice?

Writers considering the way forward with human rights invariably call attention to the grievous economic inequity in the world, but they vary on what action should be taken. Some scholars, including Helen Meekosha, Jasbir Puar, and Karen Soldatic, argue that focusing on rights diverts attention from the struggles of impoverished people, including disabled people, in low-income nations and suggest we should move beyond rights themselves. Samuel Moyn, however, advocates retaining human rights but supplementing them with long overdue attention to global injustice. "Human rights . . . are essential—but they are not enough," he says in *Not Enough: Human Rights in an Unequal World* (xii). He calls human rights necessary because they stigmatize states and communities that fail to provide sufficient protection of residents, which he sees as an indisputably positive contribution. But pointing to the fact that the international human rights movement rose to global prominence alongside neoliberalism, he ruefully notes that human rights guarantee status equality but not distributive equality. "Human rights, even perfectly realized human rights, are compatible with inequality," he notes (213). Moyn goes on to argue that we need to find ways to put a ceiling on what one individual can amass and to provide a minimum floor of protection for those in poverty. However, achieving that will be exceptionally difficult, especially on a global scale. As Moyn acknowledges, welfare policies have long been organized nationally.

In our current moment in the midst of a global pandemic, it is hard to know what is to come, but the post-pandemic era seems sure to feature more inequality. As noted in the Introduction, global capitalism has led to laudable progress, as some people have escaped extreme poverty. The United Nations achieved its Millennium Development Goal of cutting in half the number of people living in extreme poverty in 2010, five years ahead of schedule. Yet many other people remain impoverished, and the writer and CNN commentator Fareed Zakaria recently predicted that in a post-pandemic world we will have more inequality as large corporations and companies do better and everyone else does worse. Far from being an equalizer, the internet encourages the creation of monopolies, he notes. "While disease can sometimes erase inequalities, most of the time it exacerbates them," he concludes (166). Affluent people have enjoyed relative success, but the pandemic has revealed the economic challenges and vulnerability of many poor people throughout the world, including disabled people in the Global South, pointing to challenges ahead.

Moreover, scholars in the new field of posthumanism insightfully argue that true justice requires even more effort.[1] Pointing out that the category of human is increasingly problematic in a world that destroys the environment and nonhuman animal life and where nonhuman artificial intelligence technology makes an increasingly large difference, they together show that one injustice is caught up in others. If we continue to delay on global warming, that will have dire consequences for people everywhere, including disabled people in the Global South who may lack adequate shelter or health care. If we expand into wildlife habitats where we have increased risk of disease and pandemic jumping from animals to humans, as apparently happened with COVID-19, that would negatively affect all humans, disabled and nondisabled alike. As we consider what could make human rights even more effective, a holistic approach, instead of just focusing on one group or issue, seems increasingly necessary.

If these challenges seem overly daunting, we might remember Chris Abani's poignant but encouraging words on the difficulty of achieving justice:

> One of my earliest spiritual advisers told me that to be human is to accept that there will never be world peace, but to live life as though it is possible. This is the core of my aesthetic: belief in a deeper humanness that is beyond race, class, gender, and power, even as I know

that it is not possible. And yet I strive for it in every way, even when I fail. ("Ethics")

Knowing one will fail, Abani suggests, is not a reason to back down from the effort. We could also expand on his concept of "deep humanness" to include human care for the well-being of nonhuman animals and the natural environment. Big, even intimidating, goals, to be sure, but worth attention and effort, because that will make a good life more possible for everyone. One lesson that this literature shows repeatedly is that we are all interdependent, our fates entwined. By focusing on disabled people in the Global South and lifting them up, we could lift up many people. Since World War II, Anglophone postcolonial literature has helped to make disabled people in the South visible, important, and consequential and seen as fully human with rights. That is another reason this great writing gives hope and should be celebrated.

Acknowledgments

I am especially grateful to the readers of one or more chapter drafts, whose trenchant comments and questions made this a much better book: Michael Bérubé, Mrinalini Chakravorty, Michael Davidson, Rita Felski, Susan Fraiman, Debjani Ganguly, Robert McRuer, Caroline Rody, Matthew Rubery, Ellen Samuels, my brother Peter, and the very helpful anonymous reviewers at Temple University Press. Thanks, too, to Rachel Adams, Ellen Contini-Morava, Nirmala Erevelles, Ato Quayson, Jahan Ramazani, Rebecca Sanchez, Carol Stevens, Michael Ashley Stein, and Kirk VanGilder for their encouragement and generosity with their knowledge and insights.

My gratitude goes to the University of Virginia (U.Va.) in a number of ways, including for creating a stimulating intellectual environment with people doing interdisciplinary work. Particular thanks go to my invigorating, supportive colleagues in the English Department and in our small American Sign Language (ASL) Program. The Institute of the Humanities and Global Cultures at U.Va. gave me a Mellon Humanities Fellowship; thanks to its director, Debjani Ganguly, for creating a space for me and other fellows to develop and share our work. Moreover, the Buckner W. Clay Dean of Arts & Sciences and the Vice President for Research at U.Va. gave me support that allowed me to join groups going to China (in 2011) and Zimbabwe and Kenya (in 2016). I was able to gain invaluable real-world experience with disabled people in these places. Further thanks go to U.Va. for sesquicentennial leaves and summer stipend awards, which freed up time for writing.

I need a separate paragraph to extend my deep appreciation to U.Va. for its commitment to diversity and for employing a late-deafened faculty member like me. I have benefited from working with exceptional sign language interpreters, including Rene DeVito, Elaine Hernandez, Kate O'Regan, and Laurie Shaffer, who made classes and meetings accessible. Faculty from all over Grounds belonging to the U.Va. Disability Studies Initiative added valuable collaboration and community. I also thank the committed members of the Disability Advocacy and Action Committee, founded by Dr. Marcus Martin, for making countless improvements for disabled students, faculty, staff, and visitors at U.Va. over the past decade.

For their interest, ideas, and stimulation, I thank audiences at the conventions of the Modern Language Association and the Society for Disability Studies, as well as at disability studies symposia and faculty lectures at U.Va.

I am indebted to the smart and motivated students, both graduate and undergraduate, at U.Va. who helped me to develop my ideas over the years. In addition, I am grateful to the graduate students Jordan Burke, Eva Hoenigess, and, especially, Julianne McCobbin for their research assistance.

I also extend my appreciation to Cindy Wu for helping me to take this project to Temple University Press. Shaun Vigil, my editor at Temple, has expertly guided this book along, and the conscientious production team has made the whole process a pleasure.

My elderly parents continue to take active interest in my work, asking me regularly for progress reports. During production of this book, my father passed away at 93 after a full, rich life; among countless other gifts, I am thankful he showed me the rewards of engaged academic work. My wonderful siblings Peter, Michael, Elizabeth, Susie, and Matthew, as well as my in-laws and nieces and nephews, provide consistent support, too. A special pleasure during the pandemic was our daily "Corture" sessions each morning, when we did a fifteen-minute abdominal workout together on Zoom across multiple time zones. It was a great way to start a day and to stay in shape.

I started this book before my son Daniel, now eight, was born. His joyful bursting into my study to see if I could play kept me grounded and smiling. My wife, Michelle, has been a patient, loving, and kind presence, whose shared interest in sign language and in literature is always a delight. Thank you for everything you do, honey. This book is dedicated to you because you make all the difference.

Notes

INTRODUCTION

1. See African Youth with Disabilities Network, thirty-one videos, updated May 31, 2013, www.youtube.com/playlist?list=PL407C8373BB7BE5C3.

2. Statistics vary according to the source and methodology. In 2011 the disability studies scholar Dan Goodley estimated the number of disabled people in the Global South at around four hundred million (39), while that same year the World Health Organization and World Bank issued a joint report with an estimate that was almost double that: 785 million people. In many low-income nations, reliable data can be difficult to obtain. For a helpful consideration of the matter, see Eide and Loeb "Counting."

3. The Trump administration also withdrew from the United Nations Human Rights Council in 2018, a decision reversed in 2021 by President Joe Biden.

4. Some foundational texts in literary disability studies include Davis's *Enforcing Normalcy* (1995); Garland-Thomson's *Extraordinary Bodies* (1997); and Mitchell and Snyder's *Narrative Prosthesis* (2000), as well as Davis's edited editions of *The Disability Studies Reader*.

5. See, e.g., journals such as *Wagadu* (in 2007) and the *Journal of Literary & Cultural Disability Studies* (in 2010).

6. In addition, interdisciplinary collections such as Shaun Grech and Karen Soldatic's *Disability in the Global South* and Michael Gill and Cathy Schlund-Vials's *Disability, Human Rights, and the Limits of Humanitarianism* have added to the burgeoning attention to disability around the world. Because new scholarship in this area is frequently appearing, my listing is not exhaustive or complete.

7. Some notable works here include Slaughter's *Human Rights Incorporated* (2007); Anker's *Fictions of Dignity* (2012); Parikh's *Writing Human Rights* (2017); Dawes's *Novel of Human Rights* (2018); and several edited collections, such as Goldberg and Moore's *Theoretical Perspectives on Human Rights and Literature* (2012); McClennen and Moore's *Routledge Companion to Literature and Human Rights* (2016); and Parikh's *Cambridge Companion to Human Rights and Literature* (2019).

8. Although Anker does not explicitly consider disability, she sees fiction as reclaiming the body and embodiment. Her discerning analysis of how postcolonial writers "reanimate registers of corporeal engagement" sets the stage for my study (*Fictions* 3).

9. By "neoliberalism," I mean the global capitalism favored by corporations in the North and often promoted by international organizations such as the World Bank and the International Monetary Fund. Although the term can seem to mean many different things to different people, it helpfully describes the current world order that frequently puts capital above democracy and social justice. For helpful elucidation of the concept, see, e.g., Erevelles "Disability"; Nixon *Slow Violence*; Slobodian *Globalists*.

10. In *Nothing About Us Without Us*, James Charlton notes that he first heard this expression in South Africa in 1993, and sources there said they learned it at an international disability rights conference in Eastern Europe, which suggests its currency among the global disability activists at the end of the twentieth century.

11. Unfortunately, the ratifiers do not include the United States, whose Congress has declined to agree to an international convention that might interfere with national sovereignty (although the United States does already have the ADA in force). For the same reason, the United States has not ratified such foundational treaties as the Convention on the Rights of the Child or the Convention on the Elimination of All Forms of Discrimination against Women (CEDAW).

12. In the late 1970s, the head of the World Bank, Robert McNamara, announced the establishment of the Independent Commission on International Development Issues. Former German Chancellor Willy Brandt agreed to head the group, which consisted of experienced politicians and economists. The report that the commission released in 1980, now commonly referred to as the Brandt Report, was formally titled *North-South: A Program for Survival*.

13. As another alternative, some critics have used the phrase "majority world" for the Global South, since most of the world's people are there, but this nomenclature has not caught on.

14. In 1995, the anthropologists Benedicte Ingstad and Susan Reynold Whyte even noted that "the disabled" as a general term does not translate easily into many languages, which may have words for blind people and lame people and cognitively "slow" people, but not for the category of disability (*Disability and Culture* 7).

15. The field of deaf studies explores this rich heritage of cultural and linguistic

uniqueness. Still, it's important to note that some deaf people have embraced the disability category and been leaders in the disability community. For example, the late Frank Bowe (who became deaf at age three but did not have the opportunity to learn sign language until he was an adult) served as the founding director of the American Coalition of Citizens with Disabilities. In 1977 he conceived and led a nationwide disability protest that pressured the government into finally issuing regulations for Section 504, which banned discrimination against disabled people by organizations receiving federal funding and has been called America's first federal disability rights law. Culturally deaf leaders such as Frederick Schreiber, executive secretary of the National Association of the Deaf, and T. J. O'Rourke were also involved in the Section 504 protests. Today, the World Federation of the Deaf has a position paper on its website that supports *both* a linguistic/cultural model and a disability model for deaf people who use sign language.

16. To be sure, such an alliance did not just suddenly materialize. With reason, people sometimes refer to an invisible hierarchy within the disability community and disability studies, where wheelchair users are at the top and those with cognitive disabilities are at the bottom; white disabled people receive more attention than disabled people of color; and disability in the Global South is largely left out of the critical conversation. Fortunately, such glaring omissions have been receiving more attention.

17. I note somewhat ruefully that such unity has special appeal in our current, extremely polarized moment in the twenty-first century, reminding us that people with important differences can still join together when they have a sense of common purpose.

18. I do not use "crip" in this study, though, because I want to be careful to avoid clapping a Euro-American theory onto the complex and different postcolonial literature.

19. This negative view makes me suspect that Puar probably has never experienced the warmth or happiness of a group of deaf people signing, whether in Zimbabwe or China, or the tangible joy of a Society for Disability Studies convention dance in America.

20. For example, in the Chinese *Analects*, Confucius upholds the value of *shu*, the practice of never imposing on others what one would not choose for oneself. Similarly, in the New Testament of the Bible, Jesus says, "Do unto others as you would have them do unto you" (Matthew 7:12), the "golden rule" of ethics. Such rules of reciprocity show up in various ways in almost all of the world's religions: see Humphreys.

21. For more on how the World Bank creates the dependence that its policies were supposed to prevent, see McRuer "Bank." In his recent *Crip Times*, McRuer also insightfully critiques how neoliberal austerity measures in North America, Europe, and Brazil negatively affect disability communities through cuts to social services, welfare, and the like.

22. To cite one example of such activism, Ghai refers to a 1996 campaign of disabled people in India and their families that pushed successfully for legislation ensuring equal opportunity (92).

23. I got a glimmer of potential transnational disability identity recently on a trip to Kenya, where I visited what was called a "special" school and a nine-year-old deaf girl eagerly asked whether there really are deaf people in America. Yes, I assured her in my mishmash of American Sign Language and gesture. I quickly drew a world map on the chalkboard as the eight other deaf students in the classroom looked on with interest. There are deaf people in America (pointing at the map), in China, in France, in Brazil, everywhere, I told them. The students' faces brightened, and we smiled at one another happily.

Perhaps this was an example of global deaf transnationalism, as Joseph Murray has described it, a shared identity that unites deaf people despite national boundaries and different sign languages ("Co-equality"). I found this deaf connection when I traveled to China, Zimbabwe, and Israel; across Europe; and elsewhere. But this may also have been evidence of international bonds that started to emerge globally during the United Nations Decade of Disabled Persons, from 1983 to 1992, and the period leading up to the ratification of the CRPD in 2008, in which disabled people conceive of themselves not only as national citizens with unique cultures, but also as a global group united across borders and bodily conditions. At that school in Kenya, there were also cognitively impaired students and several with mobility impairments, who were at once distinct from deaf students (taking separate classes) and simultaneously part of a larger collective group that wore the same uniforms and ate together in the cafeteria.

24. I am well aware that the politics of international literary awards are fraught. How are winners chosen? The Nobel Prize in Literature (awarded in Sweden) and Man Booker Prize (England) could well be charged with having a Northern, European bias, of selecting books that readers in Europe and North America especially like. Still, some of their selections have been quite critical of the North. They remain the main global literary awards and continue to carry enormous prestige. By publishing in English, these writers make it clear they are seeking a Northern Anglo-American audience, as well as English-speaking readers in their home countries.

25. True, I could have included a well-known early female author such as Nadine Gordimer, but I'm not aware of a central disability figure in her work. Again, I don't pretend to be exhaustive or definitive and hope more scholarship on the topic will follow.

26. For an insightful consideration of postcolonial literature and its relation to global market expansion in the publishing industry, see Brouillette.

27. Examples here include Chen's *Animacies* (2012); Taylor's *Beasts of Burden* (2017); Liddiard et al.'s "A DisHuman Manifesto" (2019); Linett's *Literary Bioethics* (2020); and Murray's *Disability and the Posthuman* (2020). Most recently, Michael

Lundblad was the guest editor of the provocative "Animality/Posthumanism/Disability" issue of *New Literary History* (Autumn 2020).

CHAPTER 1

1. For that reason, Adichie stresses the importance of having multiple stories and perspectives to break simplistic, stereotypical thinking. "The problem with stereotypes," she says, "is not that they are untrue, but that they are incomplete."

2. Vermeule makes this point especially clearly in Carter.

3. Many studies of child development have connected reading with children's brain development, suggesting that reading fosters stronger language and social skills, helps children do better at school, gives them more awareness of the world around them, and makes them kinder, promoting understanding of others. For example, the educator Jerry Diakiw argues that reading fiction in an engaged way at primary-school age is an important predictor of children's future life success: "It appears from [a] growing body of research that individuals who read fiction are better able to understand other people, empathize with them and see the world from their point of view."

4. For more on the connection between readers and characters, see esp. Dawes "Human Rights, Literature, and Empathy"; Felski.

5. See, e.g., Kidd and Castano.

6. Huggan explores this aspect of postcolonial literature.

CHAPTER 2

1. For the seventieth anniversary of the UDHR in 2018, people around the world recorded themselves reading an article of the declaration in their native language. The videos—in more than eighty languages from 130 countries—were posted by the United Nations and testify to how the UDHR has affected people in many different places (UN "Universal").

2. For a helpful recent analysis of how Achebe conveys the expressive oral dimensions of the indigenous Igbo culture even as he uses written English, see Chakravorty.

3. For example, Wahneema Lubiano maintains that insisting on the ethnographic value of *Things Fall Apart* is reductive and "represses the structure and form of black texts" (107). Similarly, Graham Huggan extensively critiques what he calls an anthropological exotic with regard to the novel.

CHAPTER 3

1. The United Nations issued the Declaration on the Granting of Independence to Colonial Countries and Peoples in 1960. Sometimes called "third-generation" human rights, such rights go beyond the framework of individual rights to

focus on collective concepts, including self-determination, group and communal rights, and so on.

2. Barker is one of the few scholars who has written about disability in *Midnight's Children*. She focuses on representations of exceptional children in *Postcolonial Fiction and Disability*. In this chapter, I seek to build on that by considering treatment of disabled adults, too.

3. The British colonial presence in India endured for centuries, running from 1612 to 1947.

4. In his semiautobiographical story "The Courter" in *East, West*, for instance, Rushdie memorably writes of feeling he has ropes pulling on his neck commanding him to choose between East and West. "I choose neither of you, and both," he declares. "Do you hear? I refuse to choose" (211).

5. For more information on Campbell, see Krentz "Duncan Campbell."

6. I explore this paradoxical representation of Funes and other instances of disability in Borges's stories in "Borges." Borges, who became blind later in his life, represents disability in interesting ways.

7. Juan Manuel Espinosa usefully approaches García Márquez's *One Hundred Years of Solitude* from a literary disability studies angle in his chapter in *Libre Acceso*.

8. Grass's novel contains a narrator, Oskar, who retains the stature of a child (during World War II he performs with a troupe of dwarfs) and later is housed in a mental hospital, while Morrison's work includes the minor characters the three deweys who never grow up and, despite physical differences, have their individual identities merge into one. Such celebrated novels reveal the literary intersection of magic realism and disability around the globe. The technique is profoundly transnational, including authors in the North and the South.

9. While it has sometimes been controversial when able-bodied actors portray disabled people on screen, no such issues seem to surround able-bodied authors writing disabled characters, any more than there is unease at, say, Willa Cather writing from a man's point of view in *My Antonia*. The acts of reading and writing seem to be about the imagination in ways that film is not, where writers are free to explore other subjectivities and points of view.

10. This is also the title of a revealing study of disability oppression and empowerment around the world that James Charlton published in 1998.

11. See, e.g., "The Political Rushdie: An Interview by Ashutosh Varshney," in Herwitz and Varshney.

12. Rushdie returns to the theme of intentional disabling in his later story "The Prophet's Hair." "With a parent's absolute love," we're told, a criminal "had made sure [his four sons] were all provided with a lifelong source of high income by crippling them at birth, so that, as they dragged themselves around the city, they earned excellent money in the begging business" (*East, West* 53). When the sons are miraculously cured by a religious relic at the end of the story, they are "very properly furious, because the miracle had reduced their earning power by 75 per cent" (58).

13. Drawing on his interviews with disability rights activists throughout the world, Charlton declares that, in reality, disabled people are usually outsiders and "peripheral everywhere" across the globe.

CHAPTER 4

1. For more on this colonial wound trope, see esp. Barker 16; Quayson "Looking Awry"; Ramazani 50; Titchkosky.

2. Derek Walcott's essays "Tribal Flutes" (1967) and "The Muse in History" (1974) provide examples of this critique, as do his lines about people who "nurture the scars of rusted chains" near the end of his autobiographical poem "Another Life" (1973) (in *Collected Poems* 269). Ramazani uses "the wound motif" rather than disability to describe the impairments in *Omeros*, but Walcott's characters have what we would term disabilities today. For example, the Black St. Lucian Philoctete has a painful injury that tortures him to the point of making him consider amputating his leg while the white British Major Plunkett experiences symptoms of post-traumatic stress disorder from his participation in World War II.

3. We could debate the issue of authorial intent—whether they deliberately create such an effect—but the fact remains that their literary portrayals are inventive and productive.

4. In making this argument, I am especially indebted to Ramazani's discussion of Walcott and to Barker, who points to the empathy postcolonial authors frequently have toward their disabled characters (20).

5. Simi Linton writes, "I am not willing or interested in erasing the line between disabled and nondisabled people, as long as disabled people are devalued and discriminated against, and as long as naming the category serves to call attention to that treatment" (13).

6. Coetzee's parents were of Afrikaner descent, and his ancestors go back to the first Dutch settlers in South Africa in the seventeenth century. His parents were also bilingual, speaking English. Coetzee grew up speaking English at home; he is also fluent in Afrikaans. His fictional autobiography *Boyhood* circles around questions of identity, and much of his fiction deals with ethical questions of individual choice in a corrupt society.

7. Coetzee's notion is reminiscent of African American writers from Frederick Douglass to Ralph Ellison arguing that racism hurts both white and Black people.

8. I take the phrase "hermeneutical impasse" from Quayson, who discusses it as one type of disability representation in literature (*Aesthetic* 49–50). Coetzee's disabled characters fulfill other of Quayson's categories, including "interface with otherness (including race, class, sexuality, and social identity)" (39). They also serve to critique social hypocrisy and institutions, another feature that Quayson identifies (52). As he notes, his typology is provisional, and categories can and do overlap.

9. Perhaps Coetzee settles on this strategy because of censorship under the apartheid regime, which had become more intense after the Soweto student upris-

ing of 1976. In 1996, Coetzee wrote, "The censor is an intrusive reader, a reader who forces his way into the intimacy of the writing transaction [and] reads your words in a disapproving and *censorious* fashion" (*Giving Offense* 38).

10. K's cleft lip aligns him with images of children in the Global South with cleft lips in fundraising appeals, particularly in Europe and North America, making his impairment potentially more familiar to readers and giving it a certain immediate pathos, despite the narrative's unsentimental tone. See, e.g., the Smile Train charity website at www.smiletrain.org, which reports that a baby with a cleft lip is born somewhere in the world every three minutes, so it is not uncommon.

11. The South African apartheid government commonly used pass laws, which required travel passes, to regulate and control the movement of Black South Africans.

12. The deserted farm suggests actual farms abandoned by whites in South Africa in the late 1970s and early 1980s as racial tensions escalated and they sensed the end of apartheid coming.

13. Attwell has an especially trenchant discussion of these matters related to voice (116–117).

14. As Bérubé puts it, K desires to avoid "*being narrated*," which makes his relationship to the text all the more ironic (*Stories* 69).

CHAPTER 5

1. See Table I.1 in the Introduction for a list.

2. The committee is a body of twenty-three independent experts from around the world that monitors implementation of the CEDAW. States that have become parties to the treaty make regular reports to the committee on their progress.

3. See African Youth with Disabilities Network, "Ruth Nabasirye, Uganda" video, posted March 7, 2012, www.youtube.com/watch?v=WM3_7fDmIiM&list =PL407C8373BB7BE5C3&index=21.

4. For relevant sources here, see Rawls's *A Theory of Justice* (1971); Kittay's "Human Dependency and Rawlsian Equality" (1997) and *Love's Labor* (1999); and Kittay and Feder's *The Subject of Care* (2002).

5. Unfortunately, the issue remains quite charged for the field. Deep emotion surrounds the topic. When I presented an early version of this section on Danticat and trauma at the Society of Disability Studies convention several years ago, several attendees walked (or wheeled) out, in stark contrast to the mutual supportiveness and encouragement that usually characterizes the field.

6. Another example of this perverse legacy occurs in "Nineteen Thirty-Seven," a story from Danticat's *Krik? Krak!* In it, a prison originally built by U.S. Marines during the occupation in the early twentieth century later becomes a place where Haitians incarcerate women accused of witchcraft. There they are forced to shave their heads, are fed little food, and often die.

CHAPTER 6

1. For an incisive discussion of the global organ transplant market, where organs are typically placed in ice chests and shipped around the world, see Davidson *Concerto*.

2. As I explain in the Introduction, I have some reservations about Puar's views, but they warrant serious consideration, especially into how global capitalist forces *produce* disability and debility around the world.

3. See African Youth with Disabilities Network, "Victoria Davis: Liberia," video, posted April 16, 2012, www.youtube.com/watch?v=haQrwIqMVCc&list=PL4 07C8373BB7BE5C3&index=2&t=0s.

4. For more on the famine, see Association for Diplomatic Studies and Training.

5. Abani distinguishes this improvised sign system from the full, grammatically complex sign languages that deaf people use. My Luck says, "Our form of speech is nothing like the kind of sign language my deaf cousin studied in a special school before the war" (20).

6. In this way the novel usefully pairs with Achebe's *Things Fall Apart*, discussed in Chapter 2.

7. An optional protocol added to the Convention of the Rights of Child in 2000 raised the minimum age for members of armed forces in conflicts to eighteen.

8. In 1999, Union Carbide merged into Dow Chemical, ceasing to exist as a separate identifiable entity.

EPILOGUE

1. See n. 27 in the Introduction for provocative recent work in this field.

Works Cited

Abani, Chris. "Ethics and Narrative: The Human and Other." *Witness* 22 (2009). wit
  ness.blackmountaininstitute.org/issues/dismissing-africa-volume-22-2009/ethics
  -and-narrative-the-human-and-other.
———. *GraceLand*. New York: Picador, 2004.
———. "On Humanity." *TED*. 2008. www.ted.com/talks/chris_abani_on_humanity.
———. *Song for Night*. New York: Akashic, 2007.
Achebe, Chinua. "The Black Writer's Burden." *Présence Africaine* 31.59 (1966): 135–
  140.
———. *Morning Yet on Creation Day*. New York: Anchor, 1975.
———. "The Role of the Writer in a New Nation." *African Writers on African Writing*.
  Ed. G. D. Killam. 1964; Evanston, IL: Northwestern University Press, 1973. 7–13.
———. *Things Fall Apart*. 1958; New York: Anchor, 1994.
Adams, Rachel, Benjamin Reiss, and David Serlin. "Disability." *Keywords for Disabil-
  ity Studies*. Ed. Rachel Adams, Benjamin Reiss, and David Serlin. New York: New
  York University Press, 2015. 5–11.
Adichie, Chimamanda Ngozi. "The Danger of a Single Story." *TED*. 2009. www.ted
  .com/talks/chimamanda_adichie_the_danger_of_a_single_story.
African Youth with Disabilities Network. YouTube. 2012. www.youtube.com/playlist
  ?list=PL407C8373BB7BE5C3.
Agboola, Issac. "Opening Doors: The Legacy of Andrew Foster." *Dr. Andrew Jackson
  Foster: The Most Courageous Educator and the Most Visionary Missionary to Deaf
  Africans*. By Emmanuel Ilabor. Dugbe, Nigeria: Christian Mission for the Deaf,
  2009. 180–186.
Aggarwal, Mayank, and Sayantan Bera. "Thirty-two Years after the Bhopal Gas Tragedy, Gov[ernmen]t Apathy Intensifies Victims' Pain." *Livemint*, Dec. 2, 2016. www
  .livemint.com/Politics/sBzgTl9ogcYcRJPDLVuj1L/32-years-after-the-Bhopal-gas
  -tragedy-govt-apathy-intensifi.html.

Anker, Elizabeth. *Fictions of Dignity: Embodying Human Rights in World Literature.* Ithaca, NY: Cornell University Press, 2012.

———. "Narrating Human Rights and the Limits of Magic Realism in Salman Rushdie's *Shalimar the Clown.*" *Theoretical Perspectives on Human Rights and Literature.* Ed. Elizabeth Swanson Goldberg and Alexandra Schultheis Moore. New York: Routledge, 2012. 149–164.

Ashcroft, Bill. "Is That the Congo? Language as Metonymy in the Post-colonial Text." *World Literatures Written in English* 29.2 (Autumn 1989): 3–10.

Association for Diplomatic Studies and Training. "The Famine in Biafra—USAID's Response to the Nigerian Civil War." adst.org/2014/05/the-famine-in-biafra-usaids-response-to-the-nigerian-civil-war.

Attwell, David. *J. M. Coetzee and the Life of Writing: Face-to-Face with Time.* New York: Viking, 2015.

Bakhtin, Mikhail. *Rabelais and His World.* Trans. Helene Iswolsky. 1965; Bloomington: Indiana University Press, 1984.

Barker, Clare. *Postcolonial Fiction and Disability: Exceptional Children, Metaphor and Materiality.* New York: Palgrave Macmillan, 2011.

Barker, Clare, and Stuart Murray. "Disabling Postcolonialism: Global Disability Cultures and Democratic Criticism." *Journal of Literary & Cultural Disability Studies* 4.3 (2010): 219–236.

Barris, Ken. "Miscegenation, Desire and Rape: The Shifting Ground of *Disgrace.*" *Journal of Literary Studies* 26.3 (2010): 50–64.

Bell, Michael. "García Márquez, Magical Realism and World Literature." *The Cambridge Companion to Gabriel García Márquez.* Ed. Philip Swanson. Cambridge: Cambridge University Press, 2010. 179–195.

Berger, James. "Trauma without Disability, Disability without Trauma: A Disciplinary Divide." *JAC: Rhetoric, Writing, Culture, Politics* 24.3 (2004): 563–582.

Bérubé, Michael. "Disability and Narrative." *PMLA* 120.2 (2005): 568–576.

———. *The Secret Life of Stories: From Don Quixote to Harry Potter, How Understanding Intellectual Disability Transforms the Way We Read.* New York: New York University Press, 2016.

Bhabha, Homi K. *The Location of Culture.* London: Routledge, 1994.

Boehmer, Elleke. *Stories of Women: Gender and Narrative in the Postcolonial Nation.* Manchester, UK: Manchester University Press, 2009.

———. "Transfiguring: Colonial Body into Postcolonial Narrative." *Novel: A Forum on Fiction* 26.3 (1993): 268–277.

Borges, Jorge Luis. *Ficciones.* Trans. Alastair Reid, Anthony Kerrigan, Anthony Bonner, Helen Temple, and Ruthven Todd. 1944; New York: Knopf, 1993.

Bowe, Frank. *Comeback: Six Remarkable People Who Triumphed over Disability.* New York: HarperCollins, 1981.

Brouillette, Sarah. *Postcolonial Writers in the Global Literary Marketplace.* Basingstoke, UK: Palgrave Macmillan, 2007.

Buelens, Gert, and Dominick Hoens. "'Above and Beneath Classification': *Bartleby, Life and Times of Michael K,* and Syntagmatic Participation." *Diacritics* 37.2–3 (2007): 157–170.

Carter, Stephen. "The Characters Aren't Real. Your Rage at Them Is." *Bloomberg View*

blog. Nov. 6, 2015. www.bloomberg.com/view/articles/2015-11-06/the-characters
-aren-t-real-your-rage-at-them-is-.

Chakravorty, Mrinalini. "Never Kill a Man Who Says Nothing: *Things Fall Apart* and
the Spoken Worlds of African Fiction." *Ariel* 43.4 (2013): 11–47.

Charlton, James. *Nothing About Us Without Us: Disability, Oppression and Empowerment.* Berkeley: University of California Press, 1998.

———. "Peripheral Everywhere." *Journal of Literary & Cultural Disability Studies* 4.2
(2010): 195–200.

Chen, Mel. *Animacies: Biopolitics, Racial Mattering, and Queer Affect.* Durham, NC:
Duke University Press, 2012.

Clare, Eli. *Brilliant Imperfection: Grappling with Cure.* Durham, NC: Duke University
Press, 2017.

Coetzee, J. M. *Boyhood: Scenes from Provincial Life.* London: Secker & Warburg, 1997.

———. *Disgrace.* New York: Penguin, 1999.

———. *Doubling the Point: Essays and Interviews.* Ed. David Atwell. Cambridge, MA:
Harvard University Press, 1992.

———. *Foe.* 1986; New York: Penguin, 1987.

———. *Giving Offense: Essays on Censorship.* Chicago: University of Chicago Press,
1996.

———. *Life & Times of Michael K.* New York: Penguin, 1983.

———. *Lives of Animals.* Princeton, NJ: Princeton University Press, 1999.

———. *Waiting for the Barbarians.* New York: Penguin, 1980.

Comaroff, Jean, and John L. Comaroff. *Theory from the South; or, How Euro-America
Is Evolving toward Africa.* Boulder, CO: Paradigm, 2012.

Cooper, Audrey C., and Khadijat Rashid, eds. *Citizenship, Politics, Difference: Perspectives from Sub-Saharan Signed Language Communities.* Washington, DC: Gallaudet
University Press, 2015.

Dangarembga, Tsitsi. *Nervous Conditions.* 1988; London: Ayebia Clarke, 2004.

Danticat, Edwidge. *Breath, Eyes, Memory.* New York: Vintage, 1994.

———. "Caroline's Wedding." *Krik? Krak!* New York: Vintage, 1995. 155–204.

Davidson, Michael. *Concerto for the Left Hand: Disability and the Defamiliar Body.* Ann
Arbor: University of Michigan Press, 2008.

———. *Invalid Modernism: Disability and the Missing Body of the Aesthetic.* Oxford:
Oxford University Press, 2019.

Davis, Lennard J. *The End of Normal: Identity in a Biocultural Era.* Ann Arbor: University of Michigan Press, 2013.

———. *Enforcing Normalcy: Disability, Deafness, and the Body.* New York: Verso, 1995.

Davis, Lennard J., ed. *The Disability Studies Reader.* 3d ed. London: Routledge, 2010.

Dawes, James. "Human Rights in Literary Studies." *Human Rights Quarterly* 31 (2009):
394–409.

———. "Human Rights, Literature, and Empathy." *The Routledge Companion to Literature and Human Rights.* Ed. Sophia A. McClennen and Alexandria Schultheis
Moore. Abingdon, UK: Routledge, 2016. 427–432.

———. *The Novel of Human Rights.* Cambridge, MA: Harvard University Press, 2018.

Desai, Anita. *Fasting, Feasting.* New York: Houghton Mifflin, 1999.

Devlieger, Patrick. "Why Disabled? The Cultural Understanding of Physical Disability in an African Society." *Disability and Culture.* Ed. Benedicte Ingstad and Susan Reynolds Whyte. Berkeley: University of California Press, 1995. 94–106.

Diakiw, Jerry. "Reading and Life Success." *HuffPost* contributor blog. May 4, 2017. www.huffingtonpost.ca/jerry-diakiw/reading-and-life-success_b_16404148.html.

Douglas, Mary. *Purity and Danger.* 1966; London: Routledge, 2004.

Durosomo, Damola. "Nigerian Government to Pay $245 Million to Victims of Biafran War." *Okayafrica*, Oct. 31, 2017. www.okayafrica.com/nigerian-government-to-pay-biafra-war-victims-245-million.

Eide, Arne H., and Benedicte Ingstad, eds. *Disability and Poverty: A Global Challenge.* Bristol, UK: Policy, 2011.

Eide, Arne H., and Mitchell Loeb. "Counting Disabled People: Historical Perspectives and the Challenges of Disability Statistics." *Disability in the Global South: The Critical Handbook.* Ed. Shaun Grech and Karen Soldatic. Cham, Switzerland: Springer, 2016. 51–68.

Erevelles, Nirmala. *Disability and Difference in Global Contexts: Enabling a Transformative Body Politic.* New York: Palgrave Macmillan, 2011.

———. "Disability in the New World Order." *Color of Violence: The INCITE! Anthology.* Ed. INCITE! Women of Color against Violence. Cambridge, MA: South End, 2006. 25–31.

Espinosa, Juan Manuel. "The Blur of Imagination: Asperger's Syndrome and *One Hundred Years of Solitude.*" *Libre Acceso: Latin American Literature and Film through Disability Studies.* Ed. Susan Antebi and Beth Jörgensen. Albany: State University of New York Press, 2016. 245–258.

Fanon, Frantz. *Black Skin, White Masks.* Trans. Charles Lam Markmann. 1952; New York: Grove, 1967.

———. *The Wretched of the Earth.* Trans. Constance Farrington. 1961; New York: Penguin, 1990.

Felski, Rita. *Hooked: Art and Attachment.* Chicago: University of Chicago Press, 2020.

Francis, Donette A. "'Silences Too Horrific to Disturb': Writing Sexual Histories in Edwidge Danticat's *Breath, Eyes, Memory.*" *Research in African Literatures* 35.2 (2004): 75–90.

Freeman, Michael. *Human Rights.* 3d ed. Cambridge: Polity, 2017.

Gallagher, Susan VanZanten. *A Story of South Africa: J. M. Coetzee's Fiction in Context.* Cambridge, MA: Harvard University Press, 1991.

Ganguly, Debjani. *This Thing Called the World: The Contemporary Novel as Global Form.* Durham, NC: Duke University Press, 2016.

Gappah, Petina. *The Book of Memory.* New York: Farrar, Straus & Giroux, 2015.

Garland-Thomson, Rosemarie. *Extraordinary Bodies: Figuring Physical Disability in American Culture and Literature.* New York: Columbia University Press, 1997.

———. *Staring: How We Look.* Oxford: Oxford University Press, 2009.

Ghai, Anita. "Disability in the Indian Context: Post-colonial Perspectives." *Disability/ Postmodernity: Embodying Disability Theory.* Ed. Mairian Corker and Tom Shakespeare. London: Continuum, 2002. 88–100.

Gibbon, Margaret. *Feminist Perspectives on Language.* London: Longman, 1999.

Gikandi, Simon. *Reading Chinua Achebe: Language and Ideology in Fiction.* London: James Currey, 1991.

Gill, Michael, and Cathy Schlund-Vials, eds. *Disability, Human Rights, and the Limits of Humanitarianism*. Farnham, UK: Ashgate, 2014.

Gilligan, Carol. *In a Different Voice: Psychological Theory and Women's Development*. Cambridge MA: Harvard University Press, 1982.

Gilman, Sander. "Literature/Empathy." Email to the author. Feb. 22, 2021.

Goffman, Erving. *Stigma: Notes on the Management of a Spoiled Identity*. New York: Simon and Schuster, 1963.

Goldberg, Elizabeth Swanson, and Alexandra Schultheis Moore, eds. *Theoretical Perspectives on Human Rights and Literature*. New York: Routledge, 2012.

Goodley, Dan. *Disability Studies: An Interdisciplinary Introduction*. London: Sage, 2011.

Gorra, Michael. "'This Angrezi in Which I Am Forced to Write': On the Language of *Midnight's Children*." *Critical Essays on Salman Rushdie*. Ed. M. Keith Booker. New York: G. K. Hall, 1999. 188–204.

Grech, Shaun, and Karen Soldatic, eds. *Disability in the Global South: The Critical Handbook*. Cham, Switzerland: Springer, 2016.

Greco, Gian Maria, and Elena Di Giovanni, eds. *Journal of Literary & Cultural Disability Studies*. Special issue on disability and human rights. 11.3 (2017).

Haidt, Jonathan. *The Happiness Hypothesis: Finding Truth in Ancient Wisdom*. New York: Basic, 2006.

Hall, Alice. *Disability and Modern Fiction: Faulkner, Morrison, Coetzee and the Nobel Prize for Literature*. Houndmills, UK: Palgrave Macmillan, 2012.

———. *Literature and Disability*. London: Routledge, 2016.

Harpham, Geoffrey Galt. "The Grotesque: First Principles." *Journal of Aesthetics and Art Criticism* 34.4 (1976): 461–468.

Held, Virginia. *Feminist Morality: Transforming Culture, Society, and Politics*. Chicago: University of Chicago Press, 1993.

Herwitz, Daniel, and Ashutosh Varshney, ed. *Midnight's Diaspora: Critical Encounters with Salman Rushdie*. Ann Arbor: University of Michigan Press, 2008.

Herzfeld, Michael. "Global Kinship: Anthropology and the Politics of Knowing." *Anthropological Quarterly* 80.2 (Spring 2007): 313–323.

Heumann, Judith. *Being Heumann: An Unrepentant Memoir of a Disability Rights Activist*. Boston: Beacon, 2021.

Hickel, Jason. "Global Inequality May Be Much Worse than We Think." *The Guardian*. Apr. 8, 2016. www.theguardian.com/global-development-professionals-network/2016/apr/08/global-inequality-may-be-much-worse-than-we-think.

Hoegberg, David. "Principle and Practice: The Logic of Cultural Violence in Achebe's *Things Fall Apart*." *College Literature* 26.1 (Winter 1999): 69–79.

Hollington, Andrea, Tijo Salverda, Tobias Schwarz, and Oliver Tappe. "Introduction: Concepts of the Global South." Global South Studies Center, Cologne, Germany. 2015. gssc.uni-koeln.de/node/451.

Huggan, Graham. *The Postcolonial Exotic: Marketing the Margins*. London: Routledge, 2001.

Humphreys, Joe. "Unthinkable: Which 'Golden Rule' of Ethics Is Best, the Christian or the Confucian?" *Irish Times*. Jan. 31, 2014. www.irishtimes.com/culture/unthinkable-which-golden-rule-of-ethics-is-best-the-christian-or-confucian-1.1674003.

Hunt, Lynn. *Inventing Human Rights: A History*. New York: W. W. Norton, 2007.

Ignatieff, Michael. *Human Rights as Politics and Idolatry.* Princeton, NJ: Princeton University Press, 2001.

Ingstad, Benedicte, and Susan Reynolds Whyte, eds. *Disability and Culture.* Berkeley: University of California Press, 1995.

Jameson, Frederic. "Third-World Literature in the Era of Multinational Capitalism." *Social Text* 15 (1986): 65–88.

Kafer, Alison. *Feminist, Queer, Crip.* Bloomington: Indiana University Press, 2013.

Keen, Suzanne. *Empathy and the Novel.* Oxford: Oxford University Press, 2007.

Kidd, David Comer, and Emanuele Castano. "Reading Literary Fiction Improves Theory of Mind." *Science* 342, Oct. 18, 2013. 377–380.

Kittay, Eva Feder. "Human Dependency and Rawlsian Equality." *Feminists Rethink the Self.* Ed. Diana T. Meyers. Boulder: Westview, 1997. 219–266.

———. *Love's Labor: Essays on Women, Equality, and Dependency.* Lanham, MD: Rowman and Littlefield, 1999.

Kittay, Eva Feder, and Ellen K. Feder, eds. *The Subject of Care: Feminist Perspectives on Dependency.* Lanham, MD: Rowman and Littlefield, 2002.

Kortenaar, Neil ten. *Self, Nation, Text in Salman Rushdie's* Midnight's Children. Montreal: McGill-Queen's University Press, 2004.

Krentz, Christopher. "Borges in the Mind's Eye." *Journal of Literary & Cultural Disability Studies* 10.1 (2016): 37–51.

———. "Duncan Campbell and the Discourses of Deafness." *Prose Studies* 27.1–2 (April–August 2005): 39–52.

Krishna, Sankaran. *Globalization and Postcolonialism: Hegemony and Resistance in the Twenty-first Century.* Lanham, MD: Rowman & Littlefield, 2009.

Lahiri, Jhumpa. "The Treatment of Bibi Haldar." *Interpreter of Maladies.* New York: Mariner, 1999. 158–172.

Lawler, Dave. "The Decade of the Very Poor and the Super Rich." *Axios,* Dec. 30, 2019. www.axios.com/worlds-richest-and-poorest-countries-growth-trends-570972f9-4ded-4405-b16f-f8f7620d77f7.html.

Liddiard, Kirsty, Katherine Runswick-Cole, Rebecca Lawthom, and Dan Goodley. "A DisHuman Manifesto." *Manifestos for the Future of Critical Disability Studies.* Ed. Katie Ellis, Rosemarie Garland-Thomson, Mike Kent, and Rachel Robertson. New York: Routledge, 2019. 156–165.

Linett, Maren Tova. *Literary Bioethics: Animality, Disability, and the Human.* New York: New York University Press, 2020.

Linton, Simi. *Claiming Disability: Knowledge and Identity.* New York: New York University Press, 1998.

Longmore, Paul. "Screening Stereotypes: Images of Disabled People in Television and Motion Pictures" (1985). *Why I Burned My Book and Other Essays.* Philadelphia: Temple University Press, 2003. 131–146.

Lubiano, Wahneema. "Narrative, Metacommentary, and Politics in a 'Simple' Society." *Approaches to Teaching* Things Fall Apart. Ed. Bernth Lindfors. New York: Modern Language Association, 1991. 107–111.

Lundblad, Michael, ed. "Animality/Posthumanism/Disability." *New Literary History.* Special issue 51.4 (Autumn 2020).

Mansfield, Nick. "Human Rights as Violence and Enigma: Can Literature Really Be of Any Help with the Politics of Human Rights?" *Theoretical Perspectives on Human*

Rights and Literature. Ed. Elizabeth Swanson Goldberg and Alexandra Schultheis Moore. New York: Routledge, 2012. 201–214.

Márquez, Gabriel García. *One Hundred Years of Solitude*. Trans. Gregory Rabassa. 1967; New York: Perennial Classics, 1998.

McClennen, Sophia, and Alexandra Schultheis Moore, eds. *The Routledge Companion to Literature and Human Rights*. Abingdon, UK: Routledge, 2016.

McRuer, Robert. *Crip Theory: Cultural Signs of Queerness and Disability*. New York: New York University Press, 2006.

———. *Crip Times: Disability, Globalization, Resistance*. New York: New York University Press, 2018.

———. "Taking It to the Bank: Independence and Inclusion on the World Market." *Journal of Literary & Cultural Disability Studies* 1.2 (2007): 5–14.

Meekosha, Helen. "Decolonising Disability: Thinking and Acting Globally." *Disability and Society* 26.6 (2011): 667–682.

Meekosha, Helen, and Karen Soldatic. "Human Rights and the Global South: The Case of Disability." *Third World Quarterly* 32.8 (2011): 1383–1398.

Mehrotra, Nilika. "The Gender and Disability Interface within Disability Rights Discourses in India." Lecture at the University of Virginia. Apr. 10, 2014.

Melbourne, Roy M. "The American Response to the Nigerian Conflict, 1968." *Issue* 3.2 (Summer 1973): 33–42.

"Millions Have Come Out of Poverty. It's a Reason to Hope." Editorial. *Washington Post*. July 16, 2019. www.washingtonpost.com/opinions/millions-have-come-out-of-poverty -its-a-reason-to-hope/2019/07/16/76204c36-a7f4-11e9-9214-246e594de5d5_story.html.

Minich, Julia Avril. "The Decolonizer's Guide to Disability." *Junot Díaz and the Decolonial Imagination*. Ed. Monica Hanna, Jennifer Harford Vargas, and José David Saldívar. Durham, NC: Duke University Press, 2016. 49–68.

———. "Who Is Human? Disability, Literature, and Human Rights." *The Routledge Companion to Literature and Human Rights*. Ed. Sophia A. McClennen and Alexandria Schultheis Moore. Abingdon, UK: Routledge, 2016. 46–52.

Mitchell, David T., and Sharon L. Snyder. *The Biopolitics of Disability: Neoliberalism, Ablenationalism, and Peripheral Embodiment*. Ann Arbor: University of Michigan Press, 2015.

———. "Disability Haunting in American Poetics." *Journal of Literary & Cultural Disability Studies* 1.1 (2007): 1–12.

———. *Narrative Prosthesis: Disability and the Dependencies of Discourse*. Ann Arbor: University of Michigan Press, 2000.

Moore, Alexandra Schultheis. "'Disaster Capitalism' and Human Rights: Embodiment and Subalternity in Indra Sinha's *Animal's People*." *Theoretical Perspectives on Human Rights and Literature*. Ed. Elizabeth Swanson Goldberg and Alexandra Schultheis Moore. New York: Routledge, 2012. 231–246.

Morris, David, and Lennard J. Davis. "The Biocultural Manifesto." *The End of Normal: Identity in a Biocultural Era*. By Lennard J. Davis. Ann Arbor: University of Michigan Press, 2013. 121–128.

Moskowitz, Moses. *The Politics and Dynamics of Human Rights*. New York: Oceana, 1968.

Moyn, Samuel. *The Last Utopia: Human Rights in History*. Cambridge, MA: Harvard University Press, 2010.

————. *Not Enough: Human Rights in an Unequal World*. Cambridge, MA: Harvard University Press, 2018.

Mullins, Greg. "Paradoxes of Neoliberalism and Human Rights." *Theoretical Perspectives on Human Rights and Literature*. Ed. Elizabeth Swanson Goldberg and Alexandra Schultheis Moore. New York: Routledge, 2012. 120–132.

Murray, Joseph J. "Co-equality and Transnational Deaf Studies: Understanding Deaf Lives." *Open Your Eyes: Deaf Studies Talking*. Ed. H.-Dirksen L. Bauman. Minneapolis: University of Minnesota Press, 2008. 100–110.

Murray, Stuart. *Disability and the Posthuman: Bodies, Technology and Cultural Futures*. Liverpool: Liverpool University Press, 2020.

Nayar, Pramod K. *Human Rights and Literature: Writing Rights*. New York: Palgrave Macmillan, 2016.

Ndlovu, Hebron L. "African Beliefs Concerning People with Disabilities: Implications for Theological Education." *Journal of Disability & Religion* 20.1–2 (2016): 29–39. www.tandfonline.com/doi/full/10.1080/23312521.2016.1152942.

Nixon, Rob. *Slow Violence and the Environmentalism of the Poor*. Cambridge, MA: Harvard University Press, 2011.

"The Nobel Prize in Literature 2003: John Maxwell Coetzee." www.nobelprize.org /nobel_prizes/literature/laureates/2003/press.html.

Noddings, Nel. *Caring: A Feminine Approach to Ethics and Moral Education*. Berkeley: University of California Press, 1984.

Nussbaum, Martha. *Frontiers of Justice: Disability, Nationality, and Species Membership*. Cambridge, MA: Harvard University Press, 2006.

O'Grady, Siobhán. "U.N. Human Rights Office Calls on U.S. Police to Limit Use of Force." *Washington Post*. July 24, 2020. www.washingtonpost.com/world/2020/07/24 /un-human-rights-office-calls-us-police-limit-use-force.

Okoye, Emmanuel. *The Traditional Religion and Its Encounter with Christianity in Achebe's Novels*. New York: Peter Lang, 1987.

Okpewho, Isidore, ed. *Chinua Achebe's* Things Fall Apart: *A Casebook*. Oxford: Oxford University Press, 2003.

Omelsky, Matthew. "Chris Abani and the Politics of Indifference." *Research in African Literatures* 42.4 (Winter 2011): 84–96.

Oxfam. "Summary: An Economy for the 1%." Jan. 18, 2016. oxfam.org/sites/www.oxfam .org/files/file_attachments/bp210-economy-one-percent-tax-havens-180116-summ en_0.pdf.

Parekh, Pushpa Naidu. "Gender, Disability, and the Postcolonial Nexus." *Wagadu* 4 (Summer 2007): 142–168.

Parikh, Crystal. *Writing Human Rights: The Political Imaginaries of Writers of Color*. Minneapolis: University of Minnesota Press, 2017.

Parikh, Crystal, ed. *The Cambridge Companion to Human Rights and Literature*. Cambridge: Cambridge University Press, 2019.

Posner, Eric. "The Case against Human Rights." *The Guardian*. Dec. 4, 2014. www.the guardian.com/news/2014/dec/04/-sp-case-against-human-rights.

Price, Janet, and Nidhi Goyal. "The Fluid Connections and Uncertain Spaces of Women with Disabilities: Making Links across and beyond the Global South." *Disability in the Global South: The Critical Handbook*. Ed. Shaun Grech and Karen Soldatic. Cham, Switzerland: Springer, 2016. 303–321.

Puar, Jasbir. *The Right to Maim: Debility, Capacity, Disability*. Durham, NC: Duke University Press, 2017.

Quayson, Ato. *Aesthetic Nervousness: Disability and the Crisis of Representation*. New York: Columbia University Press, 2007.

———. "Looking Awry: Tropes of Disability in Postcolonial Writing." *Relocating Postcolonialism*. Ed. David Theo Goldberg and Ato Quayson. Oxford: Blackwell, 2002. 217–230.

———. "Realism, Criticism, and the Disguises of Both: A Reading of Chinua Achebe's *Things Fall Apart* with an Evaluation of the Criticism Relating to It." *Chinua Achebe's* Things Fall Apart: *A Casebook*. Ed. Isidore Okpewho. Oxford: Oxford University Press, 2003. 221–248.

Quayson, Ato, and David Theo Goldberg. "Introduction: Scale and Sensibility." *Relocating Postcolonialism*. Ed. David Theo Goldberg and Ato Quayson. Oxford: Blackwell, 2002. xi–xxii.

Ramazani, Jahan. *The Hybrid Muse: Postcolonial Poetry in English*. Chicago: University of Chicago Press, 2001.

Rawls, John. *A Theory of Justice*. Cambridge, MA: Harvard University Press, 1971.

Rhoads, Diana Akers. "Culture in Chinua Achebe's *Things Fall Apart*." *African Studies Review* 24.2 (September 1993): 61–72.

"Richest Sixty-two People as Wealthy as Half of World's Population, Says Oxfam." *The Guardian*. Jan. 18, 2016. www.theguardian.com/business/2016/jan/18/richest-62-billionaires-wealthy-half-world-population-combined.

Rorty, Richard. "Human Rights, Rationality, and Sentimentality." *On Human Rights: The Oxford Amnesty Lectures*. Ed. Stephen Shute and Susan Hurley. New York: Basic, 1993. 112–134.

Ruddick, Sara. *Maternal Thinking: Toward a Politics of Peace*. Boston: Beacon, 1989.

Rushdie, Salman. *East, West: Stories*. New York: Pantheon, 1994.

———. "Introduction to the 25th Anniversary Edition." *Midnight's Children*. New York: Random House, 2006. ix–xvi.

———. *Midnight's Children*. 1981; New York: Random House, 2006.

———. *The Moor's Last Sigh*. New York: Vintage, 1995.

Russell, Marta, and Ravi Malhotra. "Capitalism and Disability." *Socialist Register* 38 (2002): 211–228.

Sabatello, Maya, and Marianne Schulze. "Introduction." *Human Rights and Disability Advocacy*. Ed. Maya Sabatello and Marianne Schulze. Philadelphia: University of Pennsylvania Press, 2014. 1–13.

Said, Edward W. *Culture and Imperialism*. New York: Vintage, 1993.

Sedgwick, Eve Kosofsky. *Epistemology of the Closet*. Berkeley: University of California Press, 1990.

Shakespeare, Tom. *Disability Rights and Wrongs*. New York: Routledge, 2006.

———. "The Social Model of Disability." *The Disability Studies Reader*. 3d ed. Ed. Lennard J. Davis. New York: Routledge, 2010. 131–138.

Shattuck, Sandra D. "Dis(g)race, or White Man Writing." *Encountering Disgrace: Reading and Teaching Coetzee's Novel*. Ed. Bill McDonald. Rochester, NY: Camden House, 2009. 138–147.

Sherry, Mark. "(Post)colonizing Disability." *Wagadu* 4 (Summer 2007): 10–22.

———. "The Promise of Human Rights for Disabled People and the Reality of Neoliberalism." *Disability, Human Rights, and the Limits of Humanitarianism.* Ed. Michael Gill and Cathy Schlund-Vials. Farnham, UK: Ashgate, 2014. 15–26.

Siebers, Tobin. *Disability Theory.* Ann Arbor: University of Michigan Press, 2008.

Sinha, Indra. *Animal's People.* New York: Simon & Schuster, 2007.

———. "Animal's People." *Footnotes: Indra Sinha.* www.indrasinha.com/books-2/animals-people.

———. "A Conversation with Indra Sinha." Reprinted in *Animal's People.* New York: Simon & Schuster, 2007.

———. "Life and Death of a Mad Bhopali Child: A Tribute to Sunil." *Footnotes: Indra Sinha.* www.indrasinha.com/books-2/animals-people/a-tribute-to-sunil.

Slaughter, Joseph. *Human Rights, Inc.: The World Novel, Narrative Form, and International Law.* New York: Fordham University Press, 2007.

Slobodian, Quinn. *Globalists: The End of Empire and the Birth of Neoliberalism.* Cambridge, MA: Harvard University Press, 2018.

Snyder, Carey. "The Possibilities and Pitfalls of Ethnographic Readings: Narrative Complexity in *Things Fall Apart.*" *College English* 35.2 (2008): 154–174.

Snyder, Sharon L., and David T. Mitchell. *Cultural Locations of Disability.* Chicago: University of Chicago Press, 2006.

Spivak, Gayatri Chakravorty. "Can the Subaltern Speak?" *Colonial Discourse and Postcolonial Theory: A Reader.* Ed. Patrick Williams and Laura Chrisman. New York: Columbia University Press, 1994. 66–111.

Stein, Michael Ashley. "China and Disability Rights." *Loyola of Los Angeles International & Comparative Law Review* 7 (2010): 7–26.

———. "Disability Human Rights." *California Law Review* 95 (2007): 75–121.

Taylor, Sunaura. *Beasts of Burden: Animal and Disability Liberation.* New York: New Press, 2017.

Titchkosky, Tanya. "Life with Dead Metaphors: Impairment Rhetoric in Social Justice Praxis." *Journal of Literary & Cultural Disability Studies* 9.1 (2015): 1–18.

Trivedi, Harish. "Salman the Funtoosh: Magic Bilingualism in *Midnight's Children.*" *Rushdie's* Midnight's Children: *A Book of Readings.* Ed. Meenakshi Mukherjee. Delhi: Pencraft, 1999. 69–94.

Tronto, Joan C. *Moral Boundaries: A Political Argument for an Ethic of Care.* New York: Routledge, 1993.

United Nations (UN). "Guiding Principles of the Convention." www.un.org/development/desa/disabilities/convention-on-the-rights-of-persons-with-disabilities/guiding-principles-of-the-convention.html.

———. "The International Year of Disabled Persons, 1981." www.un.org/development/desa/disabilities/the-international-year-of-disabled-persons-1981.html.

———. "Sustainable Development Goals." www.un.org/sustainabledevelopment/poverty.

———. "Toolkit on Disability in Africa: Culture, Beliefs, and Disability." www.un.org/esa/socdev/documents/disability/Toolkit/Cultures-Beliefs-Disability.pdf.

———. "Universal Declaration of Human Rights Multilingual Video Collection." www.un.org/en/udhr-video.

———. "Women with Disabilities Fact Sheet." www.un.org/development/desa/disabilities/resources/women-with-disabilities-fact-sheet.html.

United Nations Enable. "World Programme of Action Concerning Disabled Persons." 2006, www.un.org/disabilities/default.asp?id=23.

Uprety, Sanjeev Kumor. "Disability and Postcoloniality in Salman Rushdie's *Midnight's Children* and Third-World Novels." *The Disability Studies Reader*. 1st ed. Ed. Lennard J. Davis. New York: Routledge, 1997. 366–381.

Vermeule, Blakey. *Why Do We Care about Literary Characters?* Baltimore: Johns Hopkins University Press, 2010.

Vidali, Amy. "Seeing What We Know: Disability and Theories of Metaphor." *Journal of Literary & Cultural Disability Studies* 4.1 (2010): 33–54.

Vital Signs: Crip Culture Talks Back. Dir. Sharon Snyder and David Mitchell. Fanlight Productions, 1995.

Walcott, Derek. *Collected Poems*. New York: Farrar, Straus & Giroux, 1986.

———. "The Muse in History" (1974). *Poetry in Theory: An Anthology 1900–2000*. Ed. J. Cook. Blackwell: Oxford, 2004. 420–436.

———. *Omeros*. New York: Farrar, Straus & Giroux, 1990.

———. "Tribal Flutes" (1967). *Critical Perspectives on Derek Walcott*. Ed. Robert D. Hammer. Washington, DC: Three Continents, 1993. 41–44.

Wallerstein, Immanuel. *The Modern World System: Capitalist Agriculture and the Origins of the European World Economy in the Sixteenth Century*. New York: Academic, 1974.

Wendell, Susan. "Towards a Feminist Theory of Disability." *The Disability Studies Reader*. 1st ed. Ed. Lennard. J. Davis. New York: Routledge, 1997. 260–278.

World Federation of the Deaf. "Complementary or Diametrically Opposed: Situating Deaf Communities within 'Disability' versus 'Cultural and Linguistic Minority' Constructs." Position paper. May 11, 2018. wfdeaf.org/news/resources/11-may-2018-deaf-community-linguistic-identity-disability-position-paper.

World Health Organization and World Bank. *World Report on Disability*. Geneva: World Health Organization Press, 2011. www.who.int/disabilities/world_report/2011/en/index.html.

Wren, Robert. *Achebe's World: The Historical and Cultural Context of the Novels of Chinua Achebe*. Washington, DC: Three Continents, 1980.

Zakaria, Fareed. *Ten Lessons for a Post-pandemic World*. New York: W. W. Norton, 2020.

Index

Page numbers followed by the letter t *refer to tables. Page numbers followed by the letter* f *refer to figures.*

CHRISTOPHER KRENTZ is Associate Professor at the University of Virginia with a joint appointment between the English Department and the American Sign Language Program. He is the author of *Writing Deafness: The Hearing Line in Nineteenth-Century American Literature*, as well as numerous articles about disability in literature and culture, and editor of *A Mighty Change: An Anthology of Deaf American Writing, 1816–1864*. He is currently Director of the University of Virginia's Disability Studies Initiative and helped found their American Sign Language Program.